Motherhood: A Feminist Perspective

"Reminds us that our attention to diversity must be extended to our conceptualization of mothering and motherhood. This compilation of research, anecdote, poem, and critique gives us the words and tools to examine mother-blaming in ourselves and in our work; to offer clients alternatives to pathologizing mother and self-as-mother; and to experience pride in and acceptance of our own mothers and our own motherhood. This work is an historical moment, SOON TO BE A WELL WORN REFERENCE, for my colleagues, for my mothers' groups, and for me."
S. Auguste Elliott, MA, Private Practitioner, Montpelier, Vermont

"A timely collection . . . which challenges the myths of motherhood. Finally we speak the truth about this complex relationship! Phyllis Chesler, Paula Caplan, Janet Surrey, and Rachel Josefowitz Siegel offer us a new perspective on mother blaming/mother hating which, if put into practice, could revolutionize our view on human development. This book is IMPORTANT READING for clinicians and theoreticians alike."
Sharon Volansky-Gerard, RN, MA, Licensed Psychologist-Master, Associates in Obstetrics & Gynecology, University Health Center, Burlington, Vermont

"An INTELLECTUALLY AND EMOTIONALLY RIVETING book. The contributions from these talented authors expose the unidimensional myths of motherhood and delineate the multifaceted nature of being a mother. Many mothers and their children have no doubt grappled with their intuitive awareness of these issues, but the complex realities that these authors affirm have never been so clearly articulated until now. Whether you come to this book as a clinician, mother, father, daughter, or son, it will expand your understanding of being, having, or loving a mother."
Barbara Swain, PhD, Clinical Psychologist, Prescott, Arizona; Adjunct Faculty, Prescott College, Prescott, Arizona

"This is an exciting and important book that SHOULD BE READ BY ALL WOMEN AND BY MEN WHO WANT TO UNDERSTAND WOMEN. It is also a helpful book which can be used to foster understanding and reconciliation among women of different generations, socioeconomic classes, racial and ethnic backgrounds, and family lifestyles. It offers a new look, a 'revisioning' of motherhood which affirms the value of motherhood and womanhood and encourages connection and empathy. The section on mother-blaming alone is worth the purchase price."
Judith B. Rowan, PhD, Psychologist in Private Practice, Concord, New Hampshire; Member, Adjunct Faculty, Antioch/New England Graduate School, Keene, New Hampshire

"While reading this book, I felt as if I were attending a wonderfully creative workshop with new thoughts stimulated by each author. My expectations of the book were met as I explored areas which will be helpful in my clinical work, but they were exceeded as I frequently found myself pausing in my reading to look into my own roles as daughter and mother. My 85-year old mother and my 30-year old daughter are each reading the book now, and I look forward to the exciting multi-generational discussions which are sure to follow! This book EXPANDS THE POSSIBILITIES FOR PARENTING and is an important contribution to the literature."
Margery M. Noel, PsyD, Clinical Psychologist, Certified Sex Therapist, and Supervisor of Sex Therapists, Santa Fe, New Mexico

Motherhood: A Feminist Perspective

Jane Price Knowles
Ellen Cole
Editors

Routledge
Taylor & Francis Group
New York London

First Published 1990 by The Haworth Press, Inc.

Published 2013 by Routledge
605 Third Avenue, New York, NY 10017
2 Park Square, Milton Park, Abingdon, Oxon OX14 4RN

Routledge is an imprint of the Taylor & Francis Group, an informa business

Motherhood: A Feminist Perspective has also been published as *Women & Therapy*, Volume 10, Numbers 1/2 1990.

Library of Congress Cataloging-in-Publication Data

Motherhood : a feminist perspective / Jane Price Knowles, Ellen Cole, editors,
p. cm.
Simultaneously published: Woman-defined motherhood. New York : Harrington Park Press, 1990.
"Has also been published as Women & therapy, volume 10, numbers 1/2, 1990"—T.p. verso.
Includes bibliographical references.
ISBN 1-56024-044-X
1. Motherhood — Psychological aspects —Congresses. I. Knowles, Jane Price. II. Cole, Ellen.
HQ759.W585 1990b
306.874'3 —dc20 90-37913
CIP

ISBN 13: 978-0-918393-87-6 (pbk)

Motherhood: A Feminist Perspective

CONTENTS

Preface xv
Ellen Cole

SECTION I: INTRODUCTION

Woman-Defined Motherhood 1
Jane Price Knowles

SECTION II: MOTHERS AND DAUGHTERS

Two Poems:
I Was In Hawaii 9
The Gold Taloned Mirrors 11
Pat Andrus

"I Hope I'm Not Like My Mother" 13
Shere Hite

Daughters Discover Their Mothers Through Biographies and Genograms: Educational and Clinical Parallels 31
Karen G. Howe

Mourning the Myth of Mother/hood: Reclaiming Our Mothers' Legacies 41
Martha A. Robbins

SECTION III: MOTHER-BLAMING

Making Mother-Blaming Visible: The Emperor's New Clothes 61
Paula J. Caplan

Mother-Hatred and Mother-Blaming: What Electra Did to Clytemnestra 71
Phyllis Chesler

Mother-Blaming and Clinical Theory 83
Janet L. Surrey

Old Women as Mother Figures 89
Rachel Josefowitz Siegel

SECTION IV: DIVERSITY

Caught Between Two Worlds: The Impact of a Child on a Lesbian Couple's Relationship 99
Eloise Stiglitz

The Myth of the Wicked Stepmother 117
Laura V. Salwen

Feminist Considerations of Intercountry Adoptions 127
Susan E. Barrett
Carol M. Aubin

No Accident: The Voices of Voluntarily Childless Women – An Essay on the Social Construction of Fertility Choices 139
Anita Landa

Establishing the First Stages of Early Reciprocal Interactions Between Mothers and Their Autistic Children 159
Dorothy Gartner
Nancy M. Schultz

SECTION V: OPPRESSION

Mothering the Biracial Child: Bridging the Gaps Between African-American and White Parenting Styles 169
Robin L. Miller
Barbara Miller

Lesbian Parents: Claiming Our Visibility 181
Sandra Pollack

Sarah and the Women's Movement: The Experience of Infertility 195
Dina Afek

Sturdy Bridges: The Role of African-American Mothers in the Socialization of African-American Children 205
Beverly Greene

SECTION VI: RESEARCH

Motherhood and Sex Role Development 227
Mary A. Halas

ABOUT THE EDITORS

Ellen Cole, PhD, has devoted 25 years to the practice of psychology. She is currently an adjunct faculty member in the Human Development Program, Prescott College, Prescott, Arizona. An AASECT certified sex therapist and sex educator, she was formerly a professor of psychology at Goddard College in Vermont and chair of the Committee on Women and Minorities of the Vermont Psychological Association. In addition, she co-edited, with Esther Rothblum, the book *Another Silenced Trauma*, which received a 1987 Distinguished Publication Award from the Association for Women in Psychology. Dr. Cole is a co-editor of the journal *Women & Therapy*, co-editor of the Haworth Series on Women, and mother of four young adults.

Jane Price Knowles, MD, qualified as a doctor in 1974, within weeks of the birth of her first son. She works as a consultant to the National Health Service in the United Kingdom. Dr. Price's first book, *Motherhood: What It Does to Your Mind* (Pandora Press), was published in 1988.

Woman-Defined Motherhood

Preface

In September 1988, the first *Women & Therapy* conference was held at Goddard College, in Plainfield, Vermont. It was called "Woman-Defined Motherhood: A Conference for Therapists." Its intention was to define motherhood from a feminist perspective and to explore the implications of that definition for therapists; the format included experiential sharing, the examination of theoretical issues and concepts, a poetry reading, a banquet, and a performance by MATRIX, a women's group that sings songs from the Balkan countries and the Middle East.

This volume is designed to share much of the conference with a wider audience, for the sense of the participants was that it was a "trailblazing" event. As one of the organizers, I found myself moved time and again throughout the weekend, as I realized that what we – the organizers, the presenters, the participants – had collectively created was a celebration and an honoring: of ourselves as mothers, of our daughters and our sons, but most deeply, I think, of our own mothers.

When conference proceedings are published, the papers are typically submitted before the actual presentation. We decided to do it differently, and asked presenters to submit their papers after the conference. Our prediction, which proved to be correct, was that the conference would provide food for thought, that the paper written or "revisioned" after the conference wouldn't be the same as its predecessor. What you have in this volume, then, are many of the papers that were presented in an earlier form at the conference. You have two of the poems that were read. Three papers in this volume were not presented at the conference: Susan Barrett and Carol Aubin were out of the country at the time; Laura Salwen was inspired to write about stepmothering when she realized it was a serious omission at the conference; and Shere Hite called afterwards to say she had been collecting data on mothers and daughters for years that didn't seem to fit anywhere else—might we want to include it in this collection?

Fittingly, this volume, as the conference itself, begins with an introduction by my co-editor and conference co-organizer, Jane Price Knowles, who travelled to Vermont from her home in Great Britain. And fitting, too, is that an entire section is devoted to four papers that were presented as a panel at the conference, a panel about Mother-Blaming. It was, as one woman later described it, "a stunning revelation" when this panel of four—Paula J. Caplan, Phyllis Chesler, Janet L. Surrey, and Rachel Josefowitz Siegel—shocked us into the recognition that it is almost impossible to think without mother-blaming: it is everywhere. I believe even the panelists themselves were surprised at how disturbing, painful, and ultimately powerful this panel proved to be. One woman said later, "I felt overwhelmed by the sense of having been present at one of life's truly historic moments."

There are pieces missing from this collection. Some of the presenters, for instance, did not submit papers even though their presentations were central to the success of the conference. There is not space enough to include all the papers that were submitted. The panelists wrote process notes which we are unable to include because of page constraints. Jane and I asked our mothers to write about us, and now we find we are unable to include what they wrote. And we had hoped there'd be room for Freda L. Paltiel, Senior Advisor on the Status of Women in Canada, who provided the conference ice-breaker, to perform a similar task here.

There are omissions in content, too, as there were at the conference. Most notable, perhaps, is the paucity of references to teen pregnancy and parenting. [Note, for instance, that two-thirds of the children younger than three in the U.S. live in households headed by 15-21 year olds who are poor; that every 23 minutes a teenager gives birth; that the number one reason for dropping out of high school is pregnancy; that one out of five teens 16-19 years old with below average academic skills and below the poverty level is a parent—in contrast to one out of every 20 teens above the poverty level with average academic skills; that more than 470,000 babies were born to teens in 1986. (Lynn Leight, personal communication, November, 1989)]

Yet it's our hope that what we have included approximates the experience of attending this memorable conference. As a closing exercise, we asked participants to define motherhood, in writing, in their own way. Here are some of the responses:

"Woman-defined motherhood means that *all* mothers have something valuable to share, should be listened to, and appreciated, that learning about our diversity is what will enable us to feel good about our mothers and ourselves as mothers. That woman-defined motherhood is learning how to better love ourselves and our mothers."

—Sandra Pollack

"Again I find just when I thought I knew/felt/understood it all, there is more to know/feel/understand. Woman-defined motherhood is unpredictable, joyous, painful. It is a birth—painful—long—dangerous—and ultimately joyful."

—Randy Meadoff

"Mother-bashing is obsolete. We must forgive ourselves and our mothers."

—Gay Mize

"Thank god we are finally defining motherhood for ourselves. We must continue to assert the mixture of feelings and complexity of roles, so that others don't suffer from the romantic myth."

—Anonymous

"The treasured experience to me that is most new is the connection and inclusiveness with women who are different from me—lesbians, black women—who shared and taught me rather than excluding me in anger. My humanity is enlarged by this connection, healing some of the damage to the oppressor of the limited straight, white experience."

—Mary Halas

"This conference has helped me realize a direction for myself: the forgiving of my mother. I see in a greater way the need for me to do this work and the impact it can have, not only on my life, but on how I view all women."

—Anonymous

"Woman-defined motherhood feels like a gift of freedom, for me, for my mother, for my women friends. I wish my mother could know how we reclaimed what has always been."

—Joan F. Levinson

"Woman-defined motherhood is the only counter power we have against one of the worst and most pervasive types of women-abuse: mother-hating, mother-trashing. I leave this conference a little less angry with my mother, a little more forgiving of myself, a little more appreciative of my daughter, and much more aware of mother-hating."

—Jean Lathrop

"To me, woman-defined motherhood conveys a message of *affirmation* of *all* of who we are as women, and broadens the meaning of motherhood greatly."

—Lori Soule

"I have felt the pain of mother-hate—both as doer and receiver—for my whole existence. Being able to name it, explore it, and define motherhood from my own experience is life saving. It opens so many doors and connects me with my roots and history."

—Diane Bray

"The actual process and interactions between participants in this conference clarified for me what a woman-defined *conference* can be. We were able to exemplify the values of non-blaming, validation, and empathic empowerment of which the presenters spoke so eloquently. I leave stimulated emotionally as well as intellectually, and with a feeling of hopefulness and validation in my efforts to create a more loving definition of motherhood and daughterhood in my own life."

—Shoshana Zonderman

"Woman-defined motherhood is learning how to forgive my mother and myself for not being perfect. It is learning how to forgive myself for not wanting to be a mother under the current definition of motherhood. I now understand it's okay to love myself and my mother instead of hating us both for being ourselves."

—Melissa Meth

"Tears have washed my eyes throughout the weekend as thoughts of myself as mother and of my mother replace what the experts have taught, wrongly. My knowing feels affirmed by other women and, as always, sisterhood is powerful."

—Etta Bender Breit

"The joy of a woman-defined, or *women*-defined, motherhood is that when women speak the truth about their experiences as mothers and daughters, there turns out to be not one definition, but many. I can take my and your and their definitions and decide what might work for me. I'm also empowered to lighten up a bit and to let my mother have her own definition of how mothering works for her. I love you, Mom!"

—Patricia Cluss

Ellen Cole

Editors' Note: A special thank you to Elissa Brown, Paula Caplan, Michele Clark, Robin Dion, Lisa Eiker, Auguste Elliott, Carol Kennedy, Jean Lathrop, and Esther Rothblum for their valued help exactly when it was needed.

SECTION I: INTRODUCTION

Woman-Defined Motherhood

Jane Price Knowles

Everyone has an image of and some basic assumptions about what a mother is. We have all experienced being mothered in some form or another, and we have complex feelings about that experience, some of which we could discuss openly but some of which are hidden even from ourselves, in the darkest recesses of our minds. The way in which we judge or accept our own mothers colors the way in which we are likely to perceive ourselves and others as parents. What we say about mothering may not truly reflect how we feel. What we believe ourselves to feel may only be a part of what is buried in the unconscious area of the mind. Becoming a mother often challenges and then alters these images and the assumptions. . . .

Jane Price Knowles, MD, qualified as a doctor in 1974, within weeks of the birth of her first son. She has come to psychoanalysis via psychiatry and works as a full-time consultant to the National Health Service in the United Kingdom. Dr. Price's first book, *Motherhood: What It Does to Your Mind*, was published in 1988 by Pandora Press.

What becomes clear in the discussion of 'what is a mother?' is the extent to which the mother/daughter relationship is focal during pregnancy and early mothering. However, men also had mothers and have feelings, usually strong ones, on the subject of mothering. In this context men have a distinct psychological disadvantage because, unlike daughters, they cannot themselves become pregnant, experience labor or experience mothering from the perspective of providing rather than consuming it. They are prone, therefore, to find it hard to reassess the internal, mostly unconscious feelings of being mothered.

Given that men still have the powerful say in forming our culture, in literature, art, science, economics and what is 'normal' for relationships, their view of mothering without the advantage of refined, adult re-perceptions is the one that predominates. This is particularly true in the world of psychoanalysis where male notions of what constitutes a mature woman or a 'proper' family still hold sway. For several generations these theorists have defined what mothering is, what mothering should hope to achieve, what women should do in order to be good mothers, and, in their analysis of troubled adults, pointed the finger at the bad mother as if she were the cause of all evils. Such formulations ignore the fact that most mothers are remarkably socially powerless to challenge and change life for themselves, let alone their children. They are only allowed to make changes within the guidelines of what culture accepts. That culture is laid down, in the most part, by men who have childhood memories of mothering, with all its inconsistencies and misunderstandings, and who have avoided the adult reality of parenting young children which would undoubtably change and moderate their views of mothers.

—Jane Price, 1988

There are two words which I have changed in this written presentation from the original verbal delivery. Firstly I talked of maternal deprivation and was reminded quite rightly, by Paula Caplan, that we should talk now of parental deprivation. Secondly I talked of forgiveness in my closing paragraph and have later changed that to acceptance—there being nothing to forgive!

The discrepancy between the adult experience of motherhood and the child experience of being mothered is a powerful source of discontent, both for the women who have to contain both experiences and struggle to make sense within their own psyches of the contradictions and paradoxes this presents internally, and to the vast majority of fathers, protected from the practical and true psychological demands of early parenting, who are left to judge adult reality from the remembered position of the helpless and vulnerable child. Hence the discrepancy within the adult individual may also be enacted within the parental relationship.

It is important to look at the psychological cost to women, and their children, of leaving this discrepancy undiscussed and unresolved as a social issue as much as an individual one. One such cost is the reported rate of diagnosable mental illness in women with young children. The psychiatric world is gradually realizing how many young mothers are unhappy and their response to this is to see it as illness in the individual. It is surprisingly rare for the assessment to include an objective look at the marital relationship, and even if it does and it is seen to be unsupportive and even damaging to the woman, it is still more than likely that the woman will be diagnosed and treated as if the illness resides in her. This has important consequences for the design and planning of the services we are able to offer—in-patient wards versus places in child-care nurseries, for instance. It also has important consequences for mothers who eventually find themselves fighting custody battles. A past diagnosis of mental illness tends to weight Court opinion against the mother no matter how good her mothering has been. In order to make it possible to both locate the extent and intensity of the distress, provide appropriate help, and see it as part of a cultural experience of present day mothering which should not act as a judgment on the moral or psychological health of the mother, we need first of all to develop a model of what the experience of mothering is actually like—not what the hopeful child inside of us all might have wanted, but what the grown woman experiences. From that woman-defined position we can then begin a sensible exploration of the many problems experienced in mothering in ways that are healthy for mother, child, father and extended family.

The most common question I am asked by women with young

children is, "Why didn't someone tell me that it was going to be like this?" Why indeed should this common female experience be shrouded in mystery? Is it a social plot or do we simply forget? And yet can we really forget the pain of dragging ourselves from bed for the fifth time that night to a child who will not be comforted, forget the overwhelming fatigue which saps any enjoyment of life, forget the agony of bearing the brunt of our baby's projected infantile rage and depression, forget the intensity of projections from loved ones, friends and relatives, forget the sense of isolation, loneliness and abandonment? Can we really forget all that?

What is missing in the understanding of mothering is the extent to which it is a painful relationship and an exhausting, often thankless, occupation. In the world of the media, art, and literature we are exposed to happy mothers. We are reared with the idea of children fulfilling us and yet with very little idea of how that should come about. The mothers of television advertising fame are not depressed, addicted, anorexic, anxious or fiercely angry as they womanfully produce meals that delight tiny palates and deal with unbelievably dirty clothes. They represent the belief that such occupations are a joy. For a few women in fact this is totally true; for many it is sometimes true; for some it is never true. Of the many women I see in counseling, I am struck by the normality of the psyches and the ridiculous nature of the demands placed upon them. In some ways their "illness" is usually a statement that at some level they too know that what is expected of them is ridiculous but have no ideas or models of how to escape to a more self-defined existence of mothering in ways suitable to themselves.

Nobody has ever told them that each woman mothers differently depending on her own strengths and weaknesses. Not only is this all right, it is essential. It is what allows for the uniqueness of the mother/baby interaction. For as long as we try to impose any one view on mothering—whatever that view—it will be wrong for the vast majority of mothers and babies.

In the United Kingdom, research has demonstrated that up to 50% of mothers with small children (under age five) have symptoms of intense emotional distress on a regular or continual basis (Oates, 1986). Women are five times more likely to be diagnosed as mentally ill in the first year after their first child's birth than at any other time in their lives. Hence when judges ask my expert opinion on whether a woman is a fit mother because of her mental illness, it seems important to underline the fact that it was becoming a mother in our present culture which has made the woman have such distressing psychological experiences in the first place.

When research looks at the factors in a woman's life which predispose her towards the unhappy 50%, we find many factors that are preventable. For instance, in the cases of puerperal psychosis, the most intense presentation of emotional distress, we find factors like the mother being aged more than 28, having a Caesarian Section, being of a high social class (based on her occupation), and being married to a doctor just as indicated as risk factors as there being a family or personal history of mental illness. Similarly, for other major psychiatric illness (e.g., psychotic depression or mania), the loss of a previous child and/or family and marital disharmony make a woman more vulnerable (Oates, 1986).

In less severe (but still extremely debilitating) reactions the list of factors lengthens to include parental deprivation in the mother's childhood, losing her own mother prior to the age of 14, being younger than 19 or older than 30 when first a mother (perhaps because of the isolation from similarly aged peer groups these women often experience), prolonged infertility investigations, questioned termination, expressions of medical concern over the fetus in utero, admissions to hospital, major life events (e.g., deaths or moving house) and experiences of neonatal or maternal illness immediately after birth. These factors tend to cluster. They can be reduced. Of course there is a real risk involved in the adventure of becoming a parent but many of these risks are avoidable. It clearly indicates that society should be kinder and more helpfully supportive to mothers with young children.

Instead they often receive nothing but criticism for their standards of mothering. When these women say, "I do not love my baby," or, "I am a terrible mother," they are describing their own experience of disillusionment, their own abandonment, their own depression.

Motherhood seems to me to be a process of birth as much for the mother as for the child. It is unavoidable that close bonding to an infant provides psychological experiences that allow women to rework their own experiences of babyhood, infancy, childhood and adolescence all over again—and that for many if not all women this is a painful process at times as well as being unique, wonderful, and fulfilling, too. Our inner child is often hand-in-hand with the babe in our arms. On the other hand, society expects its mothers to be very grown up indeed. Of course we were all young and helpless at one time and want to believe that our mothers were always strong, could always cope, knew best and were equipped to help our survival and happiness. Mothers, however, are only human beings in a far-from-perfect world. New mothers make that startling discovery anew with each succeeding generation. Inside the potential ring of happiness of mothering for both mother and child is a black hole—the reality of the limits of the mother and of her environment.

We know, of course, that mothering is meant to be "good enough." What is "good enough" however is a mystery. Certainly women should not be forced to fall back onto male definitions of what good enough mothering is—men have their work cut out attempting to define realistic fathering and should not be either expected or allowed to define the relationship of mother to child. If they do, then they judge real mothers against the hoped-for mother of their fantasy, colored by their own bittersweet memories from childhood, unrefined by adult re-experience. Against this background, mother will often fail. And if they accept that, then they are placed in the position of "failing" in the relationship most crucial and central to them: the relationship in which they wanted to do well so much it makes their hearts ache, the relationship to which they are giving themselves body and soul twenty-four hours a day, in which they experience being invaded and digested, when they may have forgotten when they last thought, for even a second, of themselves, except to condemn. It is a small wonder that despair is not far behind.

The women gods we once had as our cultural heritage, so sadly taken over in recent centuries by male gods, were Mother Gods. They were the Good Mother Gods, the Bad Mother Gods, and then the third variety of Mother Gods who were both good and bad—and only they were called The Great Mother Gods. The challenge of mothering seems to be not how to be "good enough," but to dare to believe in our goodness enough to also be "bad enough." In a world full of adults whose inner children feel impoverished, who still yearn for the good mothering of their fantasies, how do we find the courage to fail fantasy and explore reality—not quietly behind closed doors, feeling guilty and ashamed, but noisily, even triumphantly? How to assert the central paradoxes of motherhood: it is in the failing that we succeed and in the badness that we transcend mere "good enough" and make GREAT.

Acceptance is the key word. Women are brought up to accept the men in their lives for almost everything they do or say and yet when it comes to accepting themselves and their mothers it becomes difficult. The umbilical cord continues to reach into our inner worlds, representing a wound to many women. And yet it is only by accepting our mothers for being human beings, who lived in a real world and who sometimes failed us, that we can come to accept ourselves as mothers too.

REFERENCES

Oates, M. (1986). Research presentation at the Autumn meeting of the Royal College of Psychiatrists, London, England.

Price, J. (1988). *Motherhood: What it does to your mind*. London: Pandora.

SECTION II: MOTHERS AND DAUGHTERS

Two Poems

Pat Andrus

I Was In Hawaii

My daughter had an abortion. She and her best friend and her best friend's boyfriend, drove her to the hospital two days after Christmas. I was in Hawaii, without daughter, because daughter, who had also been honoring the needle, three times a week, for six weeks, wouldn't go in for treatment, wouldn't seek out people to help her figure out why, maybe, she gave so much importance to the needle.

There were complications. The abortion wasn't completed. So two days later, when bleeding increased, she went back to the hospital, by metro bus. And this time she felt a needle, not the one that goes in her arm, but that one that keeps her from feeling surgery, the one she wasn't supposed to feel, the one she screamed out in pain from.

I was in Hawaii. My daughter is 17. My daughter tries to protect herself from AIDS when having sex. But she forgets about condoms and

---

A recent MFA graduate from Goddard College, Ms. Andrus teaches creative writing classes in the Pacific Northwest and is Manuscript Editor for Open Hand Publishing. Her most recent works have appeared in *Z Miscellaneous*, *The Amaranth Review*, and *Perspectives*. A chapbook collection of her poems, *Daughter*, was published by Olivewood, Seattle.

pregnancy rates. My daughter also forgets about the AIDS that travels from the needle to her arm.

My daughter is 17. I would have held her hand. I would have let her cry on my shoulder. I would have driven her to the hospital. I would have cushioned her head for her. I was in Hawaii.

My daughter has played with needles and pills. My daughter has loved at least one night. I have held my daughter through years of her growing. I have tried to teach her how to love and care for herself.

But there are no lessons for raising daughters. Just when you wonder if they need a hug, you must tell them they are late for school. Just when you are sure they are asking for a lullaby, you must remind them to go find their own apartment, buy a cat or dog. You must say goodbye when the cord pulls with the most pain.

I was in Hawaii.
My daughter is 17.

—Pat Andrus
1988
Seattle

The Gold Taloned Mirrors

This child, my daughter
we go blind from mirrors
jagged pieces we both wear
and it cuts my cave
and my daughter child cries
raw reflections scarring her face

but if she sings
I drop
in hunger for love
and my lost dreams
crawl toward dawn
falling into these mirrors at sunrise
now decorated with gold talons
holding pictures of sheafs of wheat

and a crystal ball
hangs from one frame
telling me it's here
it's all here
this light
this house of pain
I still call love

—Pat Andrus
1988
Seattle

"I Hope I'm Not Like My Mother"

Shere Hite

Has the feminist movement changed things? What do daughters now say about their mothers? In research conducted between 1982 and 1988, answers were collected from 874 girls and young women, ages twelve to twenty-seven, to a series of open-ended questions about their mothers. Their answers were returned anonymously. Following is a representative sample of the answers received.

What do daughters say about their mothers? Angry, poignant, longing, conflicted comments that all reflect one thing: the pain young women feel on viewing the second-class status of most women within the nuclear family, and their desire not to repeat this pattern.

• *83% of women participating in this study say they have a terrific fear of being like their mothers:*

"If I thought I was like her, I'd put a gun to my head."

"I was afraid of being anything like her—even to the point of hating myself for looking similar to her. I hate the thought of old age because I think I will get to look more and more like her. Psychologically, I am working to separate from her upbringing of me and find my own identity."

What *is* this fear we have of "being like our mothers"? Is it fear of being second-class, not important, not counting? of developing

---

Shere Hite is an internationally recognized cultural historian and researcher. *The Hite Report on Female Sexuality*, *The Hite Report on Male Sexuality* and *The Hite Report on Women and Love* have been translated into thirteen languages and are used in courses at universities around the world. Hite holds a BA and an MA in history, with further work toward her doctorate in The History of Ideas, 1789 to the Present, at Columbia University.

subservient behaviors? or is it fear of being considered "unattractive" and "old"? If anyone is going to change these attitudes about "older women"—and also the status of women, what it means to be a woman—it is going to have to be us. We cannot do this by simply joining the negativity toward women; at the same time, we have to say clearly what it is about the way we as women have been that we don't like. This is part of our continuing critique of the culture and statement of a new alternative philosophy.

• *Many women muse over how much they are like their mothers:*

"In many ways I am very much like my mother—I worry about things like she does, and like her, I try much too often to please everyone."

"I didn't like it when my mom tolerated stupid people or went along with things they said. I worry when I see myself now being a mirror of this sometimes."

• *Most women feel a sense of great ambiguity about their mothers:*

"My most important female relationship has to be with my mother. I love her and hate her the most. I would like to solve some of our differences. We are both idealists, agnostics, rebels without causes."

"Do I enjoy being 'feminine,' like my mother? NO, it's a wimpy role!"

• *Many women say they saw their mothers being too giving, or "giving in" to their fathers most of the time while they were at home growing up; most express negative feelings now of their mothers because of this:*

"Although I like my mother very much, I have always felt very sorry for her. She has stayed with a man all her life who makes her miserable and saps her self-confidence. I used to get very angry at her for accepting my father's behavior, but all I feel now is pity that she does not feel strong enough to change her life. I always felt she was a good person, and I never felt abused by her. She was a great baker, a good house maker. Thrifty too. And if there ever was only a little butter left, she made sure she was the one with the dry toast.

"But father was often emotionally abusive to both my mother and us children. He would sometimes drink and go into senseless rages. I used to get furious at both of my parents; my father for acting the way he did, and my mother for accepting it. She would always play the 'good mother' role to counteract the 'horrible father,' but she never tried to stop him from behaving the way he did. I remember so clearly wishing that she would leave him, but she never did. Now I am 22, I just stay away from home a lot, I never go there."

"My mother gives and gives with no thought to herself. She's such a giving woman that I get the feeling she doesn't think she's *worthy* of love."

• *The majority of women have distressed and confused feelings about their mothers: 73% feel a very deep love and tie, but also a great disappointment or anger about their mothers' subservience, "passivity,"—or even "cowardice"—in the face of their husbands' authority (are these compromises that daughters are often proud not to have to make, or are we still making them?).*

"I longed to be close to her but she was so repressed and dominated by my father that she rarely expressed her true feelings. She was a full-time mother and housewife. I felt very protective of her when I was young, impatient at her lack of guts when I was older. She died 5 years ago—having devolved until she was unable to make any independent decisions and seemed extremely depressed. I feel anger at the waste."

"My mother is the world's greatest victim. She never took control of her life. But I've got to say, she is getting better. She has more self-confidence now at 64 then ever in the past. I am so pleased for her. Am I like my mother? I never wanted to be like her, hate it when I am. . . . when I can be the 'victim' of life, when I get too needy, when I have high approval needs. I resent her passing those things on to me. I mostly make it okay, but not all the time."

"My mother was a doormat for my father—very passive and mousy, very little-girlish. She gave up being a nurse to raise his four children. She spent her life searching for dirt and trying to contrive the appearance in us of normal, presentable children for her lord and master. For her, we were to say thank you at the right times, match the decor, and never express ourselves. My father used to make himself feel like a big man; my mother should be pleased we fit into her fairy tale of the nuclear family, and said thank you and smiled."

"I can't relate to my mother other than to feel sorry for her—she never stands up for what she believes—she sways with the wind."

"She never taught me to have any goals of my own, and she has relationship problems she has never solved but *continues* to gripe about—25 years with this husband. She doesn't grasp the big picture of why women have so much heartache. I think I grasp the total picture and have come to know how to solve problems, not simply cope with them endlessly. I do not want to take responsibility for solving others' problems. In this way, she makes herself needed, but doesn't have to be on center stage herself."

• *Woman after woman describes how she daily watched the subservient position of her mother under her father in the household, and her father's condescending attitude toward her mother:*

"My mom tried to argue but my dad would never respond, which to me at the time made her look foolish. My father's attitude toward mom was to not get as "worked up" as her, because he was "above it." He looked superior to me. Mother's attitude: You have to work around him in order to get what you want from him."

"My father really treated my mother like dirt. The only time I ever heard him communicate with her, it was to scold her and refuse to eat his favorite Friday night supper, tuna fish because it wasn't on a bulky roll, it was on bread."

• *Women also remember with infinite sadness or anger the position of their mothers at home, often lamenting bitterly the fact that their mothers did not stand up for themselves more, were not equal members of the household—wishing they had rebelled:*

"My mother was a good mother, stable, loving, wise, patient, soft-spoken, a hard worker, never complained. In fact, a living martyr! In other words, she was not really human, never showed any weaknesses, never was overtly sexual, and was only slightly affectionate. She was responsible and dutiful. She didn't work outside the home: she was a full-time mother. She screwed me up a lot when I was a teenager. Now she is tired, resigned, slightly spaced out, very accepting. I still am not reconciled with her."

"My mother spoke too sweetly to me, continually. When I did something badly or stupid, she would say it was great. I learned not to trust her judgment because it would always be favorable. I lost respect for her. Once she gave me a home permanent, which made me look like a goose, and caused a great social embarrassment. This increased my belief that she was stupid."

"I admire her, always have, because she always does what needs to be done, and has withstood all the hard parts of her life with intelligence and grace. Still, it would have been better for us if she had stood up to my father, had been more open, less prone to try to ignore our pleas for help or communication. Back then, the prevailing philosophy was that everything was O.K. if it *looked* O.K., so we were encouraged to hide our emotions, strange or bad behavior was ignored or scorned, but not explained or discussed. If something bad happened to us, we were to pretend nothing had happened, make sure we looked O.K., and get on with life."

"My mother has let my father do her thinking for her all her life. Now that she is elderly she seems really vague and absentminded. Seems totally unused to relying on her own judgment or common sense."

"I notice she is always smiling. I sometimes didn't know whether it is what she really feels, or that she has been doing it all her life and just can't help it."

"I hated my father for being a bully, yet I felt myself more like him than anyone else in the family in terms of interests and intellectual pursuits; I hated my mother for being Pollyana, for saying things were wonderful when they weren't ever; yet her softness is probably the one thing that saved me."

Both boys and girls in the Hite Report research described their mothers in this way; see *The Hite Report on Male Sexuality* (Hite, 1981). Boys in that volume often described feelings of anger with their mothers for being too 'passive' and not standing up for themselves and their dignity. These boys did not express much understanding of the economic or historical reasons why their mothers might have found this difficult or impossible to do.

It is interesting to note that, similarly, audiences would cheer for Edith Bunker, in the famous television series, "All in the Family," when she, the stereotyped 'wimp' wife, would rebel and finally stand up for herself. The audiences went wild with enthusiastic support. We seem to want our mothers to stand up for themselves, to stop only 'giving.'

• *Are we "soft" while they (our mothers) were "weak?" Or are we "wimps" too?*

"I feel that I am soft (although I described her as weak, didn't I?). She was well-liked and I am also."

Should we blame our mothers for "passivity" in the face of such limited options? Weren't many of their compromises based on economic necessity and the pressure of centuries of attitudes toward women? How strong is *our* change? Will it last? How brave are we?

DO WE LOVE OUR FATHERS MORE?

Most women were less angry with their fathers about this situation than their mothers.

Most women are very angry at their mothers for not standing up for themselves, but they are not usually as angry at their fathers for treating their mothers as "second-class"—although when asked, 95% state that their fathers *did* have clearly condescending attitudes.

• *Most women (67%) felt closer to and admired their fathers more growing up:*

"I am closer to my mother in some ways—but if I compare it to my father, I feel I was much closer—and am much closer—to my father. Of course, by virtue of the experience of being a woman, a mother and a wife, we have a type of closeness that I don't share with my father. But she doesn't generally know my deepest, darkest secrets, whereas my father does."

"I liked her but I thought her a bit lightweight beside my father."

Shouldn't women also be angry with their fathers for not changing a system which kept their wives, who were usually economically dependent, in this psychologically imprisoned situation? But most women's replies here contain a subtle implication that at bottom, their mother was to blame, she should not have stood for it.

• *As men/fathers have more interaction with the world, and power, girls often identify—thus feeling guilty for "deserting" their mothers, for looking down on them:*

"I hated my father for his attitudes toward my mother and me, but my hatred apparently didn't evoke an intellectual critique of him. I still identified with him most and wanted to be like him."

• *Approximately 15% of women, however, do mention being angry with their fathers for their attitudes toward their mothers:*

"My father had nothing to do with anything in the house. He didn't even know how to make a pot of coffee. He went to work in the morning, he came home at night—and he was waited on by my mother, who also went to work and came home at night. I felt a great deal of contempt for him."

• *Have we picked up "male" views of our mothers?*

"My mother sold Avon part-time to help finance my college degree. I did not particularly like her—in fact I was embarrassed by her tastes and outlooks. All of her married life she was a full-time mother and housewife, which I feel was a cop-out on her potential. I don't like her. She was a success as a mother—in that role she has earned her title—but as an individual she is pretty dull and boring."

"I wasn't particularly close to my mother. I used to be ashamed of her, something father encouraged. But now I see her as having great courage."

"My parents never argued, but my father's attitude to my mother was full of disrespect and judgmentalness. But she's the spark, the interesting one, the one who talks. My mother's attitude toward my father was gently teasing—but with an underlying tone of 'he's the ultimate authority,' plus a little fear (especially of being judged or criticized); fundamentally, she seemed to think that the father-provider is mysteriously 'wonderful' in some way that only men can be."

Were our mothers "wimps," or considering the very real social and economic pressures on most of them, their choices, can we respect them as being stronger than men may have often had to be?

• *As one woman puts it perceptively:*

"Our mothers did the best they could. It wasn't them, it was the situation that stank."

WOMEN'S POSITIVE FEELINGS FOR THEIR MOTHERS

• *Most women describe their mothers as givers; but, as opposed to the previous women, 30% see this as positive in their mothers:*

"Mom was a full-time mom and home manager. I liked her a lot. I admired her beauty and sociability until I was a teenager. Like her I can't concentrate on my own pleasures until I clear the table, so to speak, get home duties out of the way; I feel I have to help everyone (less than she does)."

"What I like most about my mother is her giving, loving nature. She's never cross. She's seldom unfair. She's always there to give encouragement unless my father interferes. Like when I was pregnant, my mother had to go along with my father's decisions. She always accepted her role as second-class citizen. It wasn't until my father had a big love affair with a woman he'd gone with for years earlier that my mother got the courage to leave him."

"My mother is kind, generous, funny, beautiful, and easy going, and perhaps it was her gentle giving nature that made her such a victim. All she ever showed us was her courage."

"My mother was the perfect mother—always patient, always giving, caring, understanding, supportive, always on my side no matter what."

"My mother is the person I've loved most in my life. I'm very close to her, both physically and emotionally—still. She is warm, understanding, stable and dependable. She's much the same now, except she seems increasingly dissatisfied with her life and my father."

"My mother's affection was verbal endearment and facial understanding when my father was angry and unreasonable. She was a dedicated caretaker of others. She was always tired, but could really be there when needed. Like when one of us was sick, she could be very tender and nurturing."

"She is a great listener and should have been a therapist, she's so good at supporting. She's too traditional in that she does the cooking and cleaning while Dad does the lawn, etc., but she's always growing and can always see the bright side. I only hope I can be half the woman she is. She also has a head on her shoulders—she was a homemaker, then she went out to work when Dad went bankrupt in the early seventies."

"I am and always was emotionally and physically close to my mum. She had always shared the emotional and practical details of her life with me. We were a team, though now that she lives away, our lives are separate. Mum was a housewife while me and my sister were young. She nursed her mom (whose house we lived in) until I was eight. By the time I was hitting adolescence, she had really established herself on her own personality and will and was determined to live her own life. She took little jobs which my dad tried to persuade her were against her own interest, but she persistently held out and eventually got a responsible job with a large corporation.

"Throughout my teens, we spent a lot of time together, as friends and companions. My dad worked shifts and so we often used to have the house to ourselves in the evenings. We'd watch TV programs we wanted and then discuss the issues together. We grew politically aware and educated each other. Today her life with my father is as emotionally unsatisfying as ever and she misses our special closeness, but she also knows I have to go my own way.

"I think I am like her in terms of being a person who responds in a loving, caring way, but I'm also aware of how life has treated her and have learned not to be manipulated in the same ways—i.e., to not be as forgiving, and self-sacrificing, and hopefully not as dissatisfied on a personal level. I know I couldn't live my life through other people the way she has done."

• *6% see their mothers' giving as perhaps self-destructive, but also noble, heroic:*

"The last ten years my mother has held jobs and now is in graduate school. She is a hero and a saint, but I would not want to follow her example. She nearly wore herself out. She has only in recent years come to insist that her own needs be considered."

"I am usually hesitant to give unreservedly, because I saw what that did to mother. She was nearly drained dry and bled white, emotionally and physically. Now she is the person I give to most freely, because she needs it and deserves it."

"My mother worked full-time as long as I can remember. She was my mother *and* father. My father drank his money away, so she *had* to work to survive. I used to fantasize when I was little how someday, I could just hide in the back seat of our car and wait for her to finish work. I was deathly afraid of my father and still am, after all these years. He abused my brother physically; terribly, terribly abused. I was not spanked a lot, by lick, but mentally abused and brainwashed. I was extremely close to my brother. He was my friend and my provider, when there was no one there. He protected me and took me under his guidance.

"I used to cry when my mother would go to work at night. I never let her know though, I used to just cry to myself. She worked from about 6 P.M. to 3-4 A.M., cocktail waitress. She had many jobs after that, secretary, fashion show coordinator, real estate agent, school teacher (Sunday) switchboard operator. I remember as a child, my mother calling for jobs that called for a 'male,' and her arguing why she couldn't at least try! Although you won't see her go out of the house without lipstick on and she never wore pants before I turned 25, she knew her stuff. So there were never any sexist roles as far as she was concerned.

"Now I think she's wonderful. She had a very difficult life and tried in vain to find happiness. She is still looking, I think, for the 'ultimate' happiness."

• *And 12% of all women say they have always loved and admired their mothers and found them strong, not "wimpy":*

"My mother is the woman I love the most. She has been a tree in a storm for me and I feel a great deal for her. She has loved me unconditionally."

"She was a full-time homemaker, except for five years—but then she had a store I came to for lunch and we played games while we ate. I went there after school. My best friend's mother worked at the store next to ours. It was great. I loved my mother dearly, I always felt she was my best friend and would always be there for me. While friends took drugs and put down their mothers I never needed or wanted to."

"I am very close to my mother—she has been a role model and friend. I can't tell her everything—not about my sex life! But we always have great talks evaluating other people's and our own behavior. And I greatly respect what she has done with her life—brought up four kids, enjoys a very happy marriage and has just embarked upon a new career—because she is a more 'finished' product than any of my best friends and has a great capacity to let me grow on my own. But I always know she is behind me. She is the woman I have loved the most—she assimilates the traditional family-life-type woman with one who is never willing to stop growing or learning. I have a hard time with militant females because I don't have that animosity toward men. I think my mother is a liberated woman in a way that is compatible with "having it all.""

• *Of course, some women grew up with good family relationships all around:*

"As a child I was very close to both of my parents. They both did and still do love me. I loved the way that my mother made me feel special, being the only girl in the family. The thing that I didn't like was that she was always busy, and sometimes I felt forgotten. My father was always one to encourage family outings on the weekends, which seemed an imposition on my free time as a teenager, but looking back on it now, I realize the benefits in it. He wanted us to know that, despite the fact that he works six days a week and travels a lot, he loved us all and wanted to spend time with us. Many of my friends never had this type of close, warm family relationship; it is only now, sad to say, that I am away from them all (my family), that I can appreciate how much they did for me, and how happy we were."

"My folks were always polite to each other and friendly. I don't remember *ever* seeing them argue—they always presented a united front. Each instilled a sense of the importance of the other and they always backed up the other's authority—no chance of, "But Dad said I could. . . ." I believe very strongly that they were really happy together. I had a wonderful family life all the way through high school."

Are the answers from women under 27 years of age significantly different from answers from women in their fifties regarding their mothers' roles? In separate research including 2,191 women, it was ascertained that the answer is no, on the whole there is no difference in that both groups see their mothers as having been definitely secondary in status to their fathers, and quite frequently overworked, underappreciated and exploited. However, a larger percentage of older women have a sympathetic view of their mothers' situation, valuing the work they had done; more younger women have a somewhat naive resentment that their mothers hadn't always been home but were working outside the home—as if all those who had mothers 'at home' had had happy childhoods.

It is interesting to note that, although so many women in their forties and fifties are spending part of their time taking care of elderly mothers who are widowed and living alone, only a small percentage had turned against their mothers for this reason.

• *Stories from women under 25 tend to sound the most ambivalent and full of pain:*

"The worst clash was the summer before I left for college. She somehow discovered I was taking the pill. At the time, I was working as a teacher in a sex education project—a job which she got for me. When she found out I was on the pill she threatened to not let me go to college "If that's all I was going to do there" and would make me stay home until I learned a few things.

"It was awful. I told her that there was no way I would stay there, that I would leave whether it was college or not on my eighteenth birthday and she might as well send me to college because then at least she would know where I was. That was a bloody time. Today, we never speak on the phone. Visits are very rare, I never go to where they still live anymore. About once a month or so I get a letter. Upon seeing it and touching it I feel contaminated, I am filled with dread and loathing at the prospect of answering it, which I feel somehow obliged to do, before I even open it."

"My mother loves jerkily—here now, gone the next minute (emotionally speaking). I think she must have been afraid of physical contact. The "A" frame hug, for example. She yelled at us when she was angry, but when I was eleven, I decided I hated yelling and haven't yelled back since. I would just withdraw, act sullen and 'logical' and contemptuous. She's very vulnerable, reachable and out-there, but also quick to run away. It makes me sad to be with her, because I feel like crying and telling her I love her and want her to show more of her love for me, but I'm too scared of how she might react."

• *45% of women between ages 20 and 40 say they feel their mothers were or are jealous of the increased opportunities available to them:*

"She told me once she was jealous because she couldn't do the things I could do."

"I have never been really close to my mother. We don't discuss anything, we are worlds apart. She's been working in the restaurant since I was in the seventh grade (part-time) along with full-time housewife duties. I get the feeling that she resents the fact that I have more options about my future than she feels she had. I guess she was raised to believe that she should get married and have a family, period. Nothing else. I think that she resents the fact that I have the option of choosing my own career—that I'm going to college and she never did. I love my mother, but it's hard for me to find qualities in her that I admire in a role model."

"My mother was a farm wife, she worked farm wife work, from dawn to dark. She was curious about human nature and read the semi-psychological articles in women's magazines and *Reader's Digest* and talked to me of her dissatisfactions. She never supported me in any of my career aims, and laughed at my plans. Now, I have been away from home over twenty years. When we are together there are long, long silences. She waits until immediately before I am to leave before bringing up any subject (my divorce, for example) that particularly bothers her, so that she will have just enough time to state her opinion and I won't have time enough to refute it.

"Every few months she will write an accusatory letter (we write once a week each, as we have since I went to college) about whatever my current situation is—then I try to explain with a ten-page letter in response, to which she often does not reply, or she might respond that she ought to know better than try to give me any advice or voice her opinion anyway since I've never really paid attention to her. Still, I have finally come to believe that she really wanted me to get away from the farm (as I think she wished she could have), but couldn't help feeling envious—my climb into the middle class was always a reminder of what she didn't do. I think she is now totally unable to understand my relative contentment with my life as it is. I do not think she can begin to understand that a woman can live alone, do her work, and have warm and close relationships with her daughters. (This too is possibly a kind of accusation about what she doesn't have.)

"My most pained little moments are when I glance in a mirror and see myself making a facial expression like hers. I try very hard not to have that same bitterness she had. When I catch it in a comment, I seem to echo her and stop myself—then feel upset for hours or days as I think about it and fear having her attitude when I grow older. This long description seems to me to barely skim the surface of this relationship."

• *One woman remembers the very day when she first realized that her mother was conscious of the dominance of her father and that she would not do anything about it. She describes how disappointed and disillusioned she felt, although she and her mother have resolved things and become closer now:*

"I thought she didn't understand how badly Dad treated us, but one day when I was grown she said something that made me realize that she had known all along, and I was angry with her for years after that. I asked her why she hadn't done something about it and she shrugged. That was all. She shrugged. It took me years to get over that. But it was the way it was. Now I've been away from them for years, they've welcomed my visits, they love their grandchildren. We go on from here. I am strong enough to keep my father from treating me the way he used to, skillful enough to do it without antagonizing him, make him respect me. He likes it.

"My mother is the same now as she always was, maybe a little more able to stand up for herself. She is determined, intelligent, artistically talented, stoic, pleasant. . . . but she didn't use those traits when she needed them most. She didn't make her own solutions to things, she just let them happen, planted her feet, put blinders on and kept busy. I think I know what made her that way—I know enough about her life to make some good guesses. So she has good reason to be what she is. The important thing is that we are close now. When she dies, neither of us will have had any regrets, because now we are close, the rest is going to be nice."

"Sometimes when I am on my way to the store I have the illusion that I am her—that I look, feel, and act like she did when she was my age going to the store. In truth, I am all the things she is, but I am more aware, determined to affect things that concern me. I will never stop trying until I have fixed what needs fixing, figure out what needs figuring out, done what needs doing. But I won't put blinders on."

It is interesting to note that in so many of these cases, not a word is ever said directly, no son or daughter confronted a mother saying, "You are too subservient" or anything similar, although other insults are common. It is as if the truth of this particular situation is too terrible to mention; to say it out loud would be just too painful.

COMPARISON OF OLDER AND YOUNGER DAUGHTERS' ATTITUDES

Did women love their mothers more in the 1940's and 50's before the 'sexual revolution' and the perhaps increased general social status of "male" values? Or did they always despise their mothers for being "second-class" (and for being their disciplinarians)?

• *The majority of women over fifty seem to feel more love, and remember less hostility toward their mothers:*

"To contemplate my mother this moment brings tears to my eyes and heart. She is now ninety and we phone every Saturday morning. She has been a savior to me through my divorce and determination to keep my house and children and to survive; sent me money out of her terribly meager resources—money that made the difference for me, in scary money periods. She's got guts and today, now, I want to be just like her and I want my daughters to see me the same way, as a strong, tough role model."

"I lost my mother through her death a year ago. I miss the letters we used to write to each other. I still do write her though. She understands. I miss her, but she was ready to die and I was glad for her. I'm 63."

"I was always close to my mother, but I'm becoming even closer now. I'm 62 and she's 85. She was a full-time homemaker and mother. I like her and admire her. She dresses like an old lady. I look more and more like her."

Is this the effect of distance, or were things different? Is this just memory enhancing our thoughts, or were more mother/daughter relationships filled with less conflict—possibly because the 'sexual revolution' and women's 'emancipation' had not created such a chasm in what mothers and daughters expected?

The seeming lack of hostility among women in their fifties is especially interesting, since so many women in that age range are currently caring for their mothers, who are widowed and living alone.

But some older daughters do not speak tenderly; at times there is a tone of ridicule or condescension in women's descriptions of their mothers:

"She was kind of a sloppy housewife and not much of a cook, but she was good-natured—kind of a pushover most of the time. Now she is a really funny lady in her early seventies; a pleasure to have around, easy and comfortable to be with, not exactly eccentric but regarded humorously by the whole family. She likes dogs and caters to several poorly behaved big ones, still can't cook and the house is a mess."

Is it legitimate for women to react with hostility and contempt to their mothers' bringing them up to be "second-class," or isn't this standard anti-woman prejudice? Why shouldn't women address the same amount of rage and hurt at their fathers for not changing the situation? This is a question we must ask ourselves.

• *One mother—as many—knows how she must have appeared to her daughter, and expresses her wishes for something better for her daughter and for all women:*

"God I wish women could find a way of life that supports their needs to thrive and exist as individuals. I hope they find a way that enables them to live well in the society. And may my daughter have that opportunity and what's more, take it and find her piece of happiness. She is my hope as I've striven to break the bonds of the heritage I have had to live with. We struggle to find our way—I hope we don't have to destroy too much to get there. Each of us is entitled to do that as best we can—to find our own measure of peace."

SUMMARY AND CONCLUSIONS

It is disconcerting to note that neither the majority of women (Hite, 1987) nor the majority of men (Hite, 1981) feel angry with their fathers over the issue of their mothers' status. Women's 'passivity'—i.e., being 'wimpy' and 'not standing up for things'—is seen as the mother's problem, while little cognizance is given to the economic and social factors which may have made a woman accept humiliating situations at home. Very little blame or criticism is directed toward men who allow these situations to go on, and benefit from them.

It was found in this study that many girls see their fathers as more admirable, and identify with them, since their fathers have higher status, more privileges, and seem more important. Girls want to identify with their fathers because of their greater freedom and independence, their right to say what they think, and their money. This is not to say that fathers cannot be good fathers, of course; despite the paradoxes, the closeness and feeling of support that some women enjoy is extremely important to them, one of their deepest experiences of loving and being loved.

But having been taught so subtly and convincingly, by example, that women are less important, and that women's values' are 'unhealthy' and slightly 'silly' leaves women in a situation of having only three choices: either feeling self-hating; identifying with the father, and with 'male' values; or being psychologically bisected, alienated from the society. How seriously can we take ourselves as long as attitudes that 'female ways' are 'wimpy' are still internalized and unquestioned? This is how we learned not to take ourselves and other women as seriously as men.

REFERENCES

Hite, S. (1981). *The Hite Report on male sexuality*. New York: Knopf.

Hite, S. (1987). *Women and love: A cultural revolution in progress*. New York: Knopf.

Daughters Discover Their Mothers Through Biographies and Genograms: Educational and Clinical Parallels

Karen G. Howe

I have been teaching a Psychology of Women course for almost a decade and have been continually moved by its psychological impact on the students. During that time I have also been trying to find ways to understand the processes that account for students saying "this course has changed my life." In this paper I will discuss how the course and the assignment of writing one's mother's biography changes students' perceptions of their mothers in dramatic ways, and how similar effects are achieved in therapy with the clinical tool of the genogram.

In the Psychology of Women course, we study the male biases in traditional psychological theories, and critically examine the biological and intrapsychic explanations of psychoanalytic views of women. The rest of the course involves a strong focus on social context factors influencing the development and behavior of women. We sit in a circle, and throughout the semester use group discussions to integrate personal experience with the academic material. In addition, a number of written assignments are designed to encourage students to analyze women's experiences within the social context of the patriarchal society. Such a focus facilitates the

---

Karen G. Howe received her PhD in Social Psychology from Princeton University in 1974. Since then she has been teaching at Trenton State College in Trenton, NJ, where she is Associate Professor of Psychology and has been Coordinator of the Women's Studies Program for the past six years. Her recent research interests have developed from teaching Women's Studies, and include the mother-daughter relationship and the psychological impact of Women's Studies courses on students.

"personal is political" awareness which has been a major theme of the women's movement and consciousness-raising groups over the past two decades.

THE MOTHER BIOGRAPHY ASSIGNMENT

The written assignment that has the most dramatic impact on the students is the mother biography—which some students report as the most meaningful experience of their college careers. This assignment is based on an expanded version of Cox's (1981) structured interview questions. These questions elicit information about the mother's childhood experiences and influences, her relationship with her own parents, her work, family, and marriage experiences, and her interests. Students interview their mothers toward the end of the semester, record the answers, and write them into a narrative of the mother's life. They also answer questions regarding their own reactions to the interview and the information learned, as well as ones regarding the nature of their relationship with the mother now and in the past. If the student's mother is no longer living, the assignment can be done by interviewing relatives for the necessary information.

Once I started reading the papers I received, I realized that I had tapped into something very powerful psychologically, and therapeutic for the students. Some of the biographies were literally smudged from students' tears and some of my own. For example, one woman in her thirties used the assignment to come to terms with her feelings and information gained by what she called "a lifetime of creative eavesdropping" regarding her mother's experience of being a survivor of a Nazi concentration camp during World War II. Another student was able through the assignment to deal with her mother's death several years earlier in a house fire, and was able to go to the cemetery for the first time after writing the biography. A third student used the biography to come to a more mature understanding of her mother, who had died when the student was a young and rebellious teenager.

For most students, the primary effect of the experience was to feel like they were meeting their mothers for the first time. In fact, that particular phrase has been used by most of the students. This discovery of the mother, as a person, as a woman, has a number of interesting and important implications.

When the students interview their mothers, they learn about some aspects of their mothers' experiences for the first time, particularly those that involve their non-mothering experiences; the feminist perspective of the course allows the student to recognize the impact of the social forces and patriarchal rules on their mothers' lives. Such a perspective encourages the daughter to see the mother in a new light: she more clearly sees the *woman* and the *person* in her mother. Examples of such insights are:

> I never knew my mother had any ambitions outside of family life . . . she wanted to be a teacher.
>
> I never knew that my mother had so much pressure from her parents and society to choose a typical woman oriented career.
>
> I never knew my mother wanted to be an accomplished pianist.
>
> This was the first time I've heard of her regretting not being a microbiologist.

THE SOCIAL CONTEXT

The new perceptions of the mother, as a product of her social and family environments, often resulted in the daughter feeling less anger and blame toward the mother, which in turn enhanced communication between them. An awareness of the patriarchal context allows the daughter to see that the mother was influenced by forces that also influenced the daughter, that anger is more appropriately directed towards the patriarchal society than towards the mother who taught the rules but was also affected by them, and that social roles and stereotypes produce some inauthentic behaviors. As a result, at least for the time surrounding the interview, the mother and daughter pair move past the roles, restrictions, and stereotypes, and relate in more authentic, equal ways, sharing their commonalities as women.

In an earlier analysis of the mother biographies (Howe, 1989), I emphasized the role of social and cultural images which prevented or discouraged daughters from seeing mothers as individual women, and discussed the ways in which the mother biography assignment produced beneficial effects by encouraging the daughter to push past the societal images to more complex visions of the mother. These images, which are complex and sometimes contradictory, usually portray mothers in one-dimensional, idealized, polarized, and unrealistic ways. In doing so, they influence women's definitions and experiences of motherhood, and their relationships with their mothers. In addition, they contribute to the difficulty daughters have in seeing their mothers as individual women.

For example, society's emphasis on the centrality of the mother role in women's lives and identities discourages daughters from recognizing other aspects of their mother's lives (McBride, 1973; Oakley, 1974; Russo, 1979). In addition, the culture's idealized and polarized images of Good Mother and Bad Mother in art, literature, and film, give us unrealistic and one-dimensional portraits of motherhood (Arcana, 1979; Kaplan, 1983; Lazarre, 1976). The societal taboos about women speaking about the reality of motherhood experiences have also perpetuated the idealization (Rich, 1976).

CLINICAL PARALLELS: THE GENOGRAM

Since that earlier analysis, I have noticed a number of interesting parallels between the mother biography assignment in my Psychology of Women course and the use of the genogram in family systems therapy.

Recent work by Lerner (1985, 1988) discusses the use of the genogram, particularly in therapy involving mother-daughter relationships. The genogram was designed for use with the Bowen family systems theory and therapy. This approach involves a multigenerational orientation to therapy, an expansion of the focus beyond an individual to the broadest context of several generations. According to Lerner, this approach gives more objective views of one's parents and grandparents, and helps the individual to know the personal history and stories of the older generations.

The "family facts" about the older generation are gathered by questioning and the construction of the genogram in therapy. The genogram is a diagram that portrays the family tree of the individual, for two or three generations, and includes information such as dates of birth, adoption, miscarriages, separations, divorces, illnesses, deaths, educational and career attainments, for all members of the family tree. Within the Bowen framework for family therapy, this tool has been found to be very useful for bringing to light many issues that are central to Bowen theory and the related therapeutic process. These include differentiation-fusion issues, triangular relationships within the family, emotional cutoffs, sibling positions, multigenerational transmission of family patterns, effects of anniversary dates, and so on (Bowen, 1978; Lerner, 1988; Singleton, 1982).

Used in the therapeutic context, the genogram also brings to light the mother's personal story, in much the same way as the mother biography assignment does in the Psychology of Women course. Often the individual in therapy must ask the mother for dates and information in order to complete the genogram, and in doing so the family themes and contexts emerge. Since social rules and values are taught and played out in the family, learning about the family context in both the genogram and the biography assignment illuminates the social context as well. In her work, Lerner (1988) describes case studies in which daughters experience significant shifts in their perceptions of their mothers, and in their relationships and communication with them. As I found with my students, she reports less blaming of mothers, greater understanding of the forces influencing the mother in the past and present, and more open and authentic communication between mother and daughter. When daughters understand the family and social contexts of their mothers' experiences, they can see the mother in a new light. Instead of only seeing the mother *as* a mother, an isolated power figure responsible for everything that happens to the daughter, the mother is now seen as a woman who has also been influenced by the limitations and restrictions imposed by patriarchal systems, often transmitted through the family. As Caplan (1985) and Siegel (1988) have pointed out, mother-blaming is a prevalent theme in psychological theories, clinical judgements, and women's perceptions of their mothers. Both the use of the genogram and the mother biography assignment lessen such mother-blaming by their multigenerational orientations.

MOTHER BIOGRAPHY EXCERPTS

Some excerpts from mother biography assignments in my Psychology of Women class will illustrate a number of the themes discussed so far. The first one is by Tracy, who was the only child of a divorced mother:

> I have learned so many things from doing this assignment, many for the first time. I found many of her stories fascinating. For the first time in my life I knew how much my Mom was feeling during certain times in her life. I always perceived my Mom as being very strong and nothing could ever get her down. I guess I let those images of her get in the way of recognizing her as a real person with real emotions instead of "Supermom." I now have a better understanding about many areas of her life. Growing up I never knew how she was feeling. Now it was as if we were two old high school buddies that hadn't seen each other in twenty years and she was catching me up on all the gossip. I felt as if I knew my Mom but didn't really know her. She would tell me how she felt at a certain point in her life and I would try to remember that time and place myself back there and relate to how she was feeling all over again. It was wonderful being able to finally understand what was going on behind the scenes. It also felt wonderful that my Mom was able to share these feelings with me.

Tracy's excerpt illustrates how stereotypical images of motherhood kept her from knowing her mother's authentic feelings, but the interview allowed them to be shared. Her use of the "high school buddies" analogy is an interesting statement of equality in their relationship, stemming from the sharing of experiences in a woman-to-woman perspective.

In the next excerpt, Ginger also realizes the limitations of her knowledge of her mother, and the value of asking questions:

> From doing this assignment I have learned that I still have a lot to learn about my mother—the woman. Although after a four hour interview I learned so many new things, I also realize how many more questions need to be asked. I've learned to see my mother in other roles—especially as a daughter. I

> never knew my maternal grandparents and am ashamed of my former lack of interest in them. As a result, it was difficult imagining my mother as a daughter. I also recognize the importance of my mother's role as grandmother in helping my children see me as a daughter. She often tells them what I was like as a little girl and the funny things that happened to me.

It is interesting to note here that Ginger is able to see that the process of knowing the mother's story is a multigenerational one—and now she can encourage her own children to know her better as well.

As mentioned earlier, not only knowing the mother's story, but seeing it in the context of the family and the patriarchal society is a key to the power of the mother biographies and the genogram. The following is a very moving excerpt by Mary, who had some very negative experiences with her mother, who was recently divorced and having problems with alcohol. Prior to the interview, Mary was fearful of interactions with her mother because of earlier experiences with verbal abuse, and communication was very poor.

> I was happy to interview her because I got the chance to ask her questions that I always wanted to know, but was always afraid to ask. She opened up when I told her about the women's issues I was sure she had battled with and she seemed happy that I understood and accepted her struggles. We were able to talk more freely than we ever talked before. I can't begin to tell you how good that felt! It opened up a totally new line of communication between us. I know that I respect her a great deal more than I did in the past now because of this interview discussion we had. She told me things that I never knew before about her relationship with my father. I guess because she was the alcoholic I tended to place a lot of blame on her but now I see that his dominance and his inability to talk things out caused a lot of problems in the marriage. A lot of times, she said, she was forced into submission and she had to do things his way because he was the man. I never realized how much she had to put up with. She must have been very unhappy for a very many years. I see now her struggles and understand a little bit better why she was driven to do what she did. When I am able to take it out of the context of what it did

> to me, I can see a bit more clearly her struggles, being a woman, a good wife, a good mother, and I really feel like she did the best she could under the circumstances.
>
> I used to think that the divorce between my parents caused a great deal of pain for my mother. I now see that the marriage was where the pain was, and the divorce probably caused a great deal of relief. She was again, like when she was young, able to be independent and I am really proud of her newfound independence. During the interview, I was able to let her in on some of the women's issues we discussed in class and she seemed so grateful to be hearing them. I saw her comprehension, her pain, her agreement, her suffering. Her voice did not quiver when she talked to me after that. I think she gained some self-respect and some insights into her own life. I sat there on the couch with my mother and felt a lot of love for her. It was like I saw her for the very first time.

Here we see less blaming of the mother, more open communication, less anger, and we can almost feel the relief experienced by both Mary and her mother. This excerpt also illustrates the powerful sense of connection and empathy that emerge when both mother and daughter recognize the social context and their shared experiences as women. The sharing described by Mary and the reconciliation with her mother that is implied in the excerpt also show how important it was for this mother-daughter pair to connect as *women*. In an article on anger in the mother-daughter relationship, Herman and Lewis (1986) make the same point: "The reconciliation between mother and daughter and the establishment of a sense of continuity from one generation to the next proceed best when both mother and daughter are able to affirm the value of their common womanhood" (p. 160).

CONCLUSION

The mother biography assignment in my Women's Studies course has intense, moving, and therapeutic effects on the students' perceptions of their mothers, similar to effects of the use of genograms in therapy. As I have discussed, daughters discover the context of their mothers' lives, and as a result become less blaming, feel more closeness with the mother, develop a sense of understanding and empathy regarding the mother's experiences, and often express much affection for the mother. The papers that students hand in are usually very long and detailed; most of them indicate that the length is due to the mother's eagerness to talk, often to the daughter's surprise. Most of the papers end with an expression of thanks for having been required to do the assignment. Thus, the biography assignment becomes a powerful vehicle for enhancing mother-daughter communication and empathy.

Once the interview and biography have been done, hopefully the mother and daughter can continue to have conversations and interactions that reflect the new insights and perspectives gained from the assignment. Since the culture does not encourage us to see women or mothers in context, it becomes a continuing challenge to keep that perspective in mind. As this paper has discussed, the mother biography and genogram are useful tools for viewing the mother's life in context, and they could be used in a variety of settings. For example, individual women could interview their mothers at any time, not related to an educational or clinical setting. College and university courses in a range of academic areas could use interviews and biographies as assignments; in addition to Women's Studies, areas such as Psychology, Sociology, History, English, Multicultural Studies, and so on would be relevant. Students from Kindergarten through high school could use interviews, biographies, and family trees to explore their own family backgrounds, immigration experiences, multigenerational patterns, etc.

Asking questions, at the heart of both the genogram and the mother biographies, is a way of giving women a greater voice. As a number of feminist writers have pointed out in recent years, much of the recent explosion of material on mothers is presented from the daughter's perspective, not that of the mother herself. When we ask our mothers about themselves and their lives, we give them a voice. When we listen to them and see the commonalities, as well as the differences, in our experiences, we learn more about them and ourselves. As my student Ginger wrote at the end of her mother biography, "I see this interview as the first of many explorations leading me into deeper understandings of not only women and my mother, but also myself."

REFERENCES

Arcana, J.P. (1979). *Our mothers' daughters*. Berkeley: Shameless Hussy Press.

Bowen, M. (1978). *Family therapy in clinical practice*. New York: Jason Aronson.

Caplan, P.J. (1985). *The myth of women's masochism*. New York: E.P. Dutton.

Cox, S. (Ed.). (1981). *Female psychology: The emerging self* (2nd ed.). New York: St. Martin's Press.

Herman, J.L., & Lewis, H.B. (1986). Anger in the mother-daughter relationship. In T. Bernay, & D.W. Cantor (Eds.)., *The psychology of today's woman: New psychoanalytic visions* (pp. 139-168). Hillsdale, N.J.: The Analytic Press.

Howe, K.G. (1989). Telling our mother's story: Changing daughters' perceptions of their mothers in a women's studies course. In R.K. Unger (Ed.)., *Representations: social constructions of gender* (pp. 45-60). Amityville, N.Y.: Baywood Publishing Company.

Kaplan, E.A. (1983). *Women and film: Both sides of the camera*. New York: Methuen, Inc.

Lazarre, J. (1976). *The mother knot*. New York: McGraw-Hill.

Lerner, H.G. (1985). *The dance of anger*. New York: Harper & Row.

Lerner, H.G. (1988). *Women in therapy*. Northvale, N.J.: Jason Aronson.

McBride, A.B. (1973). *The growth and development of mothers*. New York: Harper & Row.

Oakley, A. (1974). *Women's work: The housewife, past and present*. New York: Pantheon Books, Random House.

Rich, A. (1976). *Of woman born: Motherhood as experience and institution*. New York: W.W. Norton.

Russo, N. F. (1979). Overview: Sex roles, fertility, and the motherhood mandate. *Psychology of Women Quarterly*, *4*, 7-15.

Siegel, R.J. (1988). Women's "dependency" in a male-centered value system: Gender-based values regarding dependency and independence. *Women and Therapy*, *7*, 113-123.

Singleton, G. (1982). Bowen family systems theory. In A.M. Horne, & M.M. Ohlsen (Eds.)., *Family counseling and therapy* (pp. 75-111). Itasca, IL: F.E. Peacock Publishers, Inc.

Mourning the Myth of Mother/hood: Reclaiming Our Mothers' Legacies

Martha A. Robbins

Since Adrienne Rich (1976) alerted us to the silence that surrounds the most formative relationship in the life of every woman, much research has been done about various aspects of the relationship between mothers and daughters. With the exception of personal accounts (DeBeauvoir, 1983; Lowenstein, 1981), no systematic study has explored the mother-daughter relationship from the perspective of a daughter's experience of her mother's death. To address this lack, I investigated the effect of a death of mother upon middle-aged women from psychodynamic, constructive-developmental and family systems perspectives. I was interested specifically in exploring how the ongoing process of bereavement of the mother related to the process of psychological and spiritual transformation of women in midlife within the present historical context.

PARTICIPANTS IN THE STUDY

The data used to exemplify key points in this paper were gathered from two in-depth interviews with ten white, middle-class women between the ages of 39 and 53 ($M = 46.5$ years) from the northeast-

Martha A. Robbins, ThD, is currently teaching psychology and spirituality at Pittsburgh Theological Seminary. Dr. Robbins also has a small private practice and facilitates workshops on various aspects of women's psycho-spiritual transformation. Address correspondence to: Pittsburgh Theological Seminary, 616 N. Highland Ave., Pittsburgh, PA 15206.

This article is based upon the author's doctoral research at Harvard University and forthcoming book, *Midlife women and death of mother: A study of psychohistorical and spiritual transformation* (New York: Peter Lang Publishing), 1990.

ern part of the United States. Their mothers had died from 18 months to 15 years prior to the interviews ($M = 4.7$ years). The women volunteered to participate in the study which they learned about through various sources: women's newsletters, notices posted in women's resource centers, professional meetings, referrals and personal contacts.

At the time of the interviews, eight women had lost both parents. For six of these women, the mother was the second parent to die. All ten women had attained a higher level of education than both parents. Five of the women were in their first marriages, four were divorced and one was a lesbian whose two year relationship had recently ended. With the exception of the woman who was a lesbian, all had children; three had children under 15 years of age. Nine women were working outside the home. Religious affiliations were diverse: two Catholics, two Jews, one non-practicing Quaker, one non-practicing Protestant, one Unitarian Universalist and three with no religious affiliation but who described themselves as being on a "spiritual journey." This sample is not representative of all white, middle-aged, middle class women, of course, but the range of responses encompasses much of what may be encountered in a more controlled cross-sectional study.

CATEGORIES OF FINDINGS

A surprising finding in this study was that most of the women experienced more grief over the *lives* of their mothers than their actual deaths. This finding suggests that underlying the mourning process was the unraveling and reweaving of the bonds of loyalty that gave rise to and maintained the woman's "myth of mother/hood." The function of the mother myth in the internal world of the daughter provided an interpretive key to understanding the meaning the daughter made of her loss. The metaphor "myth of mother/hood" is an overarching construct that encompasses the daughter's mythic images of self-in-relation to mother (others), world and the Divine within a particular historical context. "Myth of mother/hood" is written in this way to emphasize the dynamic interaction between the daughter's formation of her personal myth of mother and the cultural myth of motherhood.

In this paper, I will focus upon four interrelating factors that contributed to the meanings that the middle-aged women in this study made of the lives and deaths of their mothers at the time of their interviews: (1) the nature of the early mother-daughter relationship which gave rise to the daughter's "myth of mother/hood"; (2) the dimensions of grief involved in confronting the myth of mother/hood; (3) the process of mourning as unraveling and reweaving mythic images of self-in-relation to mother, self and the Divine; and (4) the developmental phases in the process of mourning and transformation. Following this discussion I will note briefly the factors that facilitated mourning and transformation and discuss their implications for women and therapy.

THE NATURE OF THE EARLY MOTHER-DAUGHTER RELATIONSHIP GIVING RISE TO THE DAUGHTER'S "MYTH OF MOTHER/HOOD"

Socio-historical contexts of mother-daughter relational patterns strongly affect the formation (and reformulation) of a woman's myth of mother/hood (Lykes, 1985). The women in this study were born between 1930 and 1944. The effects of the Great Depression and World War II on the women (and their mothers/families) differ according to the points in the life span during which women experienced these events (cf. Elder & Liker, 1982). For example, Sarah,[1] age 52, mentioned that the loyalty bonds she formed with her mother in early childhood developed in the context of the effects of the Depression on her parents who had immigrated to this country through Ellis Island. Her mother wanted to work outside the home but was not permitted to do so by her father who felt that women's role was to be in the home.

> My mother's life was *very* hard. She was married during the Depression years. My father was a difficult person. He was sort of a patriarch type and she was a very strong-willed person. They were always fighting. And I was drawn into alliances with my mother against my father. And that persisted almost until the day my father died (about five years ago).

Sarah's "pattern of intimacy and involvement" in her mother's life was shaped by her perceptions of her mother's difficult and deprived life resulting in part from the historical effects of immigration and the Great Depression on the family's life and in part by her father's attitude toward her mother and women in general.

In the same historical period but in quite a different socio-cultural context, Gail, 53, formed negative loyalty bonds with her mother. Born in Africa of missionary parents, Gail was told by her father to "be good to your mother, take care of her" while he left for several days at a time "to do God's work." "My dad was gone a lot, and my mother didn't really want to be there. She was depressed." Early on in the relationship with her mother, Gail sensed the intensity of her mother's emotional needs. "I sensed that . . . if I really got close to her I would just sort of get engulfed by her need. So I was always pretty, pretty distant. . . . I became so defended that I didn't let myself need her." Gail distanced herself from her mother to protect herself from being overwhelmed by her mother's needs. These interactional patterns were reinforced by the family myth that a small child absorbs even when she senses something is not quite right.

> I never could address this. There was a lot of "this is a wonderful family" in the midst of all this, and that was the family myth. We're a wonderful family, we laugh a lot, we all love each other.

Moreover, her father's mandate that Gail care for her mother during his prolonged absences created conflicting images of loyalty that affected her early images (or representations) of God (Rizzuto, 1979).

> Dad used to say, "God loves you *so much*, but the only way you can know about how God loves you is how we, your mother and father, love you." And my sense was that I felt pretty awful. You know my father was always leaving, my mother was depressed. And that was being loved. When we evacuated from Africa, Dad couldn't come with us because God needed him in Africa. So that was another piece of what

> God was about. . . . Like God's work and the world . . . were a whole lot more important than I was. Yet my father was talking about how wonderful God's love was. It was *very confusing*.

Both Sarah and Gail sensed the neediness of their mothers and developed different interactional patterns of response. If over the years, these interactional patterns dominated to the exclusion of others, these patterns created what I call the "myth of mother."

The daughter's personal myth of mother was developed in the context of the dynamics of the entire family system and was maintained by "invisible loyalties" (Boszormenyi-Nagy & Spark, 1973) of each family member to the family myth. Family myths were supported and undergirded by the socio-religio-cultural myth of motherhood in Western patriarchal society (cf. Keller, 1986; Lerner, 1988). The daughters' perceptions of their fathers' attitudes toward women in general and their mothers in particular became part of the formation of their sense of self as female children within this particular period of history.

Loyalty bonds between these mothers and daughters, therefore, cannot be fully understood apart from the context that bonded them together (either positively or negatively) under oppressive patriarchal realities. As such, these loyalty bonds were invisible threads that constituted the daughter's being-in-relationship and became part of the very way in which she knew herself, related to others, and gave a certain cohesiveness to her existence. What was ultimately and intimately trustworthy in the daughter's life shaped the weaving of both conscious and unconscious threads of loyalty forming the texture of her faith (Fowler, 1981; Parks, 1986). Major changes in any sphere of interaction (be it the intrasubjective, interpersonal, socio-cultural, political or religious sphere) reverberate into other spheres. Consequently, inherent in every phase of development is the woman's ongoing creation and recreation of a matrix of meaning that may connect these various spheres of interaction in ever more complex and truthful patterns.

DIMENSIONS OF GRIEF

The death of one's mother is the loss of one's oldest relationship; a fracture that exposes the underlying structure of connection (Bowlby, 1980). Consequently, the death of the mother triggered, intensified, and/or complicated the women's confrontation with and reformulation of their myth of mother/hood during their midlife period.

In describing the experience of the death of her mother two years ago, Joan, a 45 year old divorced woman said:

> In February of that year my mother died. I felt like I had sustained such a blow to my body . . . that all the life went out of me. I was already disoriented over school, I was already going through massive changes in my personal and spiritual life. But this was like I felt all of my roots were so . . . I can't think of a word that would be strong enough . . . unrooted is not strong enough. It's a 'torn' or rather a violent feeling. And I didn't know anymore if God existed. I mean a lot of this stuff was already happening, but my mother's death . . . I just didn't know any more who God was, if God was, or what God was. . . . I think that who God is for me comes through my mother . . . God is faithful. . . . My mother was faithful to me all my life. . . . Losing her meant losing that person in my life (tears). . . .

Joan was one of two of the ten women who described their mothers as being "faithfully present" to them throughout their lives. The other eight women in the study described their mothers as "sad, lonely, depressed" or "deprived, demanding, controlling." As previously noted, in most of these cases early patterns of interaction with their mothers established an intense bond wherein the daughter felt responsible either for providing emotional support for the mother, or for spending much emotional energy trying to distance herself from her mother. All eight women ascribed their mothers' depression to one or both of the following major reasons: (1) unresolved grief issues of the mother—in one case the death of her two other children, and in five cases the death of their own mothers when they (the mothers) were in their teen-age years; and

(2) unsatisfying marriages in which the mother created no other outlet to pursue her own interests.

In speaking of the effect of her mother's unresolved grief on her own grief process, Gail, 53, said:

> My mother's next youngest sister whom I was named after, died when she was 13 of diabetes. And I think that really . . . put something on my mother's life . . . . Mother talked about that all the time. You know it's like Abigail's death was a real important something that just kept on coming down to me. And I discovered much later on that my brothers didn't know about Abigail. I was the only one who heard about her. . . . I've had a lot of grief for her (my mother's) life as I've come to understand it. And really see how (tears) lost in some ways she was. But I haven't grieved for her presence.

Gail isn't able to grieve for the absence of her mother in death (which occurred 15 years previously) because she rarely felt "connected" with her in life. This leaves her with an inherent sense of vulnerability which she calls a wounding:

> I think the grief just comes through the wounding that has been in my life because of this lack—that's been the grieving—which seems to get more so as I get older rather than less so when I was younger and I had more defenses against the wound.

She later named the wound as "loneliness and feelings of abandonment."

Another 47 year old woman described how she wanted to "mother her mother" in the hope that she would heal her own felt vulnerability of "a lack of self confidence" resulting from "being sat upon by my mother":

> I didn't understand why she shut down, this smart, vital woman. I would hear her story (about her mother insisting that she go to college against her own father's will), and it wouldn't make any sense with the person I saw. Then she told me that her mother died when she was about 19 and I think that

> was very tough for her. . . . She couldn't share with me what her dreams were, cause they got stopped. But I think it was so painful for her that she couldn't face my going out and being able to accomplish what she couldn't do. The sadness that comes up for me is that I couldn't help her to get there . . . (sobbing) . . . break through her defenses . . . that deep sadness colors my life. Because it was out of her not being able to have her own personal success that she messed us up.

Both of these women speak of a core wound emerging in their early interactions with their mothers which continued to be a source of vulnerability up to and following their mothers' deaths. In the first situation, Gail illustrates what Volkan (1981) calls a "living linking object," by becoming a replacement for the longed for deceased sister of her own mother. Indeed, Gail learned, internalized and faithfully carried within herself the mother's deep disappointments and sorrows in life (cf. Williamson, 1978). The second woman points to the relevance of the cultural context of the differentiation-reconnection struggle of middle-aged women in Western society today (cf. Abramson, 1987; Baruch & Brooks-Gunn, 1984; Flax, 1978; Surrey, 1985). In coming to terms with her grief over her mother's life, what it could have been, and the effect this had on her own life, she had to come to terms with the patriarchal context of her mother's life and the changing cultural perceptions of the identity and roles of women. This cultural shifting seemed to exacerbate the process of mourning for some of the women, making the process of selectively internalizing valued aspects of the mother more difficult. Many of the women felt that they did not really know their mothers, or knowing them, devalued their lives as they judged them by their own culturally influenced perceptions of what it is to be an effective woman today (cf. Caplan, 1989).

PROCESSES OF MOURNING THE MYTH OF MOTHER/HOOD: REIMAGING SELF-IN-RELATION TO MOTHER, SELF AND THE DIVINE

What then facilitated the process of internalization and reconstruction inherent in grief work for these women? Rather than remembering the loss in order to come to terms with reality, the work of mourning focused upon remembering realistic love and finding a means for its expression in their lives (Bowlby, 1961; Raphael, 1983). For the women who felt that they did not really know their mothers because of their having "shut down," the task of grieving focused upon reconstructing their mothers' lives and "making them real" within their historical context, and, in this process differentiating themselves. Consequently, this enabled them to relate to the internal representations of their mothers from a different frame of reference. For one woman, this process was facilitated by visiting the graves of her mother's relatives, giving expression to her mother's unresolved grief. For others it was by the reading of journals, letters, or viewing pictures of their mothers (Williamson, 1978). Speaking of the importance of reading her mother's journal which her mother gave her one year before she died, Deborah stated:

> It was as if she had given me a kind of meeting ground from which we could connect with something to share. I have felt very empty of my mother: I have yearned to know more about her in life. It wasn't until after she died that I began to gain some access to information about her as a *real* person who had the kinds of emotions I had—not in an idealized sense and also not quite the way in the one-sided fashion that she presented it. And I've had an enormous period of growth in the past five years . . . I feel real.

These objects (journals, letters, pictures, etc.) served not only as "linking objects" (Volkan, 1981) to the representation of the lost mother which may be crucial links in the ability to mourn, but also as "bridges" in the process of "re-cognizing" their mothers and a concomitant recomposing of their own sense of self (Belenky, Clinchy, Goldberger, & Tarule, 1986; Gilligan, 1982; Kegan, 1982). This illustrates the importance of knowing the other (mother), of establishing an *examined felt connection* with the other, before one can truly grieve the loss of the other (cf. Lifton, 1979).

The reverse was also true. For some women it was in the process of coming to know themselves in a different way (re-cognizing themselves) through claiming their own specific abilities that enabled them to shift their perspective or relate to their mothers in a qualitatively different way as well. Six of the women were actively addressing the conflictual issues in their relationships with their mothers before they died (cf. Moss & Moss, 1983). This resulted for some in a partial healing of their felt core vulnerability. As one woman described it:

> As I feel more centered and good about what I'm doing, that if (my mother) were living, I wouldn't be as angry with her. Because some of the anger came out of the way that I felt that she handicapped me.

Renegotiation of the relationship with the actual mother, however, was not possible for some women because the shift in their own meaning-making structures occurred after the death of their mothers. Thus, the process of mourning involved dealing with the regret that they weren't able to relate to their mothers from their new developmental perspective.

> I was getting more to a place where I could just accept her for who she was, as she was. And you know, I was in that sense unfortunate. She died before I was further along in my own development and I could not be as loving as I would have liked to be with her.

The recognition and acceptance of the limits of the relationship set by her own meaning-making structures, that it couldn't have been otherwise given her underlying structures of knowing and valuing at that time in her own development, presented the task of transforming anger into regret, and regret into forgiveness of mother and self.

> I just forgave her, and I forgave myself for some of the hatred I had had toward her. I was really beginning to reckon with her as a person who had real feelings, who had been hurt and stunted and blighted in some fashion. I could separate myself from her at times enough to simply see her as that human being.

While forgiveness of mother and self were a necessary prelude to a more complex reconstruction of the myth of mother/hood, the rawness of "early vulnerabilities" for some women only began to be healed in relation to the emergence of new images of God or the Divine made possible through new significant relationships. Marian, a 45 year old divorced woman, was put into an orphanage at the age of 13 after her father deserted the family. She escaped and searched for her mother who was in another city. Upon their reunion, her mother sent Marian back to the orphanage. Anyone Marian seemed to get close to, either died or left her. She described her mother as a "brick wall" and her basic life myth as "if things go wrong, it's my fault. God is a punishing God." At the time of her mother's death, Marian developed a new relationship with an older woman whose attitudes and behavior provided new possibilities (and images) for relating. Frequently, she sought Marian out to just be with her when she was withdrawn and depressed. In the transitional space (Winnicott, 1953) of prayer and meditation, however, Marian's process of healing through internalizing the experience of being loved for herself by another woman became intensified.

> I'm coming to know a presence within. God as a loving friend, just a shining and loving being with a friend. A quality of *being there*, a rightness. . . . I'm letting go of the need to suffer and need to be unhappy. It's o.k. to start letting love in. I couldn't do any of it before, and it's still very tenuous. It's kind of a rebirth.

Other women spoke of an increasing awareness of their openness to, trust in and connectedness with a "power or energy" that they were discovering to be within themselves, between persons, among living forms and greater than the universe. In the process of "letting go and opening to the 'more' that is real, truthful and loving," some women resymbolized their self-in-relation to what they held to be intimately and ultimately trustworthy in ways that suggested a reconnecting with the "Primal Matrix" of all life (Ruether, 1983).[2] Although held and expressed in qualitatively different ways, such resymbolizations empowered many women participants to re-member broken connections with their mothers and to "give birth" to themselves. As they did so, they began to reweave their myth of mother/hood in more complex and richly textured ways.

DEVELOPMENTAL PHASES IN MOURNING AND TRANSFORMATION

In this study, there was a dynamic reciprocal relationship between *what* daughters mourned (the dimensions of grief), and *how* they mourned or made meaning of what had been lost (their underlying structures of knowing, valuing and believing). While only a longitudinal study could reveal a process of transformation of the underlying ways in which an individual woman perceives and relates to her self and others, the compiled stories of the women in this study suggested phases in the process of mourning and transformation.

By examining the underlying structure of these women's stories, I discovered five relatively progressive phases in the process of unraveling and reweaving the myth of mother/hood. Only those women who had worked through a particular phase and had moved into the next phase(s) could reflect upon the previous phase(s). This ability to reflect upon and recognize the aspects peculiar to the previous phase(s) was the criterion for phase progression. For the sake of brevity, I will present only brief descriptions of each phase.

Phase One: No Conscious Conflict

In this phase, the woman is closely identified with her mother, following in her general footsteps, adopting her values and lifestyle without critical reflection. Conflict is experienced only as a vague dissatisfaction with one's sense of self and life purposes. The ongoing process of relationship-differentiation through confronting the myth of mother/hood may be triggered by the death of mother.

Phase Two: Emergence of Conscious Conflict in the Form of Guilt

In this phase, the midlife daughter feels that she must assimilate herself into the patterns of mother-daughter relationship established earlier in life. Strong feelings of guilt in the form of abandoning the mother surface if the daughter puts more energy and time in pursuing her own interests in place of caring for the mother. Abandonment guilt may be evoked either by protestations by the mother or by feelings of betrayal within the daughter herself. Over-identification with the myth of the mother's reality does not permit direct expressions of anger. Guilt exposes while it also serves to maintain the established covert loyalties formed throughout the previous decades.

Phase Three: Entanglement in Conflict

In this phase, conflict comes inside. Still overidentified with aspects of the myth of mother's reality, the daughter repudiates her mother's life in her efforts to "re-do" her mother's life by living her own life differently. While anger is expressed, it is displaced. Forms of guilt and anger entangle the daughter in the conflict.

Phase Four: Repudiation of the Mother in Her Cultural Context

In this phase, the midlife woman understands the reasons for the guilt and anger of the previous phases, and, consequently, repudiates the earlier mother-daughter interactional patterns. While there is some recognition of the psychological and cultural factors that affected her mother's reality, the daughter resents the effects that the mother's life had on her own life and consequently blames her mother for not handling her life differently. Recognition of the conflict as internal to the woman and as reinforced by the dominant culture's myth of motherhood precipitates her search for a new way of being-in-relationship with her self, others and the world.

Phase Five: Acceptance of Mother's Life and Death

In this phase, the daughter is able to see her mother as a person in her own right. In so doing, the woman is able to accept the historical and cultural influences affecting her mother's life as well as her own with a deepening sense of respect, forgiveness and compassion. This compassion allows the daughter to selectively internalize some values of the mother and disregard others. The past relationship with the mother and others is no longer repudiated but reappropriated from a qualitatively different perspective. These daughters, consequently, experience themselves as living their own lives with authenticity or personal authority and with deepened capacities for intimacy and interdependence.

Unfavorable Outcome

Not all outcomes were favorable, however. While these phases generally describe a process of mourning that leads to psychohistorical transformation, one woman was concerned that her "life would keep shrinking" after the death of her mother. Fran's unanticipated pregnancy at 40 years of age, nine months before her mother died, became a rather literal symbolic link of the dialectic of death and life:

> I was pregnant and had a baby two weeks after my mother died. So as my mother shrunk, grew into this little shrinking person, a shell of herself, I was getting bigger and bigger with baby. . . . I felt like a life passed and a life came. . . . I felt the baby came because of my mother dying, definitely.

Speaking of the effect of the death of her mother (who died two and a half years previously) on her own life, she stated:

> Now I'm just trying to survive. I can't . . . I feel so disappointed in myself. I took more risks in my life before my mother died. I felt braver. I felt once my mother died, all I have in the world is my husband and my kids and I wouldn't do anything to risk losing any of them.

This woman spoke of being "panic stricken" with the thought of her mother dying throughout her entire life. Already suffering from chronic depression, the experience of her mother's death intensified the fragility of her own internal sense of herself apart from her mother which is consequently displaced onto her family. Her unresolved grief issues make her particularly vulnerable to pathological mourning and make her youngest son a "living linking object" (Volkan, 1981).

FACTORS FACILITATING TRANSFORMATION

Neither the age of the daughter nor the number of years since the death of the mother was related significantly to the particular phase of the daughter's reconstruction of the myth of mother/hood. Three distinct but dynamically interrelated factors significantly affected the process of mourning and transformation: (1) the strength of the self; (2) the underlying meaning-making capacities of the woman; and (3) the quality of the content and context of the images offered to the woman's ongoing creation and re-creation of images of self-in-relation to (m)others, world and her sense of ultimacy.

Insecure attachments in early childhood and the inability to tolerate ambivalence affect the resilience of a person's underlying image-making capacities in the face of loss (Marris, 1986). The development of a strong sense of self requires that the woman integrate and synthesize earlier experiences into her most mature self structure. The person must be able not only to observe these experiences but also deal with the intense affect that accompanies true recognition and ownership. The findings of this study suggest that the emergence of the underlying capacity for contextual and critical thinking is essential to being able to observe the patterns of interaction that contributed to the daughter's childhood and current myth of mother/hood. They also suggest that the deep enervating unconscious generational patterns and power structures (interpersonal and societal) can be made explicit, grieved and then reconstructed only with the emergence of the underlying capacity for dialectical and "constructivist" thinking (cf. Belenky et al., 1986). Optimally, there is a dialectical and reciprocal interaction between working through early vulnerabilities (reconstructive work) and transformation of underlying meaning-making capacities.

The effectiveness of this interaction, however, depends upon the content of the images offered to the woman in transition as well as the context through which they become experienced. "That so much depends on the search for fitting and right images and that images are so conditioned by context should give us pause" (Parks, 1986, p. 127). It is little wonder, therefore, that most of the women in this study re-storied their lives as they interacted with other women, as well as groups and ideas that presented new possibilities for being-in-relation to one's self, others and the world. This in turn influenced their re-imaging of the ultimate matrix of their lives in more complex and truthful ways. The absence of either animating images or a community of confirmation for emerging or emerged women-identified selves was a major factor hindering the process of mourning and transformation.

CONCLUDING REMARKS

In concluding, two observations are in order. The first pertains to the content of the women's grief. The woman's experience of the death of mother triggered a depth of grief that transcended the actual death of mother. That most of the women participants experienced intense grief over the lives of their mothers years after their actual deaths suggests that they were mourning the death of mother in life, that is, the absence of the mother or "maternal thinking" (Ruddick, 1980) in the personal, socio-political and religious dimensions through which life is experienced. This suggests that mother loss is more significant than the actual death of mother and that the socio-religio-political structures of Western society support mother loss while denying it at the same time. In its deepest metaphorical meaning, therefore, the death of mother in life points to the dominant culture's continued re-enactment of (and women's coparticipation) in matricide (Chesler, 1972; Keller, 1986). Daughters internalize and embody the grief of the dead mother; their grief is multidimensional, intergenerational and transgenerational.

The second observation pertains to the process of mourning and transformation. Most of the women in this study had to discover realistic love, that is, the women first had to find a basis of connection with mothers who had disconnected from their own female selves before they could adequately unravel and reweave their myth of mother/hood. The bond of connection was found in the felt awareness of a shared woundedness among women who are silenced in their grief by the dominant culture. Through the process of recognizing, owning and giving public expression to their grief, daughters may provoke others to engage their own experience of mother loss in all its forms. The potential of deep, defenseless grief when brought to public expression more than unmasks the dominant consciousness that leads people to numbness about death (especially the death of mother), it re-members. Re-membering means nothing if not re-connection; it enables us to reclaim our mothers' life-giving legacies.

IMPLICATIONS FOR THERAPY AND EDUCATION

The insights generated in this study have far reaching implications for therapeutic and educational interventions with women of all ages. Shifting cultural norms regarding the identity and roles of women intersecting with significant life crisis and/or transition (other than death of mother and midlife transition) may provoke confrontation with the myth of mother/hood and provide the opportunity for its reconstruction. The dimensions of grief that became exposed as women confront their myths of mother/hood and the progressive phases in mourning and transformation, therefore, may be relevant to women of older and younger generations. The discovery of or the reactivation of grief over mother loss during times of crises and transitions is normal and to be expected. As women become conscious of the pain of misconnections or broken connections with their mothers resulting from the dominant culture's matricide and their coparticipation in it through internalization and behavior towards other women, their awareness first provokes guilt, and then outrage and the repudiation appropriate to the recognition of such injustice as it affected their grandmothers' lives, their mothers' lives, their own lives and the lives of their children. At such times, women's grief should not be conceived either as symptomatic of "dependent attachment" to the mother, or as symptomatic of pathological grief if the mother has died, although these possibilities also may be present.

Rather, therapists and educators may facilitate the process of mourning and transformation by helping women to feelingly connect to their own past and to the world, assisting them in making conscious, selective claim to the essential relatedness of historical, intergenerational, interpersonal and spiritual life. Women may be helped to reconnect with their mothers and to reclaim their life-giving legacies by coming to understand how mother-daughter interactions are profoundly shaped by the dynamics of the entire family system, a system that is situated in a socio-cultural and religious/mythical context.

Without demythologizing and remythologizing images of self-in-relation to (m)other, world and the Divine as these images are shaped by and help to shape the contexts of development, therapeutic work may not facilitate adequately women's dealing with the multidimensional layers of grief over mother loss. The therapist's recognition and encouragement of the development of the underlying capacities for knowing, valuing and believing is crucial for this remythologizing. The strengthening of the self and transformation of meaning-making structures are related intimately to women's ability to re-cognize the mother in her psychohistorical context and to re-member realistic love.

NOTES

1. All names and places have been changed to protect the confidentiality of the participants in the study.
2. In suggesting the metaphorical image of God as the Primal Matrix, I am drawing upon the notions inherent in Ruether's (1983) metaphor of "God/ess as Matrix, as source and ground of our being" (p. 70).

REFERENCES

Abramson, J. (1987). *Mothermania: A psychological study of the mother-daughter conflict.* Lexington, MA: D.C. Heath.

Baruch, G., & Brooks-Gunn, J. (Eds.). (1984). *Women in midlife*. New York: Plenum.

Belenky, M., Clinchy, B., Goldberger, N., & Tarule, J. (1986). *Women's ways of knowing: The development of self, voice, and mind*. New York: Basic Books.

Boszormenyi-Nagy, I., & Spark, G. (1973). *Invisible loyalties*. New York: International Universities Press.

Bowlby, J. (1961). Processes of mourning. *International Journal of Psychoanalysis*, *42*, 317-340.

Bowlby, J. (1980). *Attachment and loss* (Vol.3). New York: Basic.

Caplan, P. (1989). *Don't blame mother: Mending the mother-daughter relationship*. New York: Harper & Row.

Chesler, P. (1972). *Women and madness*. New York: Doubleday.

De Beauvoir, S. (1983). *No easy death*. New York: River Press.

Elder, G. H., & Liker, J. K. (1982). Hard times in women's lives: Historical influences across 40 years. *American Journal of Sociology*, *88*, 241-269.

Flax, J. (1978). The conflict between nurturance and autonomy in mother/daughter relationships and within feminism. *Feminist Studies*, *4*, 171-189.

Fowler, J. (1981). *Stages of faith*. New York: Harper & Row.

Gilligan, C. (1982). *In a different voice*. Cambridge: Harvard University Press.

Kegan, R. (1982). *The evolving self*. Cambridge: Harvard University Press.

Keller, C. (1986). *From a broken web*. Boston: Beacon.

Lerner, H. G. (1988). *Women in therapy*. New Jersey: Jason Aronson.

Lifton, R. J. (1979). *The broken connection*. New York: Simon and Schuster.

Loewenstein, S. F. (1981). Mother and daughter—An epitaph. *Family Process*, *20*, 3-10.

Lykes, B. (1985). Gender and individualistic vs. collectivist bases for notions about the self. *Journal of Personality*, *53*, 356-382.

Parks, S. (1986). *The critical years*. New York: Harper & Row.

Raphael, B. (1983). *The anatomy of bereavement*. New York: Basic.

Rich, A. (1976). *Of woman born: Motherhood as experience and institution*. New York: W. W. Norton.

Rizzuto, A. M. (1979). *The birth of the living god*. Chicago: University of Chicago Press.

Ruether, R. (1983). *Sexism and god-talk*. Boston: Beacon Press.

Ruddick, S. (1980). Maternal thinking. *Feminist Studies*, *6*, 342-67.

Surrey, J. (1985). *The self-in-relation: A theory of women's development* (Work in Progress No. 13). Wellesley, MA: The Stone Center.

Volkan, V. (1981). *Linking objects and linking phenomena*. New York: International Universities Press.

Williamson, D. S. (1978). New life at the graveyard: A method of individuation from a dead former parent. *Journal of Marital and Family Counseling*, *4*, 93-101.

Winnicott, D. W. (1953). Transitional objects and transitional phenomena. *International Journal of Psychoanalysis*, *34*, 89-99.

SECTION III: MOTHER-BLAMING

Making Mother-Blaming Visible: The Emperor's New Clothes

Paula J. Caplan

Four of us – Phyllis Chesler, Rachel Josefowitz Siegel, Janet Surrey, and I – organized a panel on mother-blaming for the 1988 Goddard College conference on motherhood, because during the past decade each of us had been stunned and deeply pained by the degree of mother-hating we had seen – especially pained when we saw it in women, and all the more so when we saw it in feminists.

Our purpose in organizing the panel was publicly to name and begin to describe mother-blaming and mother-hating as a problem, although we knew we could not possibly explore all of its varieties or manifestations in a single session. But our aim was to raise some of the personal, clinical, social, and political issues related to

Paula J. Caplan, PhD, is Professor of Applied Psychology and former Head of the Centre for Women's Studies, Ontario Institute for Studies in Education, as well as Assistant Professor of Psychiatry and Lecturer in Women's Studies at the University of Toronto. She is author of *Don't Blame Mother: Mending the Mother-Daughter Relationship* and *The Myth of Women's Masochism*.

mother-blaming and mother-hating and to make some beginning suggestions about what kinds of action we could take to stop it.

Since I began clinical work about 20 years ago, I had been plagued by the feeling that I was like the child in the fairy tale of "The Emperor's New Clothes." The child sees that the emperor is naked but wonders why no one else seems to notice. In case conferences, I would await the final summary and formulation, the attempt to explain the causes of an emotional problem in a child whose family had been interviewed, tested, and observed with great care over a long period of time. Almost inevitably, the mother was blamed for the child's problems; and whether she was described as cold, rejecting, and castrating or as overprotective and smothering, the description of her usually bore little resemblance to the woman I had seen with my own eyes. Like many women clinicians, I attributed the difference in my perception to my lack of clinical sensitivity and judgment. Not until I read books like Phyllis Chesler's *Women and Madness* and began to find, one by one, a few other clinicians who shared my view did I realize that the problem was mother-blaming.

At the conference on motherhood, even before we presented our panel, I was aware of our need to be vigilant. For instance, the term "maternal deprivation" was used in a number of presentations. I want to suggest that that term should either never be used or should be used *only* if the following questions are raised: Was there any paternal deprivation or deprivation or mistreatment by anyone else in the child's environment? What about "cultural deprivation" in a different sense from its usual one—deprivation of mother-infant closeness by a culture that is obsessed with the importance of separation and individuation and pathologizes closeness, connection, and interdependence to the point that mothers pull away from their children out of fear that their love and closeness will damage them (Caplan, 1989). Related to this point, I would suggest that the use of terms like mother-daughter "fusion," "enmeshment," and "symbiosis" no longer be used, since they promote this kind of misguided pathologizing.

Another example of mother-blaming arose in the conference presentation by Barbara and Robin Miller on raising biracial children. A salient thread in some of the discussion from the audience was the feeling that, if the child is having problems, the mother may not have helped her child in learning to deal with them. Although it is important for the mother to help in this way, we need to ask ourselves why we automatically look to the mother. Why don't we assume that the father, alone or in addition to the mother, hasn't helped his child enough? Part of the answer is probably that we know that women are more likely to have been socialized to be sensitive to and skilled in dealing with emotional and interpersonal issues. But what we should do about that is to take great care to acknowledge what mothers *do* do and to expect fathers or other parent-figures to do an equal share.

KEEPING VIGILANT: DOCUMENTING THE PROBLEM

One example of mother-hating or mother-blaming that I experienced directly was that, when my book, *The Myth of Women's Masochism* (1987), was published, this was a typical event: I would speak about my belief that women do not really enjoy suffering but that in a sexist society we are often given a choice of two bad alternatives, and when we choose one, we're accused of enjoying our suffering. A woman would approach me after my talk and say, "I really agreed with everything you said—*except* for *my mother*! She is the one real masochist I know." North America seems to be filled with daughters, each of whom believes that her mother is the world's only masochist. What kind of culture encourages such mother-blaming? As a result of a host of experiences like these, I wrote a book called *Don't Blame Mother: Mending the Mother-Daughter Relationship* (Caplan, 1989).

Another direct experience I had which I trace to mother-blaming was that, when I was involved in a very active women's center in a major institution, although the institution rigidly limited the money, space, and personnel time available to us, because the word "women" was in the title of our center, we often became the butt of profound rage when we could not meet all of the enormous range of needs that the women students, support staff, researchers, and faculty wished we could meet. Since few women have escaped all hurt or damage that sexism inflicts, women often turn to women's organizations for healing, help, and support. And because all women are thought of as potential mothers, we tend to expect women, like mothers, to meet our needs, and we become enraged when they cannot. Women and men tend, too, to feel thoroughly justified in that rage, because they've believed the myth that mothers are capable of being endlessly nurturant, so they feel betrayed when a woman or a woman's group doesn't provide that endless nurturance: Why *didn't* she give me her all? How hard could that have been for her, since she's capable of infinite caring and selflessness?

My student Ian Hall-McCorquodale and I wrote two papers (Caplan & Hall-McCorquodale, 1985a and 1985b) in which we documented the overwhelming prevalence of mother-blaming in major clinical journals, and the fact that this has been virtually unchanged in spite of other gains the feminist movement has made. It was often shocking to see to what extremes clinicians would go in order to blame mothers. For instance, in one article the authors had wondered whether children in families whose fathers had been prisoners of war would have a higher incidence of emotional problems than children in other families, and if so, why this would be. They found that the POWs' children did have more emotional problems, and here was their explanation: The fathers were still very anxious and emotionally depleted. When they were at home with their families, they were emotionally detached. This upset their wives, and that upset interfered with their ability to mother the children properly.

Through various routes, we have come to understand that a great deal of mother-hating in women also comes from identification with the oppressor, the dominant/powerful ones, leading to the need to prove how separate we are from other people (like traditional men, like those who traditionally have held the powerful, dominant positions) and how separate we are from other women.

This pattern has had several consequences, and I want to speak briefly about some of these:

(1) A great deal of writing has been done, such as by Nancy Friday (1977), Nancy Chodorow (1978), Colette Dowling (1988), and Eichenbaum and Orbach (1988)—to name only a few—which either obviously or subtly promotes alienation of women from each other, *even though* some of these writers describe themselves as feminists. How many women eagerly read *My Mother/My Self* (Fri-

day, 1977), hoping for help with their relationships with their mothers, and ended up feeling very pessimistic about the prospects for those relationships? How many people begin to read the theoretical or therapy-oriented writings of many so-called feminists, find happily that these writers acknowledge women's oppression, but end by feeling that their problems are really all the fault of mothers who "couldn't let go," who couldn't see themselves as separate from their daughters? And the prescription is typically to pull farther away from our mothers—when as women we have been raised to *try, as Jean Baker Miller has said, to create, maintain, and improve relationships, not to back off from them (1975).*

Too much of the work on mothers and daughters has promoted the alienation of daughters from others, of women from other women, by explaining most of our problems as inadequate independence from our mothers and anyone who might be construed as a mother-type-figure—which could, of course, be any woman or the universal Woman.

The inability to see oneself as separate from another has preoccupied me for many years. As I wrote in *Between Women: Lowering the Barriers* in 1981, this inability is indeed a profound mental disorder—*but* it is exceedingly rare. It constitutes a psychosis. It does not typify mother-daughter relationships. Closeness or confusion about the dependency and independence (about which, more later) are *not* in the same league as the inability to see oneself as a separate being. And indeed, the uncanny, shivery feeling of horror that we get when we think of someone who cannot see oneself as separate is substantially produced by our culture, in which closeness is considered unhealthy, embarrassing, sick, female.

RELATED POLITICAL ISSUES

What *actually* plagues many mother-daughter relationships is the male-model-induced *fear* that we are too close, and the resulting befuddlement about how we can be both independent and connected. Otherwise brilliant, imaginative women suddenly lose their creativity, their ability to understand that *of course* one can be both, as Rachel Josefowitz Siegel has so beautifully shown in a paper in which she proposes that we scrap the terms "dependence" and "independence" in favor of a healthier, happier focus on "interdependence." Her work (1986, 1988), as well as Phyllis Chesler's revolutionary work years ago (1972) and Janet Surrey's profound writing (1985) on the self-in-relation, have unmasked the incredible power that language has to establish and maintain this dangerous, manufactured confusion.

(2) A second consequence of the obsession with separateness is the resistance of many women, even feminists, to acknowledging the intellectual debts they owe to other women. The closer one woman is to another, even intellectually, the more it seems the learner has to demonstrate her blissful unawareness of her teacher's influence on her, just as daughters feel they have to show they are independent of their mothers. This is tragic in any case and certainly has no place in the work and practice of feminists, but it happens all the time. Thus, for instance, women who say they are feminists cite object relations theorists who describe separateness as the primary goal of human development and, therefore, tend to promote mother-hating, but do not cite Jean Baker Miller (1975), Adrienne Rich (1976), Phyllis Chesler (1972), Janet Surrey (1985), or Rachel Josefowitz Siegel (1986), or any of the other *very* exciting feminist writers of whom they must surely have heard. It's hard to avoid regarding this as an uncomfortably close parallel to daughter's playing up to Daddy while they both ignore or demean Mommy.

Another political issue—one which makes it hard to be vigilant about noticing and stopping mother-blaming—concerns what I believe is a largely false dichotomy. In considering this issue in relation to mother-blaming, we need to be aware that pornographic visual displays include photographs of pregnant women and nursing women squirting their milk for the consumers of pornography. The false dichotomy is between feminists who call themselves "antipornography" and feminists who, in relation to the pornography, call themselves "anticensorship." The antipornography feminists tend to emphasize the harm that pornography does to women and children, and many believe that anyone who *has been proven to be physically or emotionally damaged* by pornography should be able to sue the pornographers for damages—just as victims of other kinds are allowed, even encouraged to sue their victimizers. This is *not* a procensorship position, but it has often been misunderstood or mislabelled in that way. Certainly most feminists would agree that censorship is to be feared and avoided, because once it is allowed, it is likely to fall into dangerous hands. But what is relevant for this topic is the disproportionate concern some "anticensorship" campaigners show for protecting the rights of mostly male, destructive pornographers and their consumers *at the expense of* the mostly female and child victims. This means that, in the name of an anticensorship position, the welfare and safety of women and children—the people associated with motherhood—have low priority. It involves a focus on some abstract principles (anticensorship) while ignoring (1) the fact that most feminists on the "other side" do not actually take a procensorship position; (2) the importance of other abstract principles (the dignity and safety of women and children); and (3) the real harm done to women and children by pornography.

My plea is that we not allow the patriarchal overvaluing of separateness and encouragement of mother-blaming and woman-blaming to divide women against each other and against our mothers and daughters on these important political issues.

TAKING ACTION: SOME BEGINNING STEPS

The initial step we can take toward overcoming mother-blaming is to become sensitive to the huge variety of forms and the depth of mother-blaming and mother-hating in our culture—simply noticing it. We need to become as aware of its manifestations as we are of other expressions of sexism. Concomitant with this, we need to ask questions that make one stop and think, that interrupt the automatic nature of mother-blaming (Caplan, 1989); for instance, when someone uses the term "maternal deprivation," the question that should immediately come to mind is, "When *mother* allegedly wasn't giving enough, what was father (or other adults) doing? What else was going on, in mother's life, in child's life, and elsewhere?"

Second, whenever anyone of either sex is having problems in

their relationships with women, we should investigate the possibility that this is a possible manifestation of mother-blaming. We should be aware also that mother-blaming is expressed through both the Perfect Mother myths and the Bad Mother myths (Caplan, 1989); myths of the first type set up expectations that no mortal mother could ever hope to meet, and therefore they set mothers up to be disappointing and infuriating for not measuring up, and myths of the second type lead us to mislabel our mothers' not-so-great behavior as horrible and their neutral behavior as bad.

Third, we should write to journal editors, offer to serve on editorial boards and to serve as reviewers for papers in the mental health fields, so that our increased awareness of mother-blaming and mother-hating can be put into action. This last suggestion will not be easy to implement, however. Let me explain why, using an example from my own experience.

Our mother-blaming documentation was published in two articles which appeared in the *American Journal of Orthopsychiatry* in 1985 (Caplan & Hall-McCorquodale, 1985a, 1985b). The second article included a list of recommendations for avoiding mother-blaming; these included, for instance, the suggestion that journal editors should screen submitted articles for unquestioning, uncritical citation of previous literature that involves mother-blaming, as well as for failures to consider factors and people other than mothers as contributors to children's emotional problems. We sent copies of our articles to the heads of every clinical training program in North America and to the editors of every clinical journal. We received only one reply, and that was from the University of Missouri program, whose director expressed pleasure at receiving our information and said that they had been concerned about this issue already.

In 1988, a deeply mother-blaming article appeared in the *American Journal of Orthopsychiatry* (Masterson, Donworth, & Williams). I wrote a letter to the editor in which I pointed out this bias. As this paper goes to press, I have no idea whether or not they plan to publish my letter, because the reply I received from the journal editor simply denied that the article was mother-blaming and then took me to task for having cited, in my letter, our own research on mother-blaming. (Needless to say, I had cited it both because it is the only quantitative survey of the phenomenon which we have been able to find and because it seemed ironic and important that the same journal that published our articles was continuing to publish mother-blaming papers.)

As this example shows, it's not going to be easy to reduce mother-blaming, because it is so well-entrenched and takes so many forms and because it fits so well into our society's women-blaming, woman-hating ideology. But the struggle to overcome mother-blaming is well worth it, because what we stand to gain is improved relationships with our own mothers and with other women, as well as a clearer sense of the true causes of problems in individuals and in our society as a whole.

REFERENCES

Caplan, Paula J. (1989). *Don't blame mother: Mending the mother-daughter relationship*. New York: Harper and Row.

Caplan, Paula J. (1985). *The myth of women's masochism*. New York: Signet.

Caplan, Paula J. (1981). *Between women: Lowering the barriers*. Toronto: Personal Library.

Caplan, Paula J., & Hall-McCorquodale, Ian. (1985a). Mother-blaming in major clinical journals. *American Journal of Orthopsychiatry*, *55*, 345-353.

Caplan, Paula J., & Hall-McCorquodale, Ian. (1985b). The scapegoating of mothers: A call for change. *American Journal of Orthopsychiatry*, *55*, 610-613.

Chesler, Phyllis. (1972). *Women and madness*. New York: Avon.

Chodorow, Nancy. (1978). *The reproduction of mothering: Psychoanalysis and the sociology of gender*. Berkeley: University of California Press.

Dowling, Colette. (1988). *Perfect women*. New York: Summit Book.

Eichenbaum, Luise, & Orbach, Susie. (1988). *Between women*. New York: Viking Press.

Friday, Nancy. (1977). *My mother/ my self*. New York: Delacorte Press.

Masterson, James, Donworth, Richard, & Williams, Nancy. (1988). Extreme illness exaggeration in pediatric patients: A variant of Munchausen's by proxy? *American Journal of Orthopsychiatry*, *58*, 188-195.

Miller, J. B. (1984). Development of women's sense of self. *Work in Progress No. 12*. Wellesley: Stone Center Working Paper Series.

Miller, J. B. (1975). *Toward a new psychology of women*. Boston: Beacon Press.

Rich, Adrienne. (1976). *Of woman born: Motherhood as experience and institution*. New York: W.W. Norton and Co.

Siegel, Rachel Josefowitz. (1988). Women's 'dependency' in a male-centered value system: Gender-based values regarding dependency and independence. *Women and Therapy*, *7*, 113-123.

Siegel, Rachel Josefowitz. (1986). Antisemitism and sexism in stereotypes of Jewish women. In Doris Howard (Ed.), *Dynamics of feminist therapy*. New York: Haworth Press.

Surrey, J. (1985). The 'self-in-relation': A theory of women's development. *Work in Progress No. 13*. Wellesley: Stone Center Working Paper Series.

Mother-Hatred and Mother-Blaming: What Electra Did to Clytemnestra

Phyllis Chesler

Clytemnestra is a queen and the mother of three children: Iphegenia, Electra and Orestes. She is also the wife of Agamemnon and the sister of Helen (better known as Helen of Troy), who marries Agamemnon's brother Menelaus. As Homer's Iliad *tells us, Helen runs off with Paris of Troy. The two brothers (Agamemnon and Menelaus), mount an expedition to win Helen back and to punish Paris for seducing her. For more than a decade, these patriarchal warriors lay seige to Troy (perhaps a matriarchal civilization). Agamemnon tricks Clytemnestra into sending their daughter Iphegenia to "visit him"–ostensibly to betroth her to a great prince; in truth, her father intends to–and does kill her as a ritual sacrifice in order to win the war. Agamemnon captures and destroys Troy, kills or enslaves the people and sets sail for home. He brings his slave-mistress Cassandra (the Trojan visionary and princess) back home with him.*

His long-abandoned queen, Clytemnestra, stabs Agamemnon to death for having killed their daughter Iphegenia; in turn, Clytemnestra's son Orestes, and her daughter Electra, conspire to kill her for having murdered their father. Ultimately Orestes is exonerated by the goddess Athena who decides that husband-murder is a more serious crime than mother-killing or matricide.

Aeschylus has immortalized this tragedy of the house of Atreus in

---

Phyllis Chesler, PhD, is Associate Professor of Psychology at the College of Staten Island City University of New York, and author of *Women and Madness; Women, Money, and Power; About Men; Mothers on Trial: The Battle of Children and Custody;* and *Sacred Bond: The Legacy of Baby M*. She has been working for a decade on a book entitled *Woman's Inhumanity to Woman*.

The Oresteia *which consists of three plays: Agamemnon, The Libation Bearers, and The Eumenides.*

* * *

We are all Electra; certainly, we are all Electra's daughters. We, and our mothers before us, have all conspired in Clytemnestra's murder. We have all committed matricide. We are therefore all mistrustful of our own daughters. (Will they one day conspire against us?)

We symbolically kill our mothers—and our daughters—every day; daily we commit sororicide. We are not conscious of what we do; when challenged, we deny it. ("I didn't do it"; "I wasn't there"; "*She* did it first"; "I don't remember any of this"; "My back was to the wall," etc.)

Electra only "conspires" in her mother's murder; her brother, Orestes, acts directly. Orestes commits matricide and is haunted and pursued by the (female) Furies. Orestes demands a public reckoning, a jury, exoneration.

Electra kills her mother indirectly; she spurs Orestes on to action but her own hands are "clean." The Furies do not pursue Electra. But why not? Is Electra unaware, amnesiac about her role in her mother's murder? Electra's suffering is private, unknown.

Electra has her side of the story. She feels spurned and shamed by Clytemnestra. For Iphigenia, Clytemnestra was willing to kill her husband; for Electra, she cannot even keep up royal, patriarchal appearances. Electra is ashamed to be the daughter of a woman who is "loathed as she deserves; my love for a pitilessly slaughtered sister turns to (Orestes)." In Electra's eyes, Clytemnestra cares more for her lover-consort Aegisthus than for her two remaining blood-children.

Electra is jealous of Clytemnestra's involvement with Aegisthus, a mere "boyfriend." Perhaps Electra is furious that because of her mother, she, Electra, is no longer respectable or marriageable in patriarchal terms. Electra addresses her murdered father Agamemnon:

> We have been sold and go as wanderers because our mother bought herself a man. Now I am what a slave is, and Orestes lives outcast with his great properties while they go proud in the high style and luxury of what you worked to win . . . grant that I be more temperate of heart than my mother, that I act with purer hand.[1]

Indeed, how is it that Clytemnestra is so attached to one blood-daughter, Iphegenia, but not to her other blood-daughter, Electra? Something is already amiss. Electra is no Persephone or "Kore" to her mother; Clytemnestra is no Demeter or mother goddess, nor is she living in a matriarchy.[2] Is this what infuriates Electra—even more than her father's murder? Is Electra outraged because she, her mother's heiress, is being dishonored—and all for the sake of a mere man, a boyfriend? In terms of earlier matriarchal and/or goddess worshipping cultures, Clytemnestra's lover Aegisthus could easily have been a son-consort. As such, his existence would never demean or shame (matriarchal) family honor.

What is amiss between Electra and Clytemnestra is what they represent: the Fall. They live after goddess-murder or matricide has been committed, after daughters and mothers have already lost each other, after daughters have come to worship fathers and brothers more than mothers or sisters. As I wrote in *Women and Madness*, and in *About Men*, since that Fall, matricide, female infanticide and sororicide are daily psychological occurrences among the daughters of Man.

Patriarchy is literally *about* the male legal ownership of children. (We carry our father's names.) It is about how we as women, learn to expect less from men, but to trust and like men more than we trust or like other women, including our mothers, from whom we expect everything and whom we do not forgive for failing us, even slightly.

It's important to remember that most mothers in the patriarchy are, in Mary Daly's words, their daughter's "token torturers,"

---

1. Aeschylus. The Libation Bearers. *The Oresteia.*

2. A Kore is one's maiden-virgin self and one's adolescent or unmarried daughter.

whose job it is to break each girl's will, to bind the feet of her mind, so that she may serve Him on earth. Mothers—no longer Mother-Goddesses—also hope to keep their daughters at home with them forever: as their truest love, their step child, servant, scapegoat. Daughters are not meant to wander off too far away or to shine too brightly. Mothers do not nurture daughters to slay their fathers or their husbands or the male state—not even symbolically, for the sake of woman's honor or freedom.

Patriarchy is also about *women* not viewing or experiencing maternity or motherhood as an existentially or politically transcendent experience. For example, in 1977, and again in 1979, most publishers whom I approached with the idea for *With Child: A Diary of Motherhood* and for *Mothers on Trial: The Battle for Children and Custody* were "not interested." Men, women, and feminists in publishing all told me that motherhood had been "done." I asked by whom: Homer, Virgil, Dante, Cervantes, Shakespeare? Emphatically, they told me that women were not interested in hearing about pregnancy, childbirth or newborn motherhood; that they were more interested in equal pay for equal work; and that anyway, it was fathers, not mothers, who were custodially oppressed.

Many feminists (both heterosexual and lesbian, mothers and not-mothers) are strongly ambivalent about female biology, pregnancy, and childbirth; as if our own biology rather than patriarchy is persecuting us. I encountered strong hostility to the very *fact* of biological motherhood when I was involved in the Baby M custody battle. I write about such female, feminist attitudes in *Sacred Bond: The Legacy of Baby M* (1988).

In 1980, when I first started interviewing women about difficulties, conflict, betrayals suffered at the hands of other women, I discovered that, like Electra, women find it hard to recall the pain they have caused another woman. Women (especially feminists) were also very worried about the kind of research I was doing. One woman told me that "some of her best friends are women"; another said that since she "had a very good relationship with her mother that what I was saying couldn't be true"; a third said that "men will use this against us so you'd better not publish anything"; a fourth asked "Are you going to name names?" ("Name names? I'd probably have to name every woman who ever existed," I replied.)

We are all Electra, and we are also Clytemnestra. We do not remember conspiring psychologically in matricide; or in female infanticide. As feminists, we only spoke of ourselves as "sisters," as if our biological sisters or "best girl friends" in grade school had actually been "sisterly" in feminist or political terms. But what ever happened to our mothers? Despite the feminist emphasis on female role-models, were we feminists entirely without mothers? Did we need to reject our mothers as too patriarchal? Did we need to deny their existence in order to create our own? Did we need to keep quiet about this? Is there any connection between this and the "difficulty" (envy, competitiveness, ambivalence, fear) that so many women have with female leadership and achievement both within themselves and in others?

I am the mother of a biological son; I have no such biological relation to a daughter. As a feminist theoretician and activist, I do have a relationship to "daughters." Often, painfully, it is like Clytemnestra's relation to Electra. I write about this briefly in Dale Spender's excellent book, *For the Record: The Making and Meaning of Feminist Knowledge* (1985). I wrote this in response to Spender's essay on my first book, *Women and Madness* (1972).

Over the years, I (along with nearly every other feminist intellectual) have been pained and mystified to find how little of my theory-making or work is mentioned (agreed or disagreed with) in the works of other feminists, especially academics; and in the works of other feminists, especially anti-academics. So many feminists (like mothers? like daughters?) feel unnamed, forgotten, unappreciated, not fully credited by those whose lives and works we have envisioned, influenced, hoped for. (Is our hunger, our egotism, our need for support bottomless? Are we insatiable? Do we expect too much? Or too much from the "wrong" people?)

Why do feminists (like other ideologues) recognize our intellectual foremothers so selectively? Why recognize personal friends—but not 'enemies' or competitors? Why write women we don't "like" out of our history even as we are making it? Why is it easier for feminists to remember a dead foremother rather than a living one; a 'minor' rather than a 'major' one? Why such amnesia—if not in the service of psychological matricide?

If Franz Fanon (1963, 1965) and James Baldwin (1956, 1963)

could write about color-prejudice among colonized Blacks; if Albert Memmi (1971, 1973) and Primo Levi (1986) could write about anti-semitism among Jews; then how can I *not* describe woman-hating among women? Would women, especially feminist psychologists and therapists, have any problem understanding that women have internalized patriarchal woman-hatred? That women are not necessarily "sisterly" within the male-dominated family; or outside the home, situated in different social classes, races, religions, etc.

Women, after all, marry and comfort the very men who wage war against *other* women (and men); women cook their food, prop them up. Women deny that they are complicit, refuse to acknowledge it, afterwards say that they "didn't know" what was going on—perhaps just as good Germans once said they "didn't know" what was going on. . . .

Both women and men—that means me and you—have an easier time blaming Mommy, than blaming Daddy; have a much harder time engaging in symbolic father-murder (patricide) or brother-murder, than in mother-murder, daughter-murder or sister-murder. Like Electra, we too forget what we've said and done; and we're not necessarily haunted by the Furies afterwards. We underestimate our power to wound, paralyze, destroy another woman. I want to share some selections from my work in progress on this subject. Begun in 1980, it's a melancholy meditation entitled *Woman's Inhumanity to Woman*. I begin with letters from an archetypal patriarchal mother to an archetypal patriarchal daughter.

A MOTHER ADDRESSES HER DAUGHTER

Oh Daughter! It is bitter to be the Mother of daughters, it is far easier with sons. Your smiles were all for your father, none for me who bore you. When you couldn't wind me around your finger, you had no use for me. Your smile terrified me. I knew you didn't mean it. For me you only had contempt. You thought that any woman who was as unhappy as I was had only herself to blame.

You wanted. You didn't want. You acted as if it was up to you. Where did you get such an idea from? Surely not from me. I told your father that if I didn't knock some sense into you you'd never get to have sons of your own. Who would protect you if not me? I did for you what my mother did for me.

You thought me a monster, a stepmother, a witch. You hated me. You wished me dead. You denounced me, you denounced me. You hated my life, yet you imagined yourself in my place. How could I trust you with any truths? You'd only run with them to your father for a trinket or two. The two of you thought me too old-fashioned, too bitter, a nag, a fool, every one's workhorse, not to be honored or obeyed, or helped. Definitely not worthy of love.

Oh Daughter mine! I tried to wash my hands of you but I couldn't. You were my flesh and blood. I never stopped trying to teach you; you never learned a thing. Whenever you got into trouble you blamed me, not your laughing father. You wanted to remain his laughing girl and you expected me to clean up your mess. What else did I have to do anyway? And when I did, you despised me as much as when I refused to. You still saved all your smiles for men, for strangers.

A DAUGHTER ADDRESSES HER MOTHER

Oh Mother, was it tenderness that drove you to prefer your sons, your "prettier" daughters, your most light-skinned children to me? Tenderness that had you pull my hair, slap my face, call me bad names, tell me I had only myself to blame, tell me that I was bad and that you were washing your hands of the whole mess?

Oh Mother, was it tenderness that drove you to order me about as if my very presence filled you with disgust? Tenderness that made you angry at my budding breasts, drove you to bind my feet, cut out my clitoris, flatten all my flesh, order me to keep my eyes lowered, my hair and all my smiles hidden?

Oh Mother, was it tender to tell me nothing of what was to come and what it meant: about marriage, motherhood, death? Tender not to whisper to me even once about resistance or escape, about honor and freedom?

Oh Mother! And when my husband beat me and left me for his mistress, when I and my children were huddled together on the floor, cold and hungry, where were you? Did you arrive with kisses, a pot of soup, a shawl, an offer that I return home with you?

"You made your bed, now lie in it" you said and also "Your father never left me! You must have done something to provoke that man—now undo it if you know what's good for you" and "You can't come and live with us, the house is too crowded, my health isn't what it once was, I have responsibilities toward your brothers' children." My mess was my own you said, I had created it, not you. You weren't about to wash my behind for me, you'd washed your hands of me long ago.

* * *

UNTITLED

A mother yells at her daughter. Her face grows huge, red. Her voice—as sharp and as flat as a knife—balloons out of control until it has her daughter completely surrounded.

"Who do you think you are?"

"How dare you?"

"Are you mocking me? Don't you ever talk to me in that tone of voice or I'll kill you myself with my bare hands. I'll show you what it is to talk back you ugly fat lazy dumb idiot . . ."

The Medusa Head shows herself to women only. Only a daughter carries the memory of Her corrosive green fury. Not only has she lost Her mother's love: she is also about to be killed. Her mother won't save her: how can she? Her mother and her murderer are one and the same.

Is this where we learn to misjudge or at least to withstand emotional abuse from men? Do we think that men are like our mothers, that they really love us, that their rage will "blow over," that we are not really being injured?

Do we so fear becoming as impotent, as tyrannical as our mothers that we are willing to rush headlong into the arms of the male tyrants, readied for them by our mothers, but feeling sufficiently safe with them because at least they are not women? Ah, but this flight into the arms of the Godfather is also how we vindicate our mothers. Our usefulness to tyranny, our refusal to rebel, is proof of our mother's ability to tame a human being into utter servility.

This is also the only way we are allowed to keep our mothers with us forever: hidden inside our own characters, alike like two peas in a pod, twins, or sisters, ageless, eternal, never-changing.

Does male fury also comfort us by reminding us of our mothers, of paradise lost and gone wild, jungled, snaked, a place suddenly too dangerous for us as women to roam in unaccompanied by men?

* * *

UNTITLED

What have they done to us? What have we done to ourselves? Each woman knows that if she sides with another woman against a man or against men's laws that "the men" will come for her, in broad daylight and in utter darkness, knows that they can hand-cuff, interrogate, rape, imprison her, knows that she might grow slowly mad and be forgotten.

A woman is brave when she knows what can be done to her but, despite such knowledge, helps other women anyway. A woman is brave *because* she chooses to withstand terror. A woman is as brave as she is willing to do combat with the "good little girl" within, the voice that tells her not to help, you'll get in trouble, you'll get caught, you'll be sorry, the grownups will punish you, they'll make you cry, *no one will like you*. . . .

Every woman (me too), has already been branded. We are unnaturally vulnerable to humiliation and threats of punishment.

But other women are only as safe as I am brave. I am only as safe as other women are brave.

Women are safe only if we are all brave.

PHYLLIS CHESLER'S SUGGESTED BIBLIOGRAPHY ON WOMAN'S INHUMANITY TO WOMAN

Aeschylus (1953). *Oresteia: Agamemnon; the Libation bearers; the Eumenides*. Translated and introduced by Richard Lattimore. Chicago: The University of Chicago Press.

Alta (1974). *Momma: A start on all the untold stories*. Oakland, CA: Times Change Press.

Arcana, Judith (1979). *Our Mothers' daughters*. Berkeley, CA: Shameless Hussey Press.

Ascher, Carol; DeSalvo, Louise; Ruddick, Sara (1984). *Between women*. Boston: Beacon Press.

Atwood, Margaret (1988). *Cat's Eye*. NY: Doubleday.

Baldwin, James (1956). *Giovanni's room*. NY: Dell.

Baldwin, James (1963). *The fire next time*. NY: Dell.

Bernard, Jessie (1974). *The future of motherhood*. NY: Dial Press.

Bernikow, Louise (1987). *Among women*. NY: Harmony Books.

Briles, Judith (1987). *Woman to woman: From sabotage to support*. NY: New Horizon Press.

Caplan, Paula J. (1981). Between women, lowering the barriers. Toronto: Personal Library.

Caplan, Paula J. (1989). *Don't blame mother: Mending the mother-daughter relationship*. NY: Harper & Row.

Chernin, Kim (1985). *The hungry self: Women, eating, and identity*. NY: Times Books.

Chesler, Phyllis (1972). *Women and madness*. NY: Doubleday; (1989) NY: Harcourt, Brace, Jovanovich.

Chesler, Phyllis (1978). *About men*. NY: Simon & Schuster; (1990) NY: Harcourt, Brace, Jovanovich.

Chesler, Phyllis (1979). *With child: A diary of motherhood*. NY: Lippincott & Crowell; (1980) NY: Berkeley.

Chesler, Phyllis (1986). *Mothers on trial: The battle for children and custody*. NY: McGraw-Hill; (1987) Seattle: Seal Press.

Chester, Phyllis (1988). Sacred bond: The legacy of baby M. NY: Times Books; (1989) NY: Vintage.

Conlon, Faith; da Silva, Rachel; Wilson, Barbara, (Eds.) (1985). *The things that divide us*. Seattle, Washington: Seal Press.

Davidson, Cathy N. and Broner, E. M. (Eds.) (1980). *The lost tradition, mothers and daughters in literature*. NY: Frederick Unger Publ. Co.

Dworkin, Andrea (1983). *Right-wing women*. NY: Perigee.

Dworkin, Andrea (1974). *Woman hating*. NY: E.P. Dutton.

dell'Olio, Anselma (1970). Divisiveness and self-destruction in the women's movement. Speech given at the Congress to Unite Women, New York City.

Eichenbaum, Luise and Orbach, Susie (1988). *Between women: Love, envy, and competition in women's friendships*. NY: Viking Penguin.

Fanon, Frantz (1963). *The wretched of the earth*. NY: Grove Press.

Fanon, Frantz (1965). *A dying colonialism*. NY: Grove Press.

Flax, Jane (1978). The conflict between nurturance and autonomy in mother-daughter relationships and within feminism. *Feminist Studies*, *4*(2).

Freeman, Jo (1972). The tyranny of structurelessness, *Second Wave 2*, No. 1; reprinted in *MS Magazine*, July, 1973.

Hammer, Signe (1976). *Daughters and mothers: Mothers and daughters*. NY: Signet.

Homer (1988). *iliad*. NY: Penguin.

Hooks, Bell (1981). *Ain't I a woman: Black women and feminism*. Boston: South End Press.

Hooks, Bell (1984). *Feminist theory from margin to center*. Boston: South End Press.

Joseph, Gloria I. and Lewis, Jill (1981). *Common differences: Conflicts in black and white feminist perspectives*. NY: Anchor Books. Especially the essay entitled, "Mothers, daughters, and feminism."

Koppelman, Susan (Ed.) (1985). *Between mothers and daughters: Stories across a generation*. NY: The Feminist Press.

Levi, Primo (1986). *The drowned and the saved*. NY: Summit Books.

Lobel, Kerry (Ed.) (1986). *Naming the violence*. Seattle: Seal Press.

Lorde, Audre (1984). *Scratching the surface, some notes on barriers to women and loving*. Trumansburg, NY: The Crossing Press.

Margolies, Eva (1985). *The best of friends, the worst of enemies: Women's hidden power over women*. NY: The Dial Press.

Meigs, Mary (1983). *The Medusa head*. Vancouver, Canada: Talon Books.

Memmi, Albert (1971). *Portrait of a Jew*. NY: Viking Press.

Memmi, Albert (1973). *The liberation of the Jew*. NY: Viking Press.

Millet, Kate (1974). *Flying*. NY: Knopf.

Millet, Kate (1977). *Sita*. NY: McGraw-Hill.

Millet, Kate (1979). *The basement: Meditations on a human sacrifice*. NY: Simon & Schuster.

Miner, Valerie and Longino, Helen (1987). *Competition, a feminist taboo?* NY: The Feminist Press.

Raymond, Janice G. (1986). *A passion for friends: Towards a philosophy of female affection*. Boston: Beacon Press.

Rich, Adrienne (1976). *Of woman born*. NY: W.W. Norton & Co.

Rubin, Lillian B. (1985). *Just friends: The role of friendship in our lives*. NY: Harper & Row.

Russ, Joanna (1985). *Magic mommas, trembling sisters, puritans & perverts*. Trumansburg, NY: The Crossing Press.

Smith, Barbara (Ed.) (1983). *Home bills: A black feminist anthology*. NY: Kitchen Table Women of Color Press.

Smith-Rosenberg, Carroll (1975). The female world of love and ritual: Relationships between women in nineteenth century America. *Signs: Journal of Women in Culture and Society*, *1*, 1-29.

Spender, Dale (1985). *For the record: The making and meaning of feminist knowledge*. London: Women's Press.

Wittig, Monique (1987). *Across the acheron*. Translated from the French by David LeVay in collaboration with Margaret Crossland. London: Peter Owen Publishers. U.S. distributor: Chester Springs, PA: DuFour Editions.

Mother-Blaming and Clinical Theory

Janet L. Surrey

While preparing for the panel at which this paper was presented, I began to review my own history, personal and professional, and my own ongoing journey into and out of "mother-blaming." My professional work has had major impact on my deepening realization of the necessity for building and strengthening my connections with other women. Slowly, and not without considerable difficulty, I have begun to work on strengthening my relationship with my mother. It continues to astound me how little professional or cultural support there has been to help develop the empathy, endurance, acceptance, forgiveness and other relational competencies (in addition to anger, assertiveness, and confrontation) that allow us to move through and beyond the frustration, hurt, and pain in this relationship without resorting to "mother-blaming" strategies.

I recalled today a watershed moment in my own life. In the context of my first therapy relationship (with a male therapist), on a snowy night in my junior year in college, the thought entered my mind: "My mother is neurotic." At that moment I crossed a dividing line. I began to assume an "objective," labeling, "blaming through diagnosis" stance, stepping out of relationship into a seemingly safer, more comfortable place. Today I can appreciate my need for help in expressing and clarifying troubling feelings and perceptions arising in this relationship which were obstacles to my growth. What frightens and angers me today is the acceptable clini-

---

Janet L. Surrey, PhD, is Research Associate at the Stone Center, Wellesley College and Director of Psychological Services at the Adult Outpatient Department, McLean Hospital, Belmont, MA. She is Instructor in Psychology, with the Department of Psychiatry, at the Harvard Medical School.

cal strategy of blaming and pathologizing mothers' behavior and how I internalized this.

My professional and clinical training further developed such culturally-sanctioned thinking and use of "blaming" formulations and diagnoses. I recently collected out-patient case reports I had written over the past ten years and listed some of the adjectives I had used to describe patients' mothers: "engulfing," "controlling," "intrusive," "enmeshed," "seductive," "overprotective," or, on the other hand, "narcissistic," "critical," "cold," "unavailable," "unempathic," "distant," "depleted," "ineffective," or "depriving." Stiver (1986) has written on the need for a language of "care" rather than such language of judgment and distancing.

I hope we can all begin to look together at the contributions our clinical and developmental theories make to such mother-blaming strategies. As clinicians we have important contributions to make; both to our clients and in raising the questions with other clinicians in whatever settings we work.

"Consciousness raising" as to the existence and prevalence of "mother-blaming" is a troubling and confusing process. We've all been clinically trained to take the perspective of the child, to view psychopathology as arising in the mother-child relationship and to value a model of growth described with separation-individuation as a primary goal. Such a model grows out of a "gender-blind," androcentric theory of human development (Gilligan, 1982).

Our work at the Stone Center, Wellesley College, has focused on articulating a developmental and clinical model based on women's experience and building on women's strengths. This model stresses the importance of growth within and through connection. The goal of relational development is described as authenticity within connectedness, which arises through the building of mutually-empathic, mutually-empowering relationships (Miller, 1986, Surrey, 1985, 1987). Separation from mother is not the primary focus, but rather the growing capacity to build and enlarge old and new relationships and relational contexts. Growing in connectedness represents the ideal of relational growth for women, (Jordan, 1986, Miller, 1984).

Jean Baker Miller (1985) has described five psychological outcomes for all participants of mutually-enhancing, growth-promoting relationships. These are increased zest or vitality, empowerment to act within and beyond the relationship, knowledge of self and other, self-worth, and a desire for more connection.

We are all aware of the degree to which our culture does not support and promote such mutual, nonhierarchical relationships. We all suffer from the failures of our culture to provide relational contexts which sustain and facilitate growth in connection (Kaplan, 1984, Stiver, 1986). Women's lives are riddled with disconnections and relational violations, yet it is our connections that sustain us and build reservoirs of strength, worth, and empowerment. As clinicians we have special responsibility for studying and facilitating healthy relational processes, and for understanding the larger cultural and systemic factors influencing women's relationships.

Such a relational model has important clinical implications for understanding and working with mother-daughter relationships. First, we need to let ourselves "see" and name the strengths emerging from mother-daughter relationships. We have been so trained in negative, pathology-focused descriptions, it is very helpful to work with a developmental model that names and builds on relational strengths. New research is beginning to suggest that healthy relational development between mothers and daughters over the life cycle can involve increasing mutuality, authenticity, and connection. This represents an ideal which may in fact be difficult to achieve in a patriarchal culture which encourages separation of mothers and daughters. We need to carefully describe the obstacles to such development and to begin to explore the diverse and illuminating experiences of different groups of women.

Second, if we hold this alternative relational vision of development, how would our therapeutic goals and strategies differ? When I speak of facilitating healthy connection, not separation, between mothers and daughters, I am only beginning to see the profound ways this might change my actual clinical work. It is always striking to me how much difficulty traditional clinicians have with this notion, as though connection seems to evoke images of unhealthy attachment or "symbiosis."

Third, if we suggest "mutual empathy" as a goal of relational development, how would we work to build empathy for mothers? Karen Howe (1988) has suggested that a woman's capacity for empathy for her mother may represent an important aspect of psychological development for women. Working to build empathy (this is not "liking" or "taking care of" or being "nice") involves facilitating complex cognitive-emotional capacities for enlarged "self-with-other" experiences, rather than self-other differentiation. Such capacities may be more complex and creative than the cognitive-affective stages of separate self/"ego" development. A whole new language and understanding is necessary. For example, Belenky, Clinchy, Goldberger, and Tarule (1986) have suggested "connected knowing" as a description of such relational growth.

These are a few of the many new and exciting challenges for clinical theory, research, and practice. I'd like to support Jean Baker Miller's (1985) suggestion that we declare a five-year moratorium on mother-blaming in order to be more creative and thoughtful in our clinical formulations and psychotherapy. It is time to embark together on this important "consciousness raising" process. This may lead us to examine how mother-blaming contributes to the psychological roots of the nuclear and ecological crises, and to the disregard and disrespect for "mother earth."

REFERENCES

Belenky, M.B., Clinchy, B.M., Goldberger, N.R. and Tarule, J.M. (1986) *Women's ways of knowing: The development of self, voice, and mind.* N.Y.: Basic Books.

Gilligan, C. (1982) *In a different voice*. Cambridge: Harvard University Press.

Howe, K. (1988) *Telling our mother's story*. In R. Unger (Ed.) *Representations: Social constructions of gender*. N.Y.: Baywood Publishing Co.

Jordan, J. (1986) The meaning of mutuality. *Work in Progress*, No. 23. Wellesley: Stone Center Working Paper Series.

Kaplan, A. (1984) The self-in-relation: Implications for depression in women. *Work in Progress*, No. 14. Wellesley: Stone Center Working Paper Series.

Miller, J.B. (1976) *Toward a new psychology of women*. Boston: Beacon Press.

Miller, J.B. (1984) The development of women's sense of self. *Work in Progress*, No. 12. Wellesley: Stone Center Working Paper Series.

Miller, J.B. (1985) Women's development in connection. Unpublished paper presented at the Stone Center, Wellesley College.

Miller, J.B. (1986) What do we mean by relationships? *Work in Progress*, No. 22. Wellesley: Stone Center Working Paper Series.

Stiver, I. (1986) The meaning of care: Reframing treatment models. *Work in Progress*, No. 20. Wellesley: Stone Center Working Paper Series.

Surrey, J. (1985) The self-in-relation: A theory of women's development. *Work in Progress*, No. 13. Wellesley: Stone Center Working Paper Series.

Surrey, J. (1987) Relationship and empowerment. *Work in Progress*, No. 30. Wellesley: Stone Center Working Paper Series.

Old Women as Mother Figures

Rachel Josefowitz Siegel

AGEISM AND MOTHER BLAMING

The rejection and oppression of old women as mother figures can best be understood in the context of our culture's pervasively sexist attitudes toward aging. Unlike other prejudices, the bias against old women is aimed at a population that will be our own reference group if we but live long enough. The avoidance of old women includes elements of avoiding our own aging. Age bias and mother blaming affect all old women, even women who have never been mothers. Black women and Asian women have told me that old women are treated with respect in their communities. In Latino families, the role of matriarch does not seem to evoke overt ambivalence. Among immigrant groups, including some Jewish communities, the treatment of old women reflects generational tensions that are caused by the differing values of separate cultures (Siegel, 1986). Old immigrant women are often perceived as holding on to or enforcing the patterns of the country of origin; they may in fact not wish to assimilate to the host country in ways that seem necessary to younger members of immigrant families. The effect of ethnicity on attitudes toward old women needs to be explored more fully (Markides & Mindel, 1987), as well as the effects of color, class, political ideology, sexual preference, physical ability and economic circumstance. Among old women, old lesbians have been the first to speak out and to write about their experience of aging in

---

Rachel Josefowitz Siegel, MSW, is a 65 year old writer, lecturer and feminist therapist in private practice in Ithaca, NY. She thanks Theo Sonderegger and Jeanne Adleman for sharing ideas on this topic while presenting together at the Association for Women in Psychology annual conference 1987, and the American Orthopsychiatric Association annual conference 1988.

a sexist, heterosexist, and ageist society (Adelman, 1986; Copper, 1988; MacDonald, 1986; MacDonald & Rich, 1983).

When I talk about old women at conferences and workshops, I invariably hear some of the following remarks: I'm not *old*; I don't feel *old*; I don't look *old*; You don't look *old*; don't call me *old*; why do you call yourself *old*; you don't look 64; 64 is not *old*; Why do you use that word? *old* is a dirty word; *old* is an ugly word.

When an old woman walks into the room, she reminds us of who we might become. She could be our mother, she could be our grandmother—she is not me, not us. *Old woman* is *mother* and *mother* is *old*; *old woman* is other. *Old woman* is a role, an image, a stereotype—she is not a person. *Old woman* is Crone, Old Witch, Old Hag, Over the Hill, Old Girl, Nice Old Lady, Role Model. *Old woman* is not me; *old woman* is not what I want to be.

I use the word *old* deliberately, in order to reclaim it. Having learned from Black women and men that *black is beautiful*, I would apply that lesson to *old*, using the word to desensitize us from the fearsome connotations of *old*. If we are to love our aging bodies, we can start by changing the language and begin to see that *old is beautiful*.

When an old woman or mother shows any signs of power or competence, she is perceived as controlling, all-powerful. When she shows any infirmities, she is perceived as needy, demanding, overly dependent.

When she wants to set limits on her ever-expected nurturing, she is perceived as cold, withholding, distancing; when she wants to get close enough for companionship or intimacy, she is perceived as intrusive, a social burden.

When she communicates less directly or overtly than younger women, she is seen as manipulative; when she expresses her needs assertively she is seen as demanding.

When she appears as a sexual person, she is perceived as ludicrous or embarrassing; when her sexuality does not show, she is perceived as disapproving of our sexuality and/or sexually dried up.

No woman can grow up in our society without learning to "pass," attempting to look and feel younger. This kind of learning starts at a very early age. In adolescence we learn that the little girl look and little girl talk are considered sexy. As we get older, the pressure to appear younger increases. Copper (1988, p. 47) said it very well:

> Somewhere in our fifties, the mass of anxieties about age, and the increase of rejection and invisibility we experience, becomes critical. This is often the time when our trained inability to identify with women older than ourselves reaches its climax. Old women cannot rely upon the midlife woman as her ally. The midlife woman, in her rage and fear, may unconsciously discharge all kinds of covert aggression against the old woman as the personification of what is threatening her.

The ambivalent mother-transference that is directed at middle-aged women becomes more frequent and more pronounced as women get older. Ageism, the fear of aging, and the fear of death now combine with unresolved feelings toward mothers and mother figures to confront the old woman with painful rejections, avoidances and invisibilities.

WE ARE NOT YOUR MOTHERS

The treatment of old women as mother figures is intertwined and blurred with the tension and friction that exist between actual mothers and daughters. Let's try to separate this tangled weave of biases against old women, and let's keep in mind that old women are not our mothers. We can change our negative attitudes and behaviors into a positive appreciation of old women and mothers, if we begin by acknowledging the powerful feelings that emerge when we focus on this topic.

We need to ask ourselves, as MacDonald (1986) has asked, why the oppression of old women has so far escaped the lens of feminist scrutiny. Why are old women practically invisible and unheard in our society, even in feminist writings and feminist gatherings? Why is the silence surrounding old women still unquestioned, when we have so effectively broken the taboos of silence surrounding other oppressions such as incest, battering and sexual harassment? Why is it so hard to love old women and to treat them with the same level of respect and empathy that we expect to receive from them?

The answers are complex. A variety of factors are involved, and I shall attempt to name some of them.

In part, it is because we have all learned to equate being lovable and successful with youth, health, and well-being, and we have learned to compete in these areas. Each of us has attempted to separate herself from her own aging and from the women who represent old age, and has thereby participated on some level in the avoidance and oppression of old women. Since the scapegoating of mothers is so deeply ingrained in society (Caplan & Hall-McCorquodale, 1985a, 1985b) and in our own psyches, we automatically perceive old women as mother-like conveyors and messengers of patriarchal culture; we now reject the old woman along with the patriarchal message. The old woman reminds us of our own areas of neediness and dependency which we have learned to dislike and to disclaim. She reminds us of our own mortality, our vulnerability, the limits of our own power. We are afraid of being swallowed up by her present or potential need for our assistance.

In addition, our own need for positive, female role models is so great that we idealize and expect perfection of those old women who have achieved some measure of feminist awareness or some level of worldly power or success.

Last, but by no means least, is the fact that we learned at a very early age to dismiss the words of our mothers and to listen to our fathers (Robbins, 1983). We have forgotten, or never realized, that the power and wisdom of old women could seriously threaten the patriarchy if it were valued and accessible to women of all ages. We may also have internalized our fathers' fears about the power of cross-generational alliances between women, which could truly change the world.

A combination of some or all of these factors are at work every time an old woman or an elderly mother is stereotyped, avoided, maligned, silenced, or ignored. If we were to ask the same questions about why the oppression of mothers has escaped the lens of feminist scrutiny, the questions and the answers would be similar; our attitudes, feelings, and behaviors towards old women and towards mothers are nearly alike. The very real and often painful issues between individual daughters and mothers need also be discussed from the mother's perspective and deserve a separate presentation, but we must remember that old women are not our mothers, nor do they wish to be.

Placing the problem in a here and now context, I am not your mother! I am not the mother who contributed to limiting the development of your full potential by teaching you patriarchal messages. I must surely have done some of this with my own daughter in my attempts to be a socially acceptable good mother, but I did not do this to you when you were growing up. If I am doing it now, it is not as your mother; it is because you and I, like all of us, are still the products of a patriarchal society, and the unlearning is never finished.

I am not the mother you wish you'd had, who can liberate and validate you with my feminist awareness and ideology. We can empower each other as allies and as equals, but we do not need to call this a mother/daughter interaction.

SOUNDING LIKE A MOTHER

How can I tell you about the treatment of old women as mother-figures, without 'sounding like a mother' to you? and why is 'sounding like a mother' a synonym for guilt-tripping? If we turn that around, how can you hear me without emotionally responding like a daughter to me? and how come 'sounding like a daughter' lacks similar negative connotations? Copper (1988) said: "Old women who find fault are seen as Bad Mothers. They are not forgiven, and they are ostracized" (p. 18). How can we, old women, name our oppression without being perceived as finding fault and without being ostracized? And is it our job to find the answer to this dilemma, are we, like other oppressed women, expected to carry the entire burden of making this relationship work? As we get older, that burden becomes heavier, our backs become weaker, we are tired, and we are angry.

Let me tell you of a woman in her late fifties who attended a workshop. In one of the first exercises, groups of three were asked to create a tableau, placing three other people into a living sculpture. Our friend was placed standing in an angry pose, pointing a punitive finger at a man and woman who were gleefully embracing and fucking on the floor in front of her. There was nothing she could say or do during or after the exercise that did not make her look and sound even more like the fault-finding figure she had been made to represent. Having been treated stereotypically, she became the stereotype. Furthermore, the woman had come to the seminar with her own agenda, which had nothing to do with finding fault in others. She was seriously diverted from attending to her own goals.

Old women and mothers are often exposed to similar or less overt assumptions of fault finding that divert us from our own issues and leave us painfully trapped in no-win situations. The automatic assumption of fault finding is often associated with the daughter's or younger woman's deep seated sense of herself as being or wanting to be central to the mother's or old woman's universe. If the daughter is at the center of her mother's psyche, then the old woman's mood, expression, or behavior cannot possibly have other sources or directions. The younger person assumes that 'she is doing it to me' rather than 'she is doing it for her own reasons.'

ROLE MODELS AND TUNING OUT

On the opposite side of fault finding, mothers and old women are frequently expected to be role models of strength and competence, even under the most trying circumstances. Our vulnerability is threatening to the women who look up to us. When this happens we feel deprived of companionship and support. The following episode happened to Joanne, a therapist in her sixties, who was going through a family crisis. Joanne could not repress her tears as she talked with a younger friend and colleague about her situation. Her friend interrupted her to say: "You know, Joanne, I see you as such a role model, it really upsets me when you cry." Joanne felt that she had to hide her vulnerability or lose her friend.

In my support group for women over sixty, we have shared similar episodes of avoidance or of being tuned out by younger women, especially when we tried to talk about death and dying, and about aging or physical disabilities (Siegel, in press). At the same time we are expected to listen empathically when younger people wish to talk about the difficulties of their stage of life.

Other incidents of rejection and distancing occur in the workplace or in women's organizations. A sixty-five year old academic tells of painful exclusions by her younger colleagues. Having fought hard to bring more women into the university, and having continued to fight for their tenure and promotions, she now finds these women dismissing her wisdom and leaving her out of positions of power. They are tuning her out in the same way that we tune out "mother noises."

AMBIVALENCE CAUSED BY THE 'GOOD ENOUGH MOTHER' CONCEPT

The 'good enough mother' (Winnicott, 1953) concept, so widely accepted even by feminists, is probably at the core of the ambivalence toward mothers and mother figures in late life. We need to look at the 'good enough mother' concept and the mother/daughter connection in light of a society that is not good enough to women, children, old people, people of color, and poor people. Our male-centered, patriarchal world provides a not 'good enough environment' for human beings, by placing the lowest priority on nurturing and care-giving, while the highest priority goes to financial growth and preparations for war.

In this not 'good enough society,' old women are still expected to nurture, to make others feel better, without making any one feel 'dependent' or guilty, even when our own capabilities are waning and our time and energy are exhausted. We are expected to provide 'good enough mothering' way beyond the age of mothering. In times of crisis, or during extended periods of need, we are expected to be the unpaid care-givers of choice, providing essential services for our parents, partners, and even adult children and grandchildren. When we are not powerful or smart enough to undo or make up for the harm caused by social, economic, or other deprivations and oppressions, or when we no longer have the energy and stamina we used to have, we are blamed and considered 'not good enough.' As old women retreat from a lifetime of care giving and endless nurturing, by choice or of necessity, as we set even minor limits on our constant availability, the rage against us intensifies. The fall from 'not good enough' is equal to the fall from perfect mother to wicked witch. We are judged by patriarchal standards that assume unlimited and unending availability.

Miller (1976) has pointed out that women are expected to provide all of the nurturing and caring functions of society without any recognition or validation of the efforts involved.

None of us can ever hope to meet all of those needs adequately, nor can we ever hope to compensate each other for the oppressive conditions that the patriarchy imposes on us. We have all made mistakes, mothers and daughters have at times demanded too much from each other and received too little, or demanded too little and provided too much. Both have been the oppressor and the oppressed. The middle aged care-giving daughter may feel guilt and self-blame for her own limitations, or she may feel anticipatory anxiety and resentment even before the care is needed. Is it easier then for the daughter to accuse the elderly mother for making demands that feel excessive than to get in touch with her own discomfort? Such situations evoke powerful and uncomfortable feelings of deprivation and injustice between mothers and daughters. Rarely are these feelings directed at the men in our lives who demand too much or provide too little, and whose absence or unavailability contribute significantly to the burdens we carry.

If we are to get beyond this impasse we must learn to accept the limits of women's ability to meet all needs, and to forgive ourselves and our mothers.

WHERE ARE THE REAL DEFICITS IN NURTURING AND CARE-GIVING?

It is time for us to turn our attention toward the fathers and the institutions that they control. Not only are individual fathers, sons and brothers rarely available to provide the kind of care that women of all ages continue to provide, but our male-dominated economic and political system does not address these needs realistically. Dinnerstein (1976) pointed out that our resentments would be less focused on mothers if men shared parenting tasks. This would be even more accurate if the care giving tasks at all stages of life were met more adequately by the institutions that men control. We can identify the real deficits in nurturing and care-giving if we but measure the paucity of funds for providing vital human services at both ends of the life cycle.

We will be miles ahead in our struggle toward a 'good enough environment' for all human beings in our society when we stop looking for 'good enough mothers,' start including old women in our alliances, and begin to treat each other as equals and individuals instead of as mythical, exaggerated mother figures.

REFERENCES

Adelman, M. (Ed.) (1986). *Long time passing: Lives of older lesbians*. Boston, MA: Alyson Press.

Caplan, P.J. & Hall-McCorquodale, I. (1985a). Mother-blaming in major clinical journals. *American Journal of Orthopsychiatry, 55*, 345-353.

Caplan, P.J. & Hall-McCorquodale, I. (1985b). The scapegoating of mothers: A call for change. *American Journal of Orthopsychiatry, 55*, 610-613.

Copper, B. (1988). *Over the hill: Reflections on ageism between women*. Freedom, CA: The Crossing Press.

Dinnerstein, D. (1976). *The mermaid and the minotaur: Sexual arrangements and human malaise*. New York, NY: Harper & Row.

MacDonald, B. (1986). Outside the sisterhood: Ageism in Women's Studies. In Alexander, J., Berrow, D., Domitrovich, L., Donnelly, M., & McLean, C. (Eds.) *Women and aging: An anthology by women*. Corvalis, OR: CALYX BOOKS.

MacDonald, B., & Rich, C. (1983). *Look me in the eye: Old women, aging and ageism*. San Francisco, CA Spinsters, Ink.

Markides, K. S. & Mindel, C. H. (1987). *Aging & ethnicity*. Newbury Park, CA: SAGE Publications.

Miller, J. B. (1976). *Toward a new psychology of women*. Boston, MA: Beacon Press.

Robbins, J. H. (1983). A legacy of weakness. In J. H. Robbins & R. J. Siegel (Eds.), *Women changing therapy: New assessments, values and strategies in feminist therapy*. New York: Haworth Press.

Siegel, R.J. (1986). Antisemitism and sexism in stereotypes of Jewish women. In D. Howard (Ed.) *The Dynamics of Feminist Therapy*. New York: Haworth Press.

Siegel, R. J. (in press). We are not your mothers. In E. Rosenthal (Ed.) *Women, aging and ageism*. New York: Haworth Press.

Winnicott, D. W. (1953). Transitional objects and transitional phenomena: A study of the first not-me possession. *The International Journal of Psychoanalysis, 34*, 89-97.

[illegible]

REFERENCES

[illegible]

SECTION IV: DIVERSITY

Caught Between Two Worlds: The Impact of a Child on a Lesbian Couple's Relationship

Eloise Stiglitz

More and more lesbians are claiming their right to motherhood through the courts, adoption and alternative insemination. While much has been written about the impact of lesbian parents on the psychological, emotional, and sexual development of children (Bozett, 1987; Harris & Turner, 1985/1986), little has been written about how children impact their lesbian parents' relationship.

From personal and clinical experience, I noticed that a seemingly disproportionate number of lesbians who were in committed relationships, who had spent months or years discussing and planning for a child, who were psychologically and socio-culturally aware, were ending their relationships by the time their child was one to three years old. While this did not hold true for all lesbian couples

Eloise Stiglitz, PhD, is Director of Student Affairs in the Department of Clinical Psychology at Antioch/New England and in private practice in Keene, NH.

The author acknowledges Joan F. Levinson for her editing and critical comments during the development of this paper.

who had a child, the numbers were higher than for the heterosexual couples with whom I had contact. Counter to the lesbian lore that lesbians "should" fare well with having a child because of their extensive planning and their tendency to have more flexible and non-traditional roles, these couples were struggling to survive. Two nurturing women caring for a child in a context of a supportive women's community was a wonderful idea whose time had come. Or was it a myth?

What does happen to a lesbian couple's dynamics when a child is introduced into the system? Do lesbian couples react differently to the birth of their first child than do heterosexual couples? Because little exists in the literature to answer these questions directly, I sought answers through an examination of related literature and by sending out questionnaires to both lesbian and heterosexual couples.

One of my basic questions was whether lesbians and heterosexuals react differently to the birth of their first child. To begin understanding what impact having a child has on these couples, I started with the largest body of available information: literature on the impact of a child on heterosexual relationship quality or satisfaction. My ultimate goals were to learn which relationship variables tend to have the strongest relationship to marital satisfaction post-birth, to review the literature on lesbian couple dynamics, and then to hypothesize about how lesbian couple dynamics might be interwoven with baby-couple dynamics. My hope was that the questionnaires would elucidate the picture.

IMPACT OF A CHILD ON A HETEROSEXUAL RELATIONSHIP

In general, having children seems to be negatively related to marital satisfaction among heterosexual couples (Belsky, Lang, & Rovine, 1985; Belsky, Spanier, & Rovine, 1983). While most couples seem to report less satisfaction with their marital relationship after the birth of their first child, there seems to be a linear relationship between pre- and post-birth marital satisfaction, with those most satisfied pre-birth reporting the greater satisfaction post-birth (Belsky, Spanier, & Rovine, 1983). Heterosexual couples generally experience a honeymoon period of a month or two after the child's birth (Miller & Sollie, 1980). This honeymoon is often followed by a significant decline in satisfaction over the next year or so (Belsky, 1985; Belsky, Lang, & Rovine, 1985; Belsky, Spanier & Rovine, 1983). Couples do not report levels of marital satisfaction equal to pre-birth years until their children all leave home (Anderson, Russell, & Schumm, 1983). Interestingly, although couples may be experiencing dissatisfaction with their relationship, divorces drop off drastically during the first year of a child's life and severely slow down during the toddler and pre-school years. Divorces apparently resume during the school years.

This pattern was noted in my clinical work with heterosexual couples and was markedly different from patterns observed in lesbian couples I was seeing. That is, heterosexual married couples, on the average, were experiencing stress and relationship dissatisfaction during the first years of the first child's life; they did not, however, tend to end their relationship, at least not until the child/children were in school. From the review of the literature on heterosexual marital satisfaction, three general areas emerged as most strongly related to marital quality in those first post-birth years: roles, intimacy, and social support. These same variables seemed, intuitively, to be significant for lesbian relationships.

Roles

While there is conflicting data regarding roles and marital satisfaction post-birth (Waldron & Routh, 1981), it appears that women have a more difficult time than men in the transition to motherhood (Steffensmeier, 1982). They report more negative changes in their personal life, less time for themselves, and more burden of the responsibility of parenting (Harriman, 1983; Waldron & Routh, 1981). A couple of findings were particularly interesting, relative to lesbian parenting. Lenz, Soeke, Rankin, and Fischman (1985) found that both men and women who had high femininity scores on the Bem Sex Role Inventory (a scale measuring traditionally masculine and feminine item endorsement) fared better after the birth of their child than did those who scored lower on femininity. This could be due to the high demand for traditionally feminine behavior of nurturing and care-taking during the early years of a child's life. On the other hand, LaRossa and LaRossa (1981) reported that chores and behaviors tended to fall along sex role lines after the birth of a child, no matter how non-traditional the couple's roles were pre-birth. Among other things, this suggests that the women may be doing the brunt of the care-taking and child care. If the mother is feminine (high femininity score on the Bem), she would likely feel more satisfied after the birth of her child. In fact, Belsky, Perry-Jenkins, and Crouter (1985) found support for this: for men and women, the sex roles which are enacted by heterosexual couples post-birth are not as important to satisfaction as is the person's comfort with the role chosen.

Intimacy

While intimacy does seem to be affected by the birth of a child, this variable is difficult to measure. Both men and women talk about having less time to spend together as a couple, enjoying fewer joint leisure activities and spending more time doing tasks such as childcare (Husten & McHale, 1983). Both men and women report that they experienced less emotional sharing with their partner after the birth of their child and women report less interest in sex (Harriman, 1983).

Since so much of intimacy is physical, separating the emotional from the physical parts of intimacy may be impossible. Both men and women talk about fatigue as one of primary stresses post-partum. In addition, women's bodies are so involved in the birth and post-birth processes of labor, delivery, and nursing that they frequently talk about feeling like their bodies are no longer their own. Without having the energy or the ownership of one's body, intimacy, especially physical intimacy, is understandably negatively affected.

Not all couples, however, are negatively affected by the birth of a child. What variables then, might differentiate those couples who are able to stay close through the stress of having a baby from those who report feeling less satisfied with their relationship? Feldman (1971) discovered that those heterosexual couples with a more companionate relationship (friendship as opposed to lover-type) tended to suffer the most after the birth of their child. From a different vantage point, Belsky (1985) discovered that the more realistic the couples' expectations are of their new life-after-baby, the greater their reported marital satisfaction. One might expect, then, that the couples with the most intimate relationship and the most realistic expectations pre-birth would be best able to maintain their relationship quality post-birth.

Social Support

Interestingly, the best predictor of women's post-partum marital adjustment was their ability to balance their social life (friendships) and motherhood (Myers-Walls, 1984). This was even more significant than their ability to balance career and motherhood. Similarly, Stemp, Turner and Noh (1986) noted that the women who were best able to alleviate their psychological distress after the birth of their child were those who perceived themselves as having social support. Support was not a factor noted in men's post-partum adjustment.

In Summary

In sum, heterosexual mothers tend to do more of the care-taking, nurturing, and traditionally feminine-type behaviors after the birth of their child. If they are comfortable with this (feminine) role, they tend to feel more satisfied after the birth of their child. While intimacy, especially physical intimacy, is bound to be interrupted, the more intimate the couple is pre-birth, the more intimate they will likely be post-partum. Thirdly, the more social support and continuity of social life that a mother experiences, the better she will feel about herself and her primary relationship. Finally, the more realistic the couple's expectations were of their new roles and relationship, the more satisfied they feel after the actual birth.

LESBIAN RELATIONSHIPS

Lesbian relationships tend to develop dynamics which are somewhat different from heterosexual couples due firstly to the fact that they are comprised of two women – bringing to the relationship the unique needs, characteristics and development of women. Secondly, but not necessarily less important, the social context in which lesbians live in our society brings to bare another set of stressors which impact and shape the relationship differently than their heterosexual counterparts.

Lesbian Relationships: Dynamics of Two Women

Research and theory supports the notion that women tend to be more nurturing, care-giving, responsible, dependent and relational than men (Chodorow, 1978; Dinnerstein, 1976; Gilligan, 1982). While many now believe that women's ways of being are different from, not less than men's, society as a whole still tends to value men's instrumentality over women's communality: acting upon is better than interacting with; being independent is better than being dependent. Women are left with the struggle of valuing themselves as women, while being devalued by social institutions, or adopting some of those socially sanctioned characteristics usually associated with men which may be alien to their sense of self as women.

The strength of a lesbian relationship is in part due to the powerful intimacy that two women are able to share due to their relatedness, orientation toward the other, and increased identification of two people who are of the same gender. Much has been written about both the beauty *and* the problems of lesbian relationship merging (Burch, 1982; Burch, 1987; Elise, 1986). As the two women come together they are able to touch upon a deep, primal bond which is at once fulfilling and frightening. Fear emerges out of each woman's anticipation of being overpowered by or dependent upon another woman. Both fear of being overpowered and fear of dependency may be viewed as developing out of the resolution of our initial symbiosis and separation from our mothers. In addition, it is impacted by our struggle with society's devaluation of women, women's relationships, and women-related traits such as dependency. When the fear overcomes the joy, the women may choose to separate, creating cycles of merging and separation within the relationship.

Separation is accomplished by various means. Some lesbians immerse themselves in their work, others spend time with hobbies or political activity. Affairs and intense friendships are a way of triangulating the relationship to both allow closeness and distance. A common problem which results out of this merging-separation cycle is a reduction in the frequency of sexual contact (Burch, 1987). Conflict, either as a result of the above stressors or as means to creating distance in and of itself, arises and maintains the needed separation/distance.

Conflict is often part of another process, the creation of an equal balance of power. The single best predictor of satisfaction in lesbian relationships is an equal power balance (Caldwell & Peplau, 1984; Peplau, Padesky & Hamilton, 1983). More lesbians than heterosexuals value an equal power balance in their relationship, and more lesbians achieve this goal (Schneider, 1986). However, many do not. The variables most commonly associated with power in a lesbian relationship are money and education. Attributes associated with lack of power are commitment to, involvement in and dependency on the relationship.

Lesbians' strong need for equal power in their relationship are once again multi-determined. Disenfranchised by the heterosexual world, lesbians do not not want to replicate within their intimate dyad what they experience outside. Similarly, many lesbian/feminists are struggling to break out of the traditional roles into which women have been cast. In another vein, however, the struggle for an equal power balance may emerge out of an old fear of being overpowered by another woman (mother). Lesbians merge and become frightened of being overpowered by another woman; each then struggles to gain her own power.

My schema for representing the dynamics of lesbian relationships has two parts. Lesbians, I believe, experience the push-pull of the merging-separation. When the women touch their cores, creating the intense joy, love, and intimacy they long for, they also touch upon the second dynamic: their fear of being overpowered by another woman. (Heterosexual couples, as a group, do not have to go through this cycle. Not only is their intimacy self-limited by men's more rigid ego boundaries, greater instrumentality and lesser relatedness, but men do not need to fear being overpowered by women because our society supports men having power over women and not vice versa. Choderow (1978), in fact, postulates that our male dominated society has developed out of this perceived fear of being overpowered by women.) Both women struggle to not be overpowered. If the women have worked out their roles, rules and power attributes, then neither woman will be overpowered and the relationship energy will remain with the merging-separation cycle, allowing for the eventual resolution of the earlier mother-daughter dynamic. If, however, the power balance is not stable and equal, whenever the women get close, they will continue to jockey for power as they struggle with their fear of being overpowered. They get close, experience their fear, and struggle not to be overpowered. The struggle itself creates the distance necessary to alleviate their fears of merger or dependency. Safe, once again, they can then remerge.

Peplau, Padesky and Hamilton (1983) report that the most common reason given for ending a lesbian relationship is too much dependency, which seems to be at the heart of this struggle. Dependency is at once a part of the closeness of the merger, the fear which is touched upon when one gets so close, and a piece of the powerlessness in the struggle for a balance of power.

Lesbian Families: Caught Between Two Worlds

Lesbians need and often seek validation from a heterosexist culture that not only does not recognize their coupleness, but discriminates against them politically, socially, economically and personally. In a world which oppresses them, many lesbians put much time and creative thought into social action—reading feminist writers, working for political organizations, marching at rallies, discussing issues with colleagues, lobbying legislators. Without the ties of nuclear family and frequently without the support and connections of an extended family of origin, lesbians, as a group, also tend to invest much physical and emotional energy into social activity—softball, concerts, dances, cultural organizations, visiting with friends. Their goal is to develop a firm and proud women's and lesbian identity.

Lesbian mothers walk a fine line between the heterosexual and lesbian worlds, not quite fitting in with their childless, politically or socially focused lesbian sisters, and still not quite comfortable with, or accepted by, heterosexuals. Even though both heterosexual and lesbian mothers have no choice but to focus inward, toward their families, their families are still quite different. The lesbian mother's alienation from her family of origin becomes more painful and poignant when children appear, as does the lack of rituals to validate the relationship and the family. While the heterosexual mother tends to receive validation from both the external world and her extended family when she births her first child, the lesbian mother is forced to look elsewhere. If she turns to her usual source of validation, the lesbian community, she is often left empty. The pre-birth support of "Isn't it wonderful that you're having a baby!" does not meet the mother's need when she's worried about how to quiet a fussy baby and all her friends are out at a rally.

As the mother is forced to interact in the mainstream world as her child grows and enters daycare and schools, she may be propelled to come out and may be forced to deal with the pain – or possibly the liberation – of the process. This may become a divisive issue in the couple, as the non-biological parent may be less willing or have less safety or energy to come out. If she does not come out, she becomes increasingly invisible, having no social or legal recognition of her role as co-parent. If neither woman comes out, their family is totally invalidated. On the other hand, if they do, they live in fear of what their child may face in response. Raising a child in a homophobic world is no easy task.

ENTER THE CHILD

The baby enters the system in the most vulnerable space: in the center of the merging-distancing/power-balance process. While the couple may not have been able to predict the complex development of feelings and experiences that emerged out of the birth, I will try to develop some hypotheses about these changes based on the above theory, research and clinical experience.

Roles

As discussed earlier relative to heterosexual couples, roles tend to change after the birth of a child, falling along classic sex role stereotypic lines. One would expect the mother, even in a lesbian relationship, to do most of the care-taking and nurturing while the co-parent would tend the yard, bills and car. If the mother is comfortable with the feminine role for herself, she may be delighted. If the co-parent enjoys her masculine-instrumental part, she, too, may be satisfied. If either is less than comfortable with the delineation of sex roles which frequently occurs, they may now become dissatisfied with their relationship. In addition, their power balance may change as roles and rules change—especially since the feminine role is often devalued or, in their own woman-identified system, the masculine role may be devalued. In any case, I would predict that for lesbian couples having a baby, roles would become less flexible and possibly less appealing, creating more difficulty when it comes time to re-negotiate power.

Intimacy

Intimacy is affected by the birth of a child. The mother bonds with the child in a way that often precludes bonding with her partner. This may exclude the co-parent; on the other hand, it could provide the triangulation necessary to maintain the closeness of the intimate relationship (Choderow, 1978). In a lesbian relationship, it could aid in the merging-separation cycle. However, unlike a hobby, it cannot be dropped when separation becomes destructive to the relationship. The mother's bonding puts her in touch with her own deep-felt dependency. Confused and scared, she may pull away from her partner, experiencing her partner's needs as a dependency overload. Or she may request, or even demand, nurturance, possibly creating a new dynamic in the relationship. The co-parent may then feel overloaded or fearful of the demands and may, in turn, back off.

Once again, new roles and rules demand new power negotiations. The mother may have less power because of her dependency; she may, on the other hand, have more because she alone has the legal right and social validation of parenthood. I would predict that the mother's dependency would emerge as an issue in the couple, along with increased struggles with maintaining intimacy and an equal power balance.

Social Support

Maintaining her social life is crucial to the heterosexual mother's well-being after the birth of her child. Lesbians are at a loss here. While a supportive women's community is what most expectant lesbian mothers look forward to, the after-birth reality may be quite different. The lesbian family lifestyle is so divergent from the childless lesbian lifestyle that the support, though possibly heart-felt, may not be perceived by the mother and her co-parent. In addition, support is often not forthcoming from either the heterosexual community or the family of origin. I would predict that the lack of support would become a stressor in the lesbian couple's relationship.

Expectations

All the above leads us to the potential of unmet expectations. As lesbian couples looked forward to having a baby in a supportive lesbian community, nurturing each other and the baby, maintaining non-traditional, flexible roles, and feeling close and intimate in their child rearing, they are soon faced with a disappointing reality. After the birth they discover that a baby is hard, tiring work which can isolate them from their support system and create havoc with their merging-separation/power-balance system. Violated expectations lower a heterosexual couple's relationship satisfaction after the birth of their child (Belsky, 1985); I would expect to find the same process in lesbian couples.

FINDINGS

The findings of McCandish (1987) support many of my predictions. She interviewed five lesbian couples who had chosen to birth children through alternative insemination. All of these couples were still together at the time of the interview (although one was contemplating ending their relationship), and all of the children were between 18 months and 7 years of age.

The couples reported an increase in hostility, particularly around nurturance. Because of new unmet needs, less time and energy for each other, and an increase in stress level, the women noted a greater need for support and nurturance—and less of it. The demand for new roles, falling into the line of biological and nonbiological mother, created new needs, experiences, and feelings. The mothers frequently felt envy of their partner's freedom; the coparents felt envy of the mother's closeness with the child. This, too, led to conflict. All of the couples had reduced their frequency of sexual contact and none had resumed to the pre-birth level. While all were working on the conflict and intimacy issues, four felt good about their progress. As noted above, one couple was considering separation. All noted that parenting superceded coupleness.

I attempted to learn more about what happens to lesbian couples after their first child was born. From the questionnaires sent out to ten heterosexual and ten lesbian couples, and returned by five heterosexual and seven lesbian couples, I gathered assessments of different components of relationship satisfaction both two years prebirth and two years post-birth. Questions focused mainly on intimacy, dependency, power, and social and community support. All heterosexual couples were married and all lesbians considered themselves to be in committed relationships at the time of the birth. They reported that they were together from three to 14 years before the birth of their child. All of the heterosexual couples were still together; three of the lesbian couples had separated and one couple was working extremely hard to stay together. All lesbians had used alternative insemination; all heterosexual couples had conceived conventionally except one that had used in vitro-fertilization. The first children ranged in age from five to two. None of the lesbians had had a second child, although one couple was in the process of trying; two heterosexual couples had had a second child and one was presently pregnant.

The most common area of dissatisfaction after the birth of their child, as reported by both heterosexual and lesbian birth-mothers and both male and female co-parents was the lack of time alone and the loss of freedom. Interestingly, every group but lesbian mothers noted that they were much less satisfied with the amount of time they had together as a couple. Lesbian mothers, on the other hand, were the only respondents to strongly report dissatisfaction with the amount and depth of their intimacy and the degree of emotional sharing with their partner. Lesbian mothers also reported struggling with the concept of mutual dependency, while lesbian co-parents complained about a lack of affection in their relationships. Co-parents as a group claimed to be unhappy about the frequency of sexual activity while a fair number of both lesbian co-parents and mothers reported dissatisfaction with the amount of passion in their lives.

A striking difference emerged between the heterosexual and lesbian couples in the areas of increased satisfaction post-birth. Heterosexual women noted that they felt more satisfied with the degree of emotional support from their families and connectedness with the community. Lesbians, on the other hand, claimed that they now felt more like a separate family.

These results partially support my predictions. The lesbian mothers, who were quite satisfied with the intensity of the intimacy experienced with their partners before the birth of their children, noted a strong dissatisfaction in this area after the birth. At the same time, and seemingly in contradiction, they were not unhappy about either the amount of time they were able to spend with their partners or with their frequency of sexual activity. A possible explanation is that they may have been content with giving their time and physical and emotional energy to their babies, which created the emotional distance needed in their dyadic relationship. While they missed the merging/intimacy with their partner, they were unwilling and/or unable to re-invest the time and energy necessary for redeveloping the closeness. Some of the most common comments on the questionnaires concerned both the fatigue and the wonderful bonding with their child. One woman specifically noted that sex was less frequent but that it was all right with her because she was afraid of intimacy. Another woman commented that her body no longer felt like her own; a co-parent noted that she felt like she had lost her partner to nursing.

The lesbian mothers were also the only group in the study that was struggling with mutual dependency. One woman wrote—"What is it? Is it possible?" Another woman noted that she felt that she and her partner were too dependent on each other after the birth of their child, while another grieved for her loss of freedom. Of those lesbians who left their relationship, discomfort with her own or her partner's dependency was the most commonly sighted reasons for separating. This supports my prediction that the birth of a child would highlight the mother's dependency issues, causing the lesbian mother to become frightened and to move away from the relationship. With most of these couples, it appears that either one or both partners became more dependent, but it was the mother's vulnerability to and fear of dependency which seemed most centrally related to dissatisfaction.

The lesbian co-parents presented themselves as feeling isolated as their partners bonded with the child. They talked about feeling left out, not knowing what role to take, and feeling jealous of the closeness their partner had with their child. They wanted more frequent sex and affection and more time together as a couple. The co-parents had a bi-modal distribution of pre-birth satisfaction with intimacy–some were very satisfied and some very dissatisfied–which did not change much post-birth. It seems as though their intimacy needs were not touched in the core way that the birth mothers' were. Instead, they struggled with their needs for inclusion, time and attention. Both mother and co-parent were looking for ways to reconnect, to re-merge. Co-parents were on the outside trying to get in; biological mothers were somewhere in the middle, with their child, searching for their partners.

Conflict or power struggles did not seem to emerge as issues in my sample. This is in contrast to the McCandish (1987) study. My questions may not have been sensitive enough or a retrospective view may have been distorting. An interview, where the respondents can develop a comfort and willingness to share more vulnerable information, may be necessary to pick up these difficult issues. Women, particularly lesbians, have difficulty with conflict (Vargo, 1987) because of their tendency to orient themselves to the other. This did seem to be the case in this study. Even those couples that had separated had difficulty expressing any hostility or anger at their partner.

Roles were not highlighted by respondents as having been changed due to the birth of their child. I would recommend the use of observational techniques to further study this area. The lesbians may be, in retrospect, unaware of the subtle changes or unwilling to admit role behavior which is contrary to their values.

Some couples did report some positive changes post-birth. All of these changes were in the social sphere. Lesbians, who have no rights or rituals to validate their relationship, felt more like a separate family after the birth of their child. They did not, however, feel the increased social support from their family of origin or connectedness with the community that the heterosexual couples enjoyed. (While they did not report loss of social support as was predicted, anecdotally, many of the lesbians talked about not fitting in with their old friends after the birth of their child and struggling to develop new social networks.) Lesbian families, as they birth children, are just at the point of development that a heterosexual couple is at the time of their marriage: becoming a separate family. Social and familial support and validation seem to be necessary ingredients which allow families to move to the next developmental stages of reconnecting with the family of origin and becoming a part of the community at large. The lesbian family, without these essential ingredients, may not be at a stage of development which can easily integrate a child into its system.

Through their comments at the end of the questionnaires, the women describe other positive changes that developed as a result of having their children: ". . . . It brought me to a new level of coming out." ". . . it was the best project we ever did together." ". . . . I learned about my ability to love and nurture . . . I love her at a depth I could not imagine." ". . . . It awakened a spiritual dimension I never knew I had." The positive impact must not be forgotten in the struggles.

On the other hand, as one women summarized. ". . . . Being a mom triggered all my mom-related issues."

A THREE-SOME

Some couples are able to maintain their relationship through the stress of birthing and raising a child while others are not. What makes the difference? In reading the questionnaires, quality of prebirth relationship, at least in my sample, does not seem to explain it. Some of the most dissatisfied couples pre-birth were the most satisfied post-birth (especially among the heterosexual couples). In reviewing the results, I note that some improvement in their relationship post-birth may actually be one of the significant variables necessary to reinforce a couple's decision to work on their relationship. The other variable seems to be commitment. Heterosexual commitment, in the form of a socially sanctioned marriage, may hold the couple together through rough months of emotional distance in the first years post-birth.

ABCX Model theory might also help to explain the differences between couples (Hill, 1949). According to this theory, a crisis (X) is determined by the number of stressors on a person/relationship/family (A), interacting with the family's supports and resources (B) and its perception of the problem or its ability to cope with the problem (C). I have reviewed numerous stressors, within the person, couple or social system. Any number of these may be impacting a particular couple at any moment in time. Similarly, I have touched upon supports. In addition, the couple or individual may choose to use therapy as a tool for dealing with the stress. One woman, who was particularly struggling with her relationship, commented that she and her partner were working together with their therapist to deal with their fears. Lastly, perception, that idiosyncratic variable, may make the difference between the couple experiencing a crisis and the couple taking all the stress in stride. While one woman admitted that their son provided an excuse not to deal with their relationship, another woman (in a heterosexual relationship) joyfully remarked that having their child was a joining in a miraculous event that deepened their commitment to each other. The demands and struggles (due largely to the lack of time) were not seen as divisive; instead they have brought them closer together and made them more flexible.

More work needs to be done to better understand, first, the dynamics of lesbian relationships and then, the impact a child has on that system. Better questionnaires, observations and more in-depth interviews should provide a means of clarifying some of the unanswered questions. Many lesbians are in the process of deciding to birth or adopt a child. Any information which will allow them to make educated decisions and develop realistic expectations will become a rich resource to aid them in the potentially stressful transition to parenthood.

REFERENCES

Anderson, S., Russell, C., & Schumm, W. (1983) Perceived marital quality and family life-cycle categories: A further analysis. *Journal of Marriage and the Family*, *45*, 127-139.

Belsky, J. (1985) Exploring individual differences in marital change across the transition to parenthood: The role of violated expectations. *Journal of Marriage and the Family*, *47*, 1037-1044.

Belsky, J., Lang, M., & Rovine, M. (1985) Stability and change in marriage across the transition to parenthood: A second study. *Journal of Marriage and the Family*, *47*, 855-865.

Belsky, J., Perry-Jenkins, M., & Crouter, A. (1985) The work family interface and marital change across the transition to parenthood. *Journal of Family Issues*, *6*, 205-220.

Belsky, J., Spanier, G., & Rovine, M. (1983) Stability and change in marriage across the transition to parenthood. *Journal of Marriage and the Family*, *45*, 567-577.

Bozett, F. (1987) *Gay and lesbian parents*, New York: Praeger.

Burch, B. (1982) Psychological merger in lesbian couples: A joint ego and systems approach. *Family Therapy*, *59*, 201-208.

Burch, B. (1987) Barriers to intimacy: Conflicts over power, dependency and nurturing in lesbian relationships. In Boston Lesbian Psychologies Collective (Eds.), *Lesbian psychologies: Explorations and challenges*, Urbana and Chicago, Illinois: University of Illinois Press, 126-141.

Caldwell, M., and Peplau, L. (1984) The balance of power in lesbian relationships. *Sex Roles*, *10*, 587-598.

Choderow, N. (1978) *The reproduction of mothering: Psychoanalysis and the sociology of gender*, Berkeley, Ca.: University of California Press.

Dinnerstein, D. (1976) *The mermaid and the minotaur*, New York: Basic Books.

Elise, D. (1986) Lesbian couples: The implications of sex differences in separation-individuation. *Psychotherapy*, *23*, 305-310.

Feldman, H. (1971) The effects of children on the family. In A. Michael, and W. Leiden (Eds.), *Family issues of employed women in Europe and America*, Netherlands: E.J. Brill.

Gilligan, C. (1982) *In a different voice: Psychological theory and women's development*, Cambridge, Mass.: Harvard University Press.

Harriman, L. (1983) Personal and marital changes accompanying parenthood. *Family Relations*, *32*, 387-394.

Harris, B., and Turner, P. (1985/86) Gay and lesbian parents. *Journal of Homosexuality*, *12*, 101-113.

Hill, R. (1949) *Families under stress*, New York: Harper & Row.

Husten, J. L. & McHale, S. M. (1983). *Changes in the topography of marriage following the birth of my first child*. Paper presented to The Society for Research in Child Development, Detroit.

LaRossa, R., and LaRossa, M. (1981) *Transition to parenthood: How infants change families*, Beverly Hills, Ca.: Sage.

Lenz, E., Soeken, K., Rankin, E., and Fischman, S. (1985) Sex-role attributes, gender and postpartal perceptions of the marital relationship. *Advances in Nursing Science*, *7*, 49-62.

McCandish, B. (1987) Against all odds: Lesbian mother family dynamics. In F. Bozett (Ed.) *Gay and lesbian parents*, New York: Praeger.

Myers-Walls, J. (1984) Balancing multiple role responsibility during the transition to parenthood. *Family Relations*, *33*, 267-271.

Peplau, L., Padesky, C., and Hamilton, M. (1983) Satisfaction in lesbian relationships. *Journal of Homosexuality*, *8*, 23-35.

Schneider, M. (1986) The relationships of cohabiting lesbian and heterosexual couples: A comparison. *Psychology of Women Quarterly*, *10*, 234-239.

Stemp, P. S. & Turner, J., & Noh, S. (1986). Psychological distress in the postpartum period: The significance of social support. *Journal of Marriage and the Family*, *48*, 271-274.

Vargo, S. (1987) The effects of women's socialization on lesbian couples. In Boston Lesbian Psychologies Collective (Eds.) *Lesbian psychologies: Explorations and challenges*, Urbana and Chicago, Illinois: University of Illinois Press.

Waldron, H., and Routh, D. (1981) The effect of the first child on the marital relationship. *Journal of Marriage and the Family*, *43*, 785-788.

The Myth of the Wicked Stepmother

Laura V. Salwen

This paper explores the myth of the wicked stepmother as it affects the position and functioning of actual stepmothers. It contains a review of some of the relevant literature on stepfamilies, comment on the prevalence of negative stereotypes of stepmothers, and preliminary ideas as to how such stereotypes may be counteracted through political and individual action. While the suggestions are aimed at stepmothers, they also imply a therapeutic direction for clinicians. The views presented owe much to the author's attendance at the Woman-Defined Motherhood Conference held at Goddard College September 16-18, 1988 and especially to the presentations of Jane Price Knowles, Paula Caplan, Janet Surrey, Rachel Josefowitz Siegel, and Phyllis Chesler.

THE STEPFAMILY: A REVIEW

High rates of divorce and remarriage in recent decades have led to an increasing number of stepfamilies. Forty-four percent of marriages that took place in 1980 were remarriages for one or both spouses. As of 1982, one in ten children lived with a stepparent and many more living in single-parent homes could expect their parents to remarry within three years (Dahl, Cowgill & Asmundsson, 1987). These figures do not include rates of remarriage for noncustodial parents which create additional stepfamilies where the

---

Laura V. Salwen is Clinical Social Worker in private practice in Buffalo, NY. She is also Clinical Assistant Professor of Social Work at SUNY Buffalo where she teaches several methods courses and a course on women and mental health. She is married and has two stepdaughters, ages 14 and 18.

children of the previous marriage spend widely varying amounts of time.

The literature related to stepfamilies comes in several forms including sociological studies (cf., Duberman, 1973; Kampara, 1980), "how to" manuals for stepfamilies (cf., Dodson, 1977; Roosevelt & Lofas, 1976) and treatment-oriented material for clinicians (cf., Johnson, 1980; Messinger & Hansen, 1982; Visher & Visher, 1979). While findings regarding the quality of functioning in stepfamily systems vary (cf., Collins & Ingoldsby, 1985), there are several consistent problems in adjustment faced by the stepfamily which are commonly agreed upon. Of primary difficulty is the "lack of specific norms for role behavior" (Kampara, 1980, p. 70) leading to role ambiguity and role confusion. The absence of clear role expectations may itself stem from the "complexity" and "variability" of stepfamily forms (Johnson, 1980, p. 305). Dodson (1977) defines a stepparent as a person who has married a spouse with one or more children and a stepfamily as a household unit where a stepchild (or stepchildren) lives or visits on a regular basis. However, these definitions actually refer to a wide assortment of living arrangements. For example, taking only those situations which include stepmothers as members, one can have the following family configurations:

1. A full-time stepmother with no biological children (i.e., the father is the custodial parent).
2. A part-time stepmother with no biological children (i.e., the father is the non-custodial or joint custodial parent).
3. A full-time stepmother with biological children from the current marriage only.
4. A part-time stepmother with biological children from the current marriage.
5. A full-time stepmother with biological children from a previous marriage only (who may be with her full or part-time).
6. A part-time stepmother with biological children from a previous marriage only (who may be with her full or part-time).
7. A full-time stepmother with biological children from both the current and a previous marriage.

8. A part-time stepmother with biological children from both the current and a previous marriage.

In addition, almost as wide a variety of stepmothering situations may occur for women living with men outside of marriage or for lesbians whose partners have children. Such a listing may seem overly fussy and obsessive. In fact, however, each of the enumerated circumstances is unique and calls for a different set of norms, role expectations, and behaviors.

Variability and complexity of family form may also affect the development of the stepfamily over time. As Brown points out, "The stages of the life cycle of a stepfamily are obviously different from the stages in a nuclear family, since, for example, there is no stage without children in a stepfamily" (1987, p. 35), and Fast and Cain (1976) discuss a number of the ways in which this changes family interactions. For example, parents have no opportunity to gradually establish a parental subsystem and solidify generational boundaries. In addition, however, specific types of stepfamilies may face particular developmental tasks which are not shared by others (e.g., incorporating "our" child into a sibling group composed of "yours" and "mine" or deciding how to handle the social stigma of a homosexual relationship with the children).

Other factors with which all stepfamilies must cope are the ambiguous or nonexistent legal status of the stepparent, the weakening of sexual taboos in step-relationships (Kampara, 1980) and the expectation of instant intimacy between stepparents and stepchildren who are, in fact, strangers (Collins & Ingoldsby, 1985).

THE UNIQUE POSITION OF THE STEPMOTHER

In addition to the complexities involved in stepfamily formation and functioning discussed above, stepmothers face several difficulties not shared by other stepfamily members. The role of the natural mother, whether dead, absent or available, becomes idealized vis-à-vis that of the stepmother. Brown (1987) notes that stepchildren assign the more desirable expressive attributes and roles to their natural mothers. The negative stereotype of the "wicked stepmother" from (supposedly) archaic fairy tales continues to have a powerful hold on contemporary imagination. It shows up in frequent allusions in the professional literature on stepfamilies (Brown, 1987; Collins & Ingoldsby, 1985; Duberman, 1973; Fast & Cain, 1976; Johnson, 1980; Kampara, 1980; and Schulman, 1972) and in anecdotal accounts whenever one broaches the subject of stepmothering. My own stepmother introduced herself to those she did not know at my wedding as "Laura's wicked old stepmother." A colleague tells me of a foster child whose care she supervises. Unwanted by his father, the adolescent boy calls his stepmother "stepmonster." One of my stepdaughters remembers that the first time I yelled at her she thought of me as "the wicked stepmother."[1] Client self-reports indicate that stepmothers continually struggle against internalizing a negative self-concept related to the connotations of evil, cruelty, jealousy, and selfishness derived from the stories of Hansel and Gretel, Snow White, and Cinderella. As one woman noted:

> I could tell immediately that my step-daughter did not want me in *her* home. Whenever I asked her to do things in the house, she made it clear that she felt just like Cinderella. It was hard to maintain my belief that this was her problem and not mine.

Bettelheim (1977) explains the persistence of the stereotype in terms of the psychological needs it meets for children. Specifically, the fantasy of the wicked stepmother allows the young child who is as yet unable to integrate her own loving and hateful feelings to manage them by splitting off anger and rage. As Bettelheim puts it:

> Although Mother is most often the all-giving protector, she can change into the cruel stepmother if she is so evil as to deny the youngster something he wants. (p. 67)

This device permits anger to be directed outward without endanger-

---

[1]Both my stepdaughters, who have recently acquired a live-in step-father, told me that the more difficult relationship is with the stepparent you live with most of the time. This observation may well apply beyond their personal experience. I suspect, however, that if views of stepparents in similar living situations were compared, as has not always been done in the research, stepmothers would still be seen more negatively than stepfathers.

ing the relationship with mother who is viewed as a different person. It allows the child to manage intense contradictory emotions which would otherwise tend to overwhelm her at this developmental stage. Further, according to the fairy tales in which the evil stepmother appears, her dominance is transitory and will be surmounted by the child herself or another good figure such as the fairy god (good) mother. This gives the child hope for smoother emotional sailing in the future.

At a later stage of development, the fairy tale enactment of triumph over the wicked stepmother is thought to allow the young girl an outlet for her "oedipal anguish" (Bettelheim, 1977, p. 15). In a girl's oedipal fantasy the mother is again split into two figures, the wonderful, loving preoedipal mother and the mean oedipal stepmother. The good preoedipal mother is not jealous of her daughter and helps her to obtain the love of the prince and to live happily ever after. The fairy tale tends to reduce the girl's guilt about what she wishes would happen to the ugly, mean (step)mother who stands in her way. The mean stepmother gets what she deserves as did Snow White's stepmother when forced to put on red-hot shoes and dance to death.

If one accepts Bettelheim's position as to the power and tenacity of, even necessity for, these fantasy figures (as I tend to), then one could begin to believe that real stepmothers must, for the good of their stepchildren, be condemned to live with the role and at times with miserable family and interpersonal situations in which they tolerate their stepchildren's negative projections. However, further analysis belies this idea.

First, one might wonder why there is no equivalent male figure of the "wicked stepfather" in fairy tales. In fact, a number of researchers have found the position of stepmother to be disadvantaged relative to that of stepfather. Duberman found that "stepfathers are more apt to achieve excellent relations with their stepchildren than stepmothers" adding that "this is in accord with the findings of all other investigators in the field" (1973, p. 290). Bowerman and Irish (1962) concluded that stepmothers are more likely to be perceived as discriminating against the children than stepfathers.

Interestingly, Bettelheim and the empirical researchers come to similar conclusions in attempting to account for the more negative image of the stepmother in both fantasy and reality. According to Bettelheim (1977), feelings about fathers are less ambivalent and intense because:

> In the usual course of family life, the father is often out of the home, while the mother, having given birth to the child and nursed him, continues to be heavily involved in childcare. (p. 114)

Or, as Duberman (1973) puts it:

> The probable reason why a step mother experiences more difficulty is that she normally spends more time with the children than the stepfather, incurring more opportunity for disharmony because of proximity and the nature of her role. (p. 283)

The key point may be the issue of role. All too often, women have sole responsibility for the rearing of children in situations where they have no other meaningful work, few satisfying emotional relationships with other adults, economic difficulties, and no network of childcare supports. We know that these conditions foster low self-esteem, depression, and feelings of isolation in women even in intact nuclear families (Weissman & Klerman, 1977). According to Chodorow (1978) and Dinnerstein (1977), such conditions also affect children in intact nuclear families by allowing only one powerfully close relationship (i.e., with mother) in which all of their intensely ambivalent feelings about themselves, their dependency needs, and the struggle of socialization must be worked out.

The current rate of failure of intact nuclear families and the creation instead of "binuclear" families (Ahrons, 1980) does not alleviate this problem. Instead, stepmothers are generally expected to fulfill the same role and functions as natural mothers without the benefit of the positive side of the ambivalent feelings—the deep and abiding love most children feel for their natural mothers.

It is my experience that over time a satisfying and positive relationship can be forged between stepmothers and their stepchildren. However, this is complicated and made more difficult by the prevailing expectation (usually shared by everyone involved) that women are supposed to be in charge of childcare and nurturing.

This is a social arrangement which is neither universal, biologically predetermined nor necessary and which may well be at the root of mother-blaming in general and of the perpetuation of the myth of the "wicked stepmother" with all its painful ramifications.

If one accepts the idea that the disadvantaged status of all women, and of stepmothers in particular, is related to their roles as the caretakers and nurturers of others, then the need for a full feminist agenda of social and political changes becomes even more acute. It serves us all to fight for pay equity legislation, parental leave benefits, and provision of adequate childcare services as a means of changing the traditional gender-based division of labor. However, there are also actions which stepmothers can take within their own personal environments to improve family dynamics.

The essential trap of stepmothering is the expectation that one will nurture but cannot do it as well as the natural mother is doing it, did it, or might have done it. One solution to the problem, at least for heterosexual couples, may be to remove oneself from the parenting role and to insist that the father, the natural parent, assume that role.[2] This does not mean that a stepmother cannot maintain a caring, concerned, involved relationship with her stepchildren. Nor does it mean that she need surrender all control over her own home or needs. However, the natural parent can more effectively deal with decision-making and arrangements necessary to provide for the child's care and socialization over time, given the stronger positive bond between them. In practice this means that the stepmother may participate in setting rules within the household around behaviors that affect her needs and well-being but would opt out of decisions that are primarily related to the child's needs or upbringing. For example, she might have a hand in decisions about household chores or appropriate behavior with guests but would not be involved in making rules about doing homework, curfews, or who the child may associate with.

---

[2]The situation is different and even more complicated for lesbian couples both because the dynamics of the couple relationship are different and because there are two socially-designed nurturing figures. There is a small but growing body of literature that addresses these issues (c.f., Eichenbaum & Orbach, 1983; Krestan & Bepko, 1980; Lyons, 1981; and Osman, 1972).

This is a fairly simple general rule to guide behavior but not an easy one and the stepmother who decides to implement this approach may encounter a number of obstacles. First, she may have to resist her own socialization as a nurturer. This is probably most difficult when she does not have her own biological children or when the stepchild initially turns to her rather than to the father for care. Secondly, this approach requires the cooperation of the father in a number of ways. He will also have to resist his own socialization to leave childcare to women. And the father will need to support the stepmother in those areas where she does participate. This presupposes a reasonable degree of communication and supportiveness within the marital relationship. In addition, the stepmother will still need to maintain generational boundaries operating as the father's partner, perhaps his advisor, but still not a parent. It may take some care not to become the child's ally in intergenerational struggles. On the positive side, there is some evidence to indicate that stepfamilies may work harder to establish viable family roles and functioning and are often successful in doing so (Brown, 1987; Dahl, Cowgill, & Asmundsson, 1987).

This is only one approach to clarifying and improving the role of the stepmother. In general, we also need more quantitative and qualitative research focused specifically on stepmothering and on the various approaches individual stepmothers have worked out to deal with their unique and potentially uncomfortable position within the family.

REFERENCES

Ahrons, C.R. (1980). Redefining the divorced family: A conceptual framework. *Social Work*, *25*, 437-445.

Bettelheim, B. (1977). *The uses of enchantment: The meaning and importance of fairy tales*. New York: Vintage Books.

Bowerman, C., & Irish, D. (1962). Some relationships of stepchildren to their parents. *Marriage and Family Living*, *24*, 113-121.

Brown, K. (1987). Stepmothering: Myth and realities. *Affilia*, *2*, 34-45.

Chodorow, N. (1978). *The reproduction of mothering: Psychoanalysis and the sociology of gender*. Berkeley: University of California Press.

Collins, L.J., & Ingoldsby, B.B. (1985). Living in step: A look at the reconstituted family. In Bloom, M. (Ed.). *Life span development: Basis for preventive and interventive helping*, 2nd edition (pp. 345-354). New York: Macmillan.

Dahl, A.S., Cowgill, K.M., & Asmundsson, R. (1987). Life in remarriage families. *Social Work, 32*, 40-45.

Dinnerstein, D. (1977). *The mermaid and the minotaur: Sexual arrangements and the human malaise*. New York: Harper Colophon Books.

Dodson, F. (1977). Weaving together two families into one. *Family Health/Today's Health, 9*, 44-51.

Duberman, L. (1973). Step-kin relations. *Journal of Marriage and the Family, 35*, 283-292.

Eichenbaum, L., & Orbach, S. (1983). *Understanding women: A feminist psychoanalytic approach*. New York: Basic Books.

Fast, I., & Cain, A. C. (1976). The step-parent role: Potential for disturbance in family functioning. In Turner, F.J. (Ed.) 2nd edition. *Differential diagnosis and treatment in social work* (pp. 676-682). New York: The Free Press.

Johnson, H.C. (1980). Working with stepfamilies: Principles of practice. *Social Work, 25*, 304-308.

Kampara, D.R. (1980). Difficulties in the socialization process of stepparenting. *Family Relations, 29*, 69-73.

Krestan, J., & Bepko, C. (1980). The problem of fusion in lesbian relationship. *Family Process, 19*, 277-289.

Lyons, T.A. (1981). *Lesbian mother families: Dynamics and interaction among mothers, lover, and children*. Paper presented at American Orthopsychiatric Association Annual Meetings, New York.

Messinger, L., & Hansen, J. (Eds.) (1982). *Therapy with remarriage families*. Rockville, MD: Aspen Systems Corp.

Osman, S. (1972). My stepfather is a she. *Family Process, 11*, 209-218.

Roosevelt, R., & Lofas, J. (1976). *Living in step*. New York: McGraw-Hill.

Schulman, G.L. (1972). Myths that intrude on the adaptation of the stepfamily. *Social Casework, 53*, 131-139.

Visher, E.B., & Visher, J. (1979). *Stepfamilies: A guide to working with stepparents and stepchildren*. New York: Brunner/Mazel.

Weissman, M.M., & Klerman, G.L. (1977). Sex differences and the epidemiology of depression. *Archives of General Psychiatry, 34*, 98-111.

Feminist Considerations of Intercountry Adoptions

Susan E. Barrett
Carol M. Aubin

Wrapped in a pink crocheted blanket and hat, she was a month old when we met. Her dark skin and blue-black hair alongside our white skin, red hair, and brown-grey hair was a significant contrast that was not lost on us. Though she had never heard the language we, her new parents, spoke to her, we three basked in our circle of pure and total love.

Deciding to parent children from another country opened a door to a world unknown to us—the world of intercountry adoption. Made up of children in need, people willing to help, agencies and shifting illusions, it was all wrapped up in constant change. One thing was very clear, very quickly, it was certainly not a feminist world. Being committed to our children and to feminism, we want to further a discussion of feminist issues and ideas around the adoption of children from a different culture.

At all levels and in all phases, adoption involves women. Most children adopted internationally are abandoned or have only one trackable birth parent, a woman. Whether in partnership or alone, women are involved as a parent-to-be in almost all adoptions, and the majority of children wanted as adoptees are girls.

Feminist considerations in the media on intercountry adoption are minimal. Several women (Aubin, 1989; Beckett, 1989; Bruining, 1989; Pastor, 1989) wrote separate articles in *Sojourner* discussing

---

Susan E. Barrett, PhD, is in private practice as a psychologist in Atlanta, GA. Carol M. Aubin is a writer. They parent two adopted children born in another country.

some feminist concerns, but the primary shapers of the adoption process are social service workers, religious groups, governmental agencies, lawyers and adoptive parents. This paper is written for ourselves and other women who want to or are parenting children born in another country. It is also for the therapists and other feminists supporting them or who are interested in this aspect of mothering.

Intercountry adoption involves many, but not all of the countries in the world. Children have been adopted into the United States since shortly after World War II. However, it wasn't until after the Korean War when Harry Holt, a born-again Christian, established Holt International to adopt children from Korea that significant numbers of adoptions have occurred. Since that time the number of intercountry adoptions has steadily increased. While only 1,612 children were adopted internationally in the U.S. in 1968, Immigration and Naturalization Service (INS) statistics show that by 1986 the number had increased to 9,946 (Kim, 1988). Approximately two-thirds of the adopted children in the United States come from Korea (Rothschild, 1988). The remaining third are from other Asian countries or from Central and South America (Kim, 1988).

Numbers alone, however, certainly cannot indicate who is adopting whom. It is a fact that essentially, white, middle class North Americans and Western Europeans are adopting poor children of color from our world's developing nations. Additionally, most adopting parents want a healthy infant (Kim, 1988), with a majority requesting a girl. Wanting a girl is particularly true in international adoption, both for couples and single parents, regardless of whether or not there already are other children of either gender in the family (Adamec, 1988).

CULTURE VS. FAMILY

Traveling all over with our daughter, we tried to soak up the very essence of her birth country. While she had the strong, stunning features of the people in the countryside, we wore the neon signs of tourists. We know a lot about her birth country. We have books, music, pictures and momentos, but we know not how to give her the deep, deep love of her birth country that can come so naturally to native people.

And, as she leaves the protective toddler years, what feelings in all of us will be nudged as she begins asking and being asked critical questions? How will she feel recognizing that she doesn't really fit in a white or a racially mixed culture, and, since she didn't grow up in her birth country, that she lacks the sense of belonging there, also. How and where will she carve out her core space?

Yet, our daughter knows how deeply she is loved and cared about by her family. She has an extensive, loving support system. We can only guess at her life had we not met, but are quite sure that she would have become one of her country's orphanage or homeless statistics.

The importance of both culture and family lie at the heart of much emotional debate over intercountry adoptions. On the one hand are those who believe that the most important thing in a child's life is for her to have a family—people who know and love her, who will raise and care for her, know her intimately and provide for her welfare. On the other hand are those who firmly believe culture and race are the primary factors to consider, for both the child and for society as a whole.

The physical and psychological benefits of a home are undeniable. It is clearly preferable to starving, living on the streets, or being raised in an institution—sometimes the only options for children. Even if physically cared for, children need specific people with whom they can bond. They need the experience of growing up with particular people who know and care for them. Self-esteem is strongly associated with a child's knowledge that significant others hold positive attitudes toward her/him (Simon & Altstein, 1987). Whole generations of people are growing up without the benefit of a person or persons to love them in particular. Individuals who believe children need families obviously believe that race and culture should not be the critical factors for the decision to adopt.

> A child without a family is a child deprived of the most fundamental human right. A child has a birthright to grow up in an atmosphere of love and family concern. A child has no birthright to protein-deficient diets, to forks or chopsticks, to a belly full of parasites, to a childhood free of caresses and parental encouragement. A child has no birthright to a particular shape of house nor to speaking a particular language. A child has a birthright to parental love. Can an orphanage ever meet the needs of any abandoned child? Should we not try . . . to meet the needs of a greater majority of homeless children by increasing the number of intercountry adoptions?
>
> The nationality or citizenship of a child is a meaningless concept to a child who is dead, or subnormal from the deprivation of institutionalization. (Taylor, 1988)

Obviously, there are very real benefits to adoption for the individual child who has no other home. There is also a more general benefit for society of not raising generations of children in mind-numbing poverty and illiteracy. As adults, instead of focusing on the source of the next meal, they might, instead, choose to eventually focus on making our world a better place.

People who believe culture and race are primary factors to consider in adoption believe removal of a child from her race or culture is not only potentially harmful for a child, but does, in fact, contribute to the end of the culture itself.

The National Association of Black Social Workers has stated clearly that it views "the placement of Black children in white homes as a hostile act against our community. It is a blatant form of race and cultural genocide" (Simon & Altstein, 1987, p. 143). Mike Jupp, executive director of the U.S. branch of Defense for Children International, a human-rights organization has said, ". . . representatives from Third World countries view [intercountry adoption] as a further example of exploitation of their natural resources. The West, they say, took their sugar, their coal, their bauzite, their gold, and their silver, and now it is taking their babies" (Rothschild, 1988).

There are obviously some strong negative consequences of intercountry and interracial adoption. A child is usually raised as a brown/black child in a white home, without parents who understand directly the impact of racism. She/he certainly is not raised in the culture into which she was born. In that sense she is a child without a community of others and having such a community is one critical factor in coming to terms with being a member of a devalued minority in a majority situation (Barrett, in press; Root, 1988).

A more general negative impact is a combination of cultural genocide and the perpetuation of the deeply entrenched patriarchal system. Allowing some abandoned and relinquished children to be adopted internationally may release just enough pressure on a society so that the country's tolerance for the status quo remains and the urgency for change is lessened. In addition, most of the children are, in all likelihood, adopted into families oriented toward maintaining the present system, not changing it.

People tend to polarize around the issues of family and culture, creating debates instead of working to see value in both sides. As feminists, we must address the total picture, delving still deeper into seemingly contradictory concepts looking for a fuller truth. For example, there is no acceptable, socially-responsible number of children to risk in the present in order to save a culture. Neither is it permissible to actively or passively contribute to the destruction of a culture on the earth.

REASONS WHY CHILDREN ARE WITHOUT FAMILIES

Strongly committed to giving something back to our daughter's country of birth, we want to help sow the seeds which will end the adoption process all together. Our beginning efforts include contributions to daycare and literacy programs, while seeking out the feminist networks within our child's birth land.

Poverty is a major reason children are without families. Both in the United States and in other countries, it is the poor who have the fewest alternatives. Often neither the birth parents/birth mother nor extended family can afford to feed and care for a child.

For instance, in Peru "every day 170 infants under the age of one year die; 80% of these deaths are the result of preventable diseases such as measles, whooping cough, respiratory infections and polio. Dehydration alone causes one death every 20 minutes" (Bisso, 1989, p. 15). Between August, 1988 and Spring, 1989, food prices rose more than 350% and gasoline prices almost 500% while the monthly minimum wage shrank to $14, covering an estimated 6% of the basic food needs for a family of six (Bisso, 1989).

The many reasons for the deadly poverty include war, natural disasters, and changes in the economic base of a country. Interwoven throughout the poverty are the influences of materialism, capitalism, and acquisitivism. Added to these is the past and present intervention and domination of foreign powers, including the United States. For instance, in Nicaragua alone there are 16,000 children orphaned by the war (Engel, 1989), a situation the United States has contributed to directly. More than a million people, including many children, are homeless because of El Salvador's 9-year-old war (Zielinski, 1989).

Sometimes, as in Argentina during the "dirty war," children of women who were political prisoners were placed for adoption by government authorities. The courageous Grandmothers of the Plaza de Mayo demonstrated and fought for information, working for custody of the grandchildren some had never seen (Arditti, 1988).

Obviously, other factors besides poverty and political turmoil influence the adoption of children. The patriarchal belief that each woman needs to be married to a man in order to have a legitimate child carries with it a stigma for both mother and child when a woman is not married. In some countries, the stigma is so strong that it is financially impossible for a woman to support a child and herself without a man (Rothschild, 1988).

Another factor influencing adoptions is the belief by white North Americans/Europeans that their cultures are preferable to all others. This racist and culturally elitist attitude definitely spills over into other countries so that many of their people believe it also. Sometimes birth mothers are coerced and/or encouraged to believe that white and industrialized is better. They are told that material and educational benefits to their children are of greater value than their love and care.

As a result of all the above, children are frequently abandoned.

They are left in public places such as parks; taken directly to governmental agencies, such as a judges' chambers; and left with child care organizations, such as church-run orphanages. Children are frequently found wandering and some live in packs on the streets. Sometimes, within a family one child is sold to pay for food so other children can eat. Some mothers relinquish a child directly to an adoptive parent or to an agency that arranges adoptions.

Throughout many countries there are thousands of children who have families unable to care for them. Many of the countries involved have neither the financial resources nor the social service mechanisms to provide even physical care for the children.

Intercountry adoption is not going to change these facts. Massive social intervention, on an international scale, is needed. Currently, large organizations such as religious groups provide some relief. Grass roots programs are also making a difference in areas such as medical care and adopt-a-school programs. Particularly now, as the economic situation of many developing countries spirals downward, international ways to meet the needs of the children are critical.

Intercountry adoption is one personal way that some of us who want to be parents can care for a particular child. However, adopting internationally brings with it certain responsibilities from a feminist perspective.

In a feminist perspective, social context makes a difference. We do not act as individuals, making decisions and choices in isolation. We live in a patriarchal, racist, capitalistic society and what we do either reinforces that or works to change it. We need to understand the social context and how it comes to bear specifically around the issues of intercountry adoption.

At the same time, each of us individually, through the way we live our lives, integrates/manifests personally the more global, long-term ideals we cherish. An interplay between the individual and society is critical. In addition to working to change the larger social context, parenting children who need parents right now is one way for adults who want to be parents to manifest/actualize/live their lives in accordance with their beliefs.

WOMEN

Adoption involves women and it is overwhelmingly women who both raise children and are a child's primary/only connection. These statements are obvious. But a discussion of them is essential to a feminist understanding of the adoption process.

Intercountry adoption in particular, but often domestic adoption as well, involves radically different economic, class, racial and cultural backgrounds for the women giving birth to children and for those of us adopting. Obviously, women adopting children have far more access to resources and far more power than the women giving birth. Inherent in this situation is the fact that these points alone become sufficient reasons for the adoptions to occur.

Economics is a horrible reason to have to let go of a child and makes a farce out of the idea that such a release is voluntary. It is not, any more than the stigma of being an "unwed" mother gives a choice. These hardly constitute situations of voluntary relinquishment (Beckett, 1989; Chesler, 1988).

Furthermore, in the United States (and not for some other countries) a child cannot be adopted into this country if she has two parents in the country of birth (INS regulations, 1986). In the vast majority of situations, if a child has only one parent available, that parent is a mother. This means that it is a woman alone who is responsible for making decisions that drastically affect her life and that of her child. This places an enormous burden on a woman who often has minimal societal support for raising a child without a man, few economic resources, and perhaps pressure to "give a child a better life."

Global feminist perspectives and actions build on the realities of women's lives, lives influenced and shaped by factors such as race and culture as well as patriarchy. One aspect of women's lives that we need to understand, in all its myriad forms and with all the variations due to culture, is giving birth and mothering. We need to build our connections to each other, in part using women's roles with children as the mortar.

Feminists who adopt internationally are in a unique position to further the active connection among women of varying cultures. We become bi-racial/cultural families immediately. Our children have strong ties to women in other countries, whether they remember them or not. We, ourselves, are inextricably bound to another woman who gave birth to the children we raise. All of this, bit by bit, can contribute to existing theory and practice of feminism on an international scope.

HEALTHY FEMALE INFANTS

While we were open to adopting a son, we now have two daughters and each has both of our names. We are a proud and joyful family of four.

What are the beliefs that result in most adoptive parents wanting a girl rather than a boy? Adamec (1988) and Dahlstrom (1988) explore a variety of reasons including a woman wanting a child most like her (and in married couples, the woman may want the child more); believing that minority women have an easier time than minority men in the U.S.; perceptions that girls are "easier" to raise; a girl often will not carry on the family name; thinking it is not manly to adopt a boy, but okay to adopt a girl; and believing that adoption is second class, they adopt the second class of the sexes. Single heterosexual women and lesbians, both single and in partnerships, are adopting children and frequently choosing girls. This choice is often a combination of wanting a child most like themselves and choosing to focus on the development of women/girls.

Sexism is inherent in the message given to women who release children for adoption that we want your daughters because they fit our fantasies better and because we think they won't challenge our world as much. On the other hand, through the same choice, we can convey a deep love and appreciation of being female and a desire to help girls directly deal with sexism. We still need to consider the boys.

Far and away, the majority of adoptive parents want to adopt infants. Having some say in the age at which a child becomes part of your family is something birth parents never have to consider; they automatically start with a newborn. Parenting children from infancy is very different from parenting children adopted when older. Parenting children with special needs is also very different from parenting healthy children. Any child can, in a split second, move from being healthy to having special needs. However, adoptive parents usually do get a choice at the start to choose what special needs they can handle.

Older children (and those with special needs) need homes and families. These children are the responsibility of all of us, not the special responsibility of adoptive parents.

THE PROCESS OF INTERCOUNTRY ADOPTION

The intercountry adoption process reflects our society in general. As feminists, if we are to participate in this process, we have to assume the responsibility for our actions and decisions. We also have the opportunity to have a positive impact by challenging the piece of the system with which we work and/or working to change the system in general.

Financially, individuals and organizations involved in facilitating intercountry adoptions run the gamut from those receiving no financial reimbursement at all to those charging and getting exorbitant fees, essentially trafficking in babies.

Entrepeneurs are motivated by money, and babies happen to be their business. Their concern is not for those most vulnerable – the child, the birth mother, and the adoptive parents – but simply, the money. Entrepeneurs charge adoption fees far in excess of what is needed. Baby brokers also sometimes recruit birth mothers, paying them minimally for their services, and only then if the child is healthy (Pastor, 1989). Recruiting poor women to bear healthy children for others must not be tolerated. People and organizations primarily designed to make a profit, buy babies or take children away from their parents absolutely need to be challenged and stopped.

Religious agencies, government agencies (such as orphanages), and adoption agencies in this country are usually examples of people motivated by service, receiving either no money or only enough to pay salaries, overhead, and fees involved. Currently, these are the organizations through whom it is most appropriate to adopt. However, we need to be aware that many of these people and organizations, some by virtue of their religious ties, are very likely to have policies that are particularly patriarchal and often racist.

Each woman considering intercountry adoption must take the

time to investigate the organizations and individuals with whom she may work. The kinds of questions that need to be asked include:

- —Are the fees of this agency in line with fees of other agencies? Where does the money go? To whom does it go?
- —Are fees higher for countries in which the children have light skin and lower for countries in which the children have dark skin?
- —Is priority given, as it should be (Ryan, 1983), to in-country adoptions by the contact in the other country?
- —If a child is being relinquished by the birth mother, what are the circumstances of her decision?
- —If a child has been abandoned, what are the circumstances of that abandonment (to be sure the child was indeed abandoned and not taken from her mother)?

Eventually, the informal connections existing among feminists interested in intercountry adoption will hopefully develop into processes that are specifically feminist in nature.

SUMMARY

It is difficult for us, being white and North American, to know what intercountry adoption would feel like if we were, for example, Hispanic and South American. The closest we can come is to imagine a world in which girl children were without homes and only men were available to adopt.

Ideally, we would live in a world in which everyone, including children, could live with a family within their own culture. People really concerned with adoption and also wanting a better world would choose that for each child now. In reality, the economic situation in developing countries is nothing like that in the United States and the resources simply do not exist to care for the children. Many people involved in intercountry adoptions in both the country of origin and in the United States believe that adoption is one viable option, one that is currently in the best interest of the child.

Adoption is an incredibly seductive process. It is very easy to lose sight of the entire adoption environment, much less the issues, when focused on wanting a child. At the very point in which we, as adoptive parents, are most emotionally vulnerable, we need to question ourselves and our intermediaries, critically raising issues that may make us uncomfortable.

The choices are difficult ones. The rewards, both in terms of parenting and in terms of being honest with ourselves, are worth it.

REFERENCES

Adamec, Christine (July/August, 1988). Adopt a boy. *Ours: The magazine of adoptive families. 21*:30-31.

Arditti, Rita (Fall, 1988). Genetics and Justice. *Women of Power. 11*:42-44.

Aubin, Carol (May, 1989). Choosing Intercountry Adoption. *Sojourner. 14*: 19-21.

Barrett, Susan (in press). Paths toward diversity: An intrapsychic perspective. *Women and Therapy*.

Beckett, Judith E. (August, 1989). Birthmarks: A birthmother's view of adoption. *Sojourner. 14*:8-9.

Bisso, Marissa (May 3, 1989). Poverty starves kids' bodies and minds. *Guardian. 41*:15.

Bruining, Anne Mi Ok (May, 1989). Made in Korea. *Sojourner. 14*:18-19.

Chesler, Phyllis (1988). *Sacred Bond: The legacy of Baby M*. New York: Random House.

Dahlstrom, Cosette (1988). Being a boy means hard to place. *Report on foreign adoption*. Boulder, CO: International Concerns Committee for Children.

Engel, Kathy (1989). Fundraising letter. *Madre, Women's Peace Network*.

Immigration and Naturalization Service, Immigration Reform and Control Act of 1986, Pub. L. No. 99-603, 315 (a).

Kim, Theodore (Spring, 1988). Congressional testimony on foreign adoption, April 26, 1988. Reprinted in *International Concerns Committee for Children*, 14-21.

Pastor, Roxanna (May, 1989). The Honduran Baby Market. *Sojourner. 14*:19.

Root, Maria P. P. (May, 1988). *Resolving "other" status: The process of identity development in biracial individuals*. Paper presented at the Advanced Feminist Therapy Institute, Seattle, WA.

Rothschild, Matthew (January, 1988). Babies for sale. *The Progressive*, 18-23.

Ryan, Angela Shen (1983). Intercountry adoption and policy issues. In Frank, Mary (Ed). *Newcomers to the United States: Children and their families*. New York: Haworth Press.

Simon, Rita J., & Altstein, Howard (1971). *Transracial adoptees and their families*. New York: Praeger Publishers.

Taylor, Rosemary (1988). Comment: Transracial adoption. *Report on foreign adoption*. Boulder, CO: International Concerns Committee for Children.

Zielinski, Mike (May 3, 1989). El Salvador. *The Guardian. 41*:14.

No Accident: The Voices of Voluntarily Childless Women – An Essay on the Social Construction of Fertility Choices

Anita Landa

This paper is divided into two parts: a section about voluntarly childlessness and a section in which voluntarily childless women speak for themselves. The former is based on a brief review of the demographic, sociological, and psychological literature; the latter draws on semi-structured clinical interviews which I conducted with sixteen voluntarily childless women (Landa, 1983), and on a poem (Fletcher, 1986) written by a woman who has chosen not to have children.

Since I am a developmental psychologist rather than a therapist, I do not feel competent to advise clinicians on the treatment of voluntarily childless women. Further, in the absence of a comprehensive theory of human reproduction, it is difficult to place voluntary childlessness in a theoretical context. While researchers have sought to illuminate the topic from their own theoretical perspectives, no conceptual framework has emerged which systematizes the insights contributed by various disciplines.

However, both researchers and their informants – the voluntarily childless women themselves – function within the early twentieth

---

Anita Landa directs the Adult Degree Option program at Lesley College where she also co-directs, with Jill Tarule, the Collaborative Learning Project. Thanks for critiquing the manuscript are offered to Mary Belenky, Judith Cohen, Susan Cohen, and Jill Tarule.

century paradigm of human development which emphasizes parents, and most especially mothers, as determinants of personality and behavior and which confounds womanhood with motherhood. Thus it is almost impossible at this time to avoid mother-centered interpretations when reporting on voluntary childlessness. Whether, and how, our views of fertility choices will change as we reconstruct our understanding of the parent-child relationship is an intriguing question. What seems clear, though, is that the etiology of voluntary childlessness is socially constructed and, as such, is culturally contextual and tentative. Within these limitations, I would like to contribute to an understanding by therapists of the small but growing population of voluntarily childless women by providing a platform from which their own voices can be heard.

I

Demographers estimate that approximately two percent of ever-married American women are currently voluntarily childless. To predict future trends, researchers examine the rate of temporary childlessness, which is the percentage of ever-married women of child-bearing age who have not decided whether to have children. The number of such women has risen dramatically over the past quarter-century, from 1-in-10 in 1960 to 1-in-4 in 1986 (*Newsweek*, 1986; U.S. Census Bureau, 1976). While some temporarily childless women will turn out to be involuntarily childless (sterile), and most will become mothers by the time they are forty-five, the increase in the rate of temporary childlessness suggests a roughly proportionate rise in the rate of voluntary childlessness in the future. Thus, by the end of the century, the rate of voluntary childlessness among ever-married women in the United States may rise to 10%. When never-married women are added to this calculation, the actual number of voluntary childless women in this country could reach three million by the year 2000 (Mosher & Bachrach, 1982; Poston & Kramer, 1981; Veevers, 1972, 1979; Glick, 1977).

A survey of the demographic, socioeconomic, and psychological literature sketches a profile of the voluntarily childless woman which has been variously characterized as "atypical but not abnormal" and "distinctive" as opposed to unique or deviant (Landa,

1983; Teicholz, 1977; Veevers, 1973, 1975, 1979, 1980). Voluntarily childless women are likely to have been first or only children, to have grown up in small or unusually large families, and to have come from Protestant or non-religious homes. The interview literature suggests that voluntarily childless women found life difficult in their families of origin.

Among the women in my own small, purposive sample, difficult childhoods were the norm rather than the exception. The women I interviewed had suffered the death or disabling illness of siblings, the institutionalization of parents, divorce in their families of origin, the disruption of war, the insecurity of economic setbacks and the upheaval of major geographic moves. The women from working class backgrounds were the first in their families to attend college, thus adding a class shift to other discontinuities. It is my impression that social discontinuity contributes to late marriage, and late marriage is firmly correlated with low fertility (Poston & Trent, 1982). Indeed, in countries such as the Peoples Republic of China, legislated late marriage is a centerpiece of population control.

Women's problematic relationships with their mothers, or a sense of having been inadequately mothered, or feeling that one's mother was not an attractive role model, are themes which run through all interview-based research. Veevers (1979, 1980) supports these findings by describing "the little mother syndrome," which I also came across in my own research (Landa, 1983), where the voluntarily childless woman, as a young girl, was called upon to care for younger siblings through the absence or inability of the mother.

My own work is the only investigation I know of which addresses voluntarily childless women's relationships with their fathers or father surrogates: such relationships were generally reported as closer and more satisfactory than relationships with mothers. However, the relationships of the voluntarily childless men whom I interviewed remembered their fathers with resentment and/or yearning. This suggests that the relationship with the same-sex parent is viewed by voluntarily childless persons as a central element in determining their fertility status.

As adults, the socioeconomic status of voluntarily childless women is high: their level of education is higher than that of either mothers or involuntarily childless women; they earn more money and have better developed careers than either of these groups and their earnings represent a significantly higher percentage of family income. The family incomes of voluntarily childless couples are equal with those of involuntarily childless couples, and are between 10% and 25% higher than the incomes of parents of small families, thus permitting a markedly higher standard of living (Fullop, 1977; Mosher & Bachrach, 1982; Poston & Kramer, 1981).

The divorce rate among the voluntarily childless has not been reliably determined, but it appears that they stay married for shorter periods of time than either the involuntarily childless or parents; most importantly, they tend to be unmarried during significant portions of their prime childbearing years (U.S. Bureau of the Census, Current Population Reports, 1976). The enduring marriages of voluntarily childless women are consistently reported in the literature as being more satisfactory than the marriages of any other group of women (Bram, 1978; Polonko, Scanzoni, & Teachman, 1982; Veevers, 1980).

Women who remain voluntarily childless are several hundred percent more likely to have agreed not to have children before marrying than are mothers and are three to four times more likely to use contraception than are any other category of married person. Oral contraception is the preferred method. The voluntarily childless tend to be mobile—they move more, change jobs more, and travel more than mothers. They tend to be non-religious, urban, and unaffiliated in the sense of belonging to social institutions (Mosher & Bachrach, 1982; Veevers, 1972, 1979, 1980).

The decision-making process among voluntarily childless women has been described in great detail by Veevers (1979, 1980) and in my own work (Landa, 1983). Veevers reports two categories, repudiators and aficionados. Repudiators "are persons who have repudiated the parenthood mystique, and actively and vehemently reject the parenthood role" while aficionados "are . . . persons who have . . . been intrigued and beguiled by some other interest" (Veevers, 1979, p. 46). I identified four types of decision-makers: the born non-parent, the surprised non-parent, the postponing or accidental non-parent, the reconfirming non-parent (Landa, 1983). The salient finding in discussions of decision-making is that voluntary childlessness is, indeed, chosen, sometimes chosen many times over the reproductive lifespan.

Studies aimed at understanding the inner lives of voluntarily childless women are rare, often informal, and generally carried out in relation to small, purposive samples of married women, and their findings should thus be viewed as tentative (Bram, 1978; Burgwyn, 1981; Cawte, 1975; Faux, 1984; Kaltreider & Margolis, 1976; Teicholz, 1977; Veevers, 1973, 1975, 1979, 1980). (My own work and the Kaltreider-Margolis research are the only two studies I know of which include never-married women.) The most persistent themes in this literature are of androgyny; of difficulty in relationships with mothers; of self-regard based on achievement rather than relationships; of psychological, moral and social development well within accepted norms; and of purposeful decision-making.

Teicholz (1977) administered a battery of personality inventories to 70 married, non-randomly assembled subjects and found no significant differences between the voluntarily childless women and other populations of women except regarding androgyny. Kaltreider and Margolis (1977) found that voluntarily childless women seeking functional contraceptives did not appear to have any psychologically distinguishing characteristics. However, those seeking contraceptive sterilization did poorly on a test measuring the quality of their relationships with their mothers, and a number of them were bisexual.

My own research (Landa, 1983) suggests that the ego and moral development of voluntarily childless women—as measured by instruments developed by Loevinger (1970, 1976) and Kohlberg (1973)—is highly evolved, but that their paths to maturity are atypical, starting with precocity in childhood and adolescence, proceeding through a long developmental moratorium in early adulthood, and accelerating again at mid-life. It is my impression, based on my understanding of life-span development and on my own personal experience and observations rather than on empirical evidence, that developmentally, voluntarily childless women in their late thirties and forties resemble mothers in their fifties whose children have grown and left home. Perhaps, whatever the route, we all arrive at the same destination. A psychotherapist, responding to my research, commented, ". . . I am left wondering whether women in any group are particularly different from each other. The interconnectedness of all comes back to me again and again" (Jane Knowles, personal communication, March, 1989).

II

Following a talk I gave several years ago, a voluntarily childless woman in the audience offered to send me a poem she had written on the occasion of her thirty-fifth birthday. When it arrived, I read it with wonder. In seven stanzas, she had touched with heart-rending honesty the major themes of voluntary childlessness. I would like to use her work as a guide for presenting the experience of voluntary childlessness in the voices of the women who have chosen it.

NO ACCIDENT

No one asks anymore.
They know. Have I taken on the look
of a childless woman?
Too tidy, too narrow,
Too dry?
Do androgynous shadows
loom behind me?

Did I forget?
birth control a habit
too well built on twenty years of caution?
Slip from too young to too old
failing to note my skin's shift
from fragile to worn?

Was I afraid for me?
to produce a child
who would become a record
of flaws physical and psychological
I labor to conceal?
Would the weight of a child
expose weak joists
in our union?

Was I afraid for the child?
Of a world so consumed by power
that other human longing starved?
Of a society so blinded by the seduction
of having
that visions of being are blinded?

Or was it a dilemma
whose import forbade
tentative or ambivalent
action?
Do other women reach a moment of clarity?
Or is the choice
to mother
inevitably
a leap of faith?

There are moments
when a sharp pain
of lost life
surprises me.
The waste of tenderness
in a man
who is no one's father.
The eyes
of some children.
The simple connectedness
of some women.

But all I know
of the truth
of my childlessness
tells me
this choice is no accident.
Rather it is born
of a need to choose.
Some things fare better reared on a diet
of doubt
than do children.

And there is only
so much time and attention
to spend.

Valerie Fletcher
7/86

Have I taken on the look/of a childless woman? Too tidy, too narrow/Too dry?

As voluntary childlessness increases, so pronatalism—prejudice against childfree women—intensifies. The words "tidy," "narrow," and "dry" capture the essence of the prejudicial stereotypes. Narrow as in the pelvis, dry as in infertile, unlubricated; dry as in acerbic, lacking the moist milkiness of motherhood; narrow as in emotionally limited, experientially confined, narrowly focused on self-gratification. Tidy, compulsively neat, over-attached to domestic rituals, obsessively concerned with self-grooming.

Nowhere in the literature is there evidence to support the stereotypes. While childless women have access to more disposable income than do mothers, this is true of both voluntarily and involuntarily childless women, and there is no reason to believe that women who have chosen not to have children are more frivolous or self-indulgent than other women. Neither is there reason to believe that childless women are frigid or narcissistic.

That the stereotypes persist says more about our culture than it does about the voluntarily childless. While raising children in our society is difficult, and many of us may envy non-parents their freedom, it also seems likely that most of us have accepted cultural formulations which define femininity in terms of fertility: a woman is a mother; a non-mothering female is an insult to her gender. While manhood is not defined in terms of fatherhood, the female archetypes remain bound to reproductive functions: Virgin, Venus, Mother Earth. Childless women—both voluntarily childless and infertile—feel defensive about the confounding of womanhood with motherhood, but they are in continual danger of internalizing the prejudicial stereotypes.

Have I taken on the look/of a childless woman?
Do androgynous/shadows loom behind me?

Both my own work and two other studies (Kaltreider & Margolis, 1977; Teicholz, 1977, 1979) indicate that voluntarily childless women tend toward androgyny. I understand that androgyny is a problematic term, and would like to define it in terms specific to this particular discussion. Androgyny here means freedom to identify with male parents, to claim some characteristics which are culturally identified as masculine, to disclaim close identification with mothers and with a number of characteristics which are culturally defined as feminine. It is my impression that the androgyny of voluntarily childless women started early in life, contributing to the decision to remain childless rather than deriving from it. One woman I interviewed told me,

> It was a matter of first I wanted to be a horse, and then I realized that was impractical. And then I was going to be a rancher . . . then a forest ranger . . . But those were not just idle images . . . they were very much part of the whole anti-frills, anti-cute little patent leather shoes. (Libby, age 36. Landa, 1983, p. 145)

Other women reported difficulty identifying with their mothers and a tendency to identify with their fathers' way of life:

> Well, I think it's that she's just one of your absolutely model mothers . . . I had a very fixed idea that I did not want to be like her . . . economically [and otherwise] dependent on a man . . . (Emily, age 38. Landa, 1983, p. 145)
>
> I got a lot of what might have been male conditioning that left me freer in some very, very subtle ways . . . My father's a lawyer, my mother's a housewife . . . and I felt, from the very beginning, if one were to identify with one of the two of them, he was the one I identified with. I identified with the person who went to work . . . I would spend days with him in the office, "helping" him. I thought about becoming a lawyer at one point. You know, I think that's important. (Beth, age 34. Landa, 1983, p. 146)

While the voluntarily childless men whom I interviewed often described themselves in terms we tend to associate with feminine self-concepts, [" . . . I'm romantic, sentimental, and cry quite a lot"; "A lot of times I try to please people when I shouldn't . . . I have difficulty saying no when somebody wants me to do something"; "I'm not a seeker of prizes or rewards . . . I'm not ambitious"; "I see myself as trusting my inner authority as regards my feelings . . . my authority doesn't come through my head, it comes from my feelings"; "I have an intuitive sense about things that I respect a lot"; "I tend to avoid confrontations . . . So part of me, I think, is cowardly . . . "] the women's self-presentations consistently reflected characteristics generally associated with male identification:

> I see myself as basically intelligent, competent, organized, capable of doing most things. . . . I have respect for my mind . . . I feel like it's a pretty good tool and I'm using it pretty much up to the capacity I have. . . . People experience me as being very blunt . . . I like to be free and honest. . . . A weak area is intimacy . . . and commitment. . . . I am most ambivalent when it comes to emotional, interpersonal things.
>
> I think I'm very competitive . . . I'm a very driven person. . . . I feel as though identification of who I am in terms of career is enormously important. . . . Essentially I feel very . . . independent and able to make choices about my life. . . . Integrity is the ultimate commitment of my life. (Landa, 1983, pp. 142-145)

The wish among voluntarily childless women to be self-determining and independent cannot be overstated. At sixty-three, toward the end of an enormously successful career, surrounded by her cats in a beautiful house she had built for herself, one of my interviewees told me,

> . . . Not wanting to become really dependent upon somebody . . . that's one of the reasons why I chose and really preferred a professional life, because it gave me self-sufficiency . . . I've seen too many women marry and become totally economically dependent. And, I suppose, emotionally so, too. (Landa, 1983, p. 146)

An interesting pattern emerges here. The mother whom voluntarily childless women do not wish to grow up like is perceived as one who stayed home, without a job or career; she was humiliatingly dependent on her husband, and simultaneously did not provide the nurturance and security which the daughter feels she needed. This mother is viewed as a negative model of both motherhood and womanhood. While the daughter doesn't want to be a man, she does feel that male characteristics are more desirable than female ones as embodied by the mother, and men, of course, don't have babies. As one of the interviewees explained, "I didn't want to be like my mother, so I didn't become a mother." So long as the concepts of womanhood and motherhood remain linked, and until our ideas about the reproduction of mothering are reconstructed, women are likely to continue viewing their perceptions of their mothers as central to both gender-identification and fertility decisions.

Was I afraid for me?
Was I afraid for the child?

Women who choose not to have children see childbearing as a risk to themselves, to their marriages and to the child. On the surface, the fears are approachable: the child would have my flaws, there wouldn't be enough money to spend on college, the world is over-populated and in danger of self-destruction. Underneath, there is another layer of fears, grounded in personal history.

One of my interviewees, growing up in a happy home, was maimed in a car accident at the age of ten.

> If you have a fear that you can be torn out of your life, especially as a child, you have the fear that if you have a child, something will happen to that child, something you have no control over. (Landa, 1983, p. 107)

Caroline, who was raised in a traditional farm family, lost two older siblings to the 1918 flu epidemic. Greta, a refugee, grew up in a large, closely-knit family. When I asked her, "Do you think that the difficulty of life in the war and transitions and this large family had anything to do with your not having kids," she answered,

> Oh, yes. . . . I still to this day feel very insecure, like how would you take care of children? My parents didn't have any money when we came to this country, they had like fifty dollars in their pockets . . . And so I have this feeling . . . that you just want to get secure before you do something . . . I just never got used to it . . . and in some ways I feel that I didn't have a childhood. (Landa, 1983, p. 53)

Women who grew up in disrupted or unhappy families, women whose models of parenting and family life were negative, hesitate to have children for both their own sakes and for the sakes of their children.

> . . . I didn't want to have kids that might be like me . . . kind of hard to get along with, temper, like my father, very sharp and sudden temper. (Caroline, age 63. Landa, 1983, p. 199)

> I felt that having children would cost me my personhood . . . I was brought up without a father . . . and with a mother who's very emotionally distant, non-nurturing. I had no model for parenthood; I had no model for family life that I could embrace and aspire to . . . So it was that I felt that having a child would require that I become the nurturer, and I hadn't had it myself. I didn't have it to give . . . Before I had words for it, before I had a vocabulary for it, I knew I didn't have the supplies to provide a child at some level. (Renee, age 38. Landa, 1983, pp. 199-200)

> I thought, "I'll be at the university and I'll be this pregnant woman . . ." And all of a sudden, I didn't know who that person was. It was almost like an identity crisis . . . So I guess I fear the loss of the old body and all. (Beth, age 34, discussing an impending abortion. Landa, 1983, pp. 133-134)

> My father humiliated my mother. I didn't want to be humiliated, so I didn't want to become a mother. (Sylvia, age 39. Landa, 1983, p. 155)

Perhaps the most extreme example with which I'm familiar, of a woman who decided not to have children because she perceived it as a multiple risk, is that of Mary. Mary is the oldest of three children. When she was seven, her alcoholic father deserted the family. Within the year, her mother was hospitalized for schizophrenia and remained institutionalized the rest of her life. Mary and her brother and sister were taken in by an unmarried, hard-working uncle whose financial and emotional resources were severely strained by caring for the children.

Mary, as the oldest, took responsibility for the care of the younger siblings and for managing the household. She was eight years old. Her brother and sister were three and five. In her late twenties, Mary became pregnant and, in spite of having been raised a Catholic, unhesitatingly sought an abortion. At that moment, she realized she did not want to have children, not then and not ever. For her, as for her mother and her uncle, raising a family would lead to anxiety, poverty, and insanity. Mary never married. She eventually became a research biologist and a lesbian—the only lesbian in the sample.

Would the weight of a child/expose weak joists/in our sturdy union?

The marriages of voluntarily childless women, like Valerie Fletcher's, tend to be "sturdy unions." Pierette, in her late forties, describes her marriage as egalitarian and supportive.

> I'd say that my husband is probably my closest friend, as well as my husband and everything else . . . I've never had the feeling that he considered anything he was doing more important than anything I was doing. And he's always had a totally sharing kind of attitude toward any kind of tasks in the marriage. (Landa, 1983, p. 239)

Pierette's sister is autistic; when her husband was seventeen, his older brother was killed in a plane crash. Would any marriage, no matter how ideal, support the weight of a death or chronic disability? While Pierette did not attribute the success of her marriage to childlessness, both she and her husband felt that children were unnecessary to their happiness. "My husband is my closest friend . . . *and everything else.*"

But all I know/of the truth/of my childlessness/tells me/this choice is no accident. Rather it is born/of a need to choose.

While the decision-making process varies from individual to individual—with a number of patterns emerging—it appears to be cyclical in nature. The decision is made many times over, most particularly during life transitions which also involve changes in marital status or career shifts.

> It's one of those choices that I don't think ever is a resolved one, in the sense that one grows and changes and therefore the substance and the texture of that choice will change. And so my choice not to have a child changes with me, but remains the same choice. (Renee, age 38. Landa, 1983, p. 249)
>
> I have periodically gotten into a big stew about it . . . felt very worried, felt under a lot of pressure to decide . . . and I feel that I can't keep on doing that forever . . . it pulsates . . . (Emily, age 38. Landa, 1983, p. 119)
>
> Well, I have thought about it. And I've almost had children. I've been pregnant twice and have had two abortions. And made very conscious decisions not to have the children . . . (Mary, age 35. Landa, 1983, p. 128)
>
> Well, I've probably been thinking about whether to have kids or not have kids ever since . . . I became conscious that people have children. (Norah, age 36. Landa, 1983, p. 128)

Women who feel they have good reason to remain childless and who have reaffirmed their decision many times during their lives, feel they have made a positive life choice. They didn't want children and they have triumphed over biocultural pressures to reproduce. Few voluntarily childless women regret their commitment.

But there are exceptions. There can come a time when each of us can break free of the lessons of childhood; we come to understand that we are not fated to reproduce our parents' lives. For voluntarily childless women, this means that they can entertain motherhood without fear of living out the negative aspects of their mothers' lives. This realization often comes at mid-life, not infrequently after the woman has tenderly nursed a dying parent.

However, fertility declines in middle age, and the struggle for motherhood is often fruitless. In such cases, the voluntarily childless become involuntarily childless and suffer all the bitterness and grief of those to whom children have been denied.

There are moments/when a sharp pain of lost life surprises me.

But grief, too, comes to an end. Ultimately, for all women—those of us who have born children, those of us who have chosen not to have children, and those of us who are involuntarily childless—reproductive fertility stops being a preoccupation, and creativity, generativity, and relatedness become our sources of positive self-regard and satisfaction.

> I spent my thirties watching friends' increasing families, grieving quietly as year by year I grew more certain I would not conceive.
>
> A year or so ago the grieving stopped: I had a hysterectomy and it galvanized my thinking. I began to celebrate the many "haves" that continually enrich my life, determined not to let this one "have not" destroy me. I found that many women I admire did not have children in their lives. From Mary Cassatt I learned you don't have to be a mother to understand the special bond between a woman and a child; from Josephine Miles, the patience and the courage that it takes to triumph over obstacles. And from the wisest, most compassionate of all, George Eliot, I learned that empathy and caring are not reserved for mothers only.
>
> I realized that for me, "barren" was a state of mind, a trick of language, just a word. That although I could not be a mother I still could be a daughter, sister, wife, and friend, and in these roles fulfill my need to share and nurture. So if others in this culture still insist on seeing me as "second rate," it doesn't matter. At my center, where it counts the most, I know that I'm first class. (Flitterman-King, 1988, p. 12)

III

Inevitably, the major question which goes begging when voluntary childlessness is discussed is why so many women whose backgrounds appear similar to those of the voluntarily childless have become parents. Intrigued by this question, I informally interviewed six women whose histories were similar to those of my childless interviewees, but who had become mothers. I found a number of differences between the two groups which perhaps begin to define the voluntarily childless more sharply.

1. The women who had children appear to have been less mature in their late adolescence and early adulthood than the voluntarily childless women. Rather than controlling their fertility, they felt that a baby might provide them with the love and security which they lacked in their childhood.

2. The women who had children were sexually active earlier and appear to have remained more sexually active during their most fertile years, which occurred while abortion was illegal. Perhaps one might say that rather than choosing motherhood, they fell into it: it just happened.

3. The women who had children appear to have been less academically successful as young students. Four of the six I interviewed reported having learning disabilities. Career paths did not appear as open to them as to their voluntarily childless counterparts. They had less to lose by having a baby.

4. The women who had children appear to have been less psychologically sturdy. They suffered from depression and bouts of despair. Creating a family of their own seemed like a buffer between themselves and psychological ruin.

5. The women who had children married men who wanted to have children and who put enormous pressure on their wives to reproduce. They found these men particularly appealing because of their "maternal" qualities; to keep their husbands, they had children. As they themselves matured, all but one left their marriages. In the remaining marriage, the husband left.

6. As a maturational pattern which did not include precocity determined much of the reproductive history of the women who had children, it also made them unable to withstand societal pressures to

reproduce. Wanting to be viewed as respected, adult women, and accepting the prevalent cultural view of womanhood as synonymous with motherhood, they became mothers.

7. The women who had children were more likely to have been father-raised, their mothers having died or deserted the family. These women either found surrogate mothers among female family members—older sisters, aunts, grandmothers—and/or they perceived their fathers as "good enough" mothers. Indeed, the pattern of androgyny persisted among these women, but parenthood was included in their model of the androgen.

These six women were passionately devoted mothers, but they had difficulty raising their children. All of them became single, working mothers; all of them were divorced from their children's fathers; some of them fought substance addiction; some took prolonged vacations from motherhood, turning their children over to the fathers or to surrogate parents; some had attempted suicide, some have struggled against persistent stress-related illnesses, two have spent time in mental hospitals and all have sought psychotherapy for prolonged periods through their lives.

While these mothers ultimately achieved professional status, completing college and, in some cases, graduate school as adults, only one of them appears to have fulfilled her career potential, earning an MBA and becoming a financial analyst. But the one who might have been a doctor became a nurse; the one who might have become a lawyer is a paralegal; the ones who seemed most creative work as middle managers in bureaucratic settings. While these women whose histories resembled those of the voluntarily childless did *not* reproduce their families of origin in all respects, they *have* lived difficult lives. Listening to their stories, I could not help feeling that women with similar histories who had decided to remain childless because they considered childbearing to be an unacceptable risk had made a positive life choice.

DEMOGRAPHIC UPDATE ON VOLUNTARY CHILDLESSNESS

In an article by Richard Berke (1989) pubished by the *New York Times*, data are reported which might shed light on the rate of voluntary childlessness between 1990 and the end of the century. According to Martin O'Connell, chief of fertility statistics for the U.S. Bureau of the Census,

> Married women in their early 30's are far more likely to plan to have children 'someday' than they were in the mid-1970's . . . The increase [is] to 54.4 percent in 1988 from 33.5 percent in 1975. (p. A16)

Thirty-four-year-old women expecting to have children at a later age:

In 1975, 31%
In 1980, 42%
In 1985, 48%
In 1988, 55% (Berke, p. A16)

From glancing at these statistics, one might expect that the rate of voluntary childlessness will fall over the next ten years. However, given that fertility declines steeply after the age of thirty-seven, and remembering that there is a correlation between women's reaching their mid-thirties and undergoing a sort of 'fertility crisis,' it is probably wise to remain cautious about predicting the final fertility outcomes for these women.

What is worth considering, in my view, is that late childbearing in a population is tied to low fertility, so that we might expect an increasing number of one-child families and, ultimately, a drop in the birth rate, which has been remarkably resistant to change, remaining around 70 births per 1,000 women between the ages of 18 and 44 for the past several decades. Additionally, *mothers have aged over the past dozen years*, the number of children born to women in their thirties having increased by about one-third over the past dozen years, so that we can expect the trend towards late childbearing to continue.

And, given that only children are more prone to becoming voluntarily childless themselves, perhaps the 'demographic timebomb' of a significant increase in voluntary childlessness and an accompanying decline in the birthrate which has been awaited in this century will actually occur in the next.

REFERENCES

Berke, R. (1989). Late childbirth is found on rise. *New York Times*, June 22, p. A16.

Bram, S. (1978). Through the looking glass: Voluntary childlessness as a mirror of contemporary changes in the meaning of parenthood. In W. B. Miller & L. F. Newman (Eds.), *The first child and family formation*. Chapel Hill, NC: Carolina Population Center.

Burgwyn, D. (1981). *Marriage without children: Childless by choice or chance*. New York: Harper & Row.

Cawte, J. (1975). Psychosexual and cultural determinants of fertility choice behavior. *American Journal of Psychiatry, 132*, 750-753.

Faux, M. (1984). *Childless by choice*. Garden City, NY: Anchor Press.

Fletcher, V. (1986). *No accident*. Unpublished poem, Boston.

Flitterman-King, S. (1988, April). [Letter to the editor]. *Ms.*, p. 12.

Fullop, M. (1977). The empirical evidence from the fertility demand functions: A review of the literature. *American Economist, 21*, 12-22.

Glick, P. C. (1977). Updating the life cycle of the family. *Journal of Marriage and the Family, 39*, 5-13.

Humphrey, M. (1969). *Hostage seekers: A study of childless and adopting couples*. (Studies in Child Development), Atlantic Highlands, NJ: Humanities Press.

Kaltreider, N. B., & Margolis, A. G. (1977). Childless by choice: A clinical study. *American Journal of Psychiatry, 134*, 179-182.

Kohlberg, L. (1973). Continuities in childhood and adult moral development revisited. In P. B. Baltes & K. W. Schaie (Eds.), *Life-span developmental psychology: Personality and socialization*. New York: Academic Press.

Landa, A. (1983). *The lives and development of voluntarily childless men and women*. Unpublished doctoral dissertation, Union Graduate School, Cincinnati, OH.

Loevinger, J. (1970). *Ego development*. San Francisco: Jossey-Bass.

Loevinger, J. (1978). *Measuring ego development*. San Francisco: Jossey-Bass.

Mosher, W., & Bachrach, C. (1982) Childlessness in the United States: Estimates from the national survey of family growth. *Journal of Family Issues, 3*, 517-543.

Newsweek. (1986, September). Three's a crowd, 11-19.

Polonko, K., Scanzoni, J., & Teachman, J.D. (1982). *Journal of Family Issues, 3*, 545-573.

Poston, D. L., & Kramer, K. B. (1981). *Patterns of voluntary and involuntary childlessness in the United States, 1955-1973* (Final Report to National Institutes of Health). Washington, DC: Government Printing Office.

Poston, D. L. & Trent, K. (1982). International variability in childlessness. *Journal of Family Issues, 3*, 473-491.

Teicholz, J. (1977). *Psychological correlates of voluntary childlessness*. Unpublished doctoral dissertation, Boston Univeresity, Boston.

U.S. Bureau of the Census. (1987). ***Fertility of American women: June 1975.*** (Current Population Reports, Series P-20, No. 301). Washington, DC: U. S. Government Printing Office.

Veevers, J. E. (1972). Factors in the incidence of childlessness in Canada: An analysis of census data. ***Social Biology, 19,*** 266-274.

Veevers, J. E. (1973). Voluntarily childless wives: An exploratory study. ***Sociology and Social Research, 57,*** 356-366.

Veevers, J. E. (1975). The moral career of voluntarily childless wives: Notes on the defense of a variant world view. *The Family Coordinator*, *24*, 473-487.

Veevers, J. E. (1979). Voluntary childlessness: A review of issues and evidence. ***Marriage and Family Review, 2,*** 2-26.

Veevers, J. E. (1980). ***Childless by choice.*** Toronto: Butterworth.

RESOURCES

Carolina Population Center
University of North Carolina
University Square 300kA
Chapel Hill, NC 27514

National Alliance for Optional Parenthood (NON)
3 North Liberty Street
Baltimore, MD 21201

Planned Parenthood World Population
Information & Education Department
810 Seventh Avenue
New York City, NY 10019

Population Reference Bureau
133 Connecticut Avenue
Washington, DC 20036

Establishing the First Stages of Early Reciprocal Interactions Between Mothers and Their Autistic Children

Dorothy Gartner
Nancy M. Schultz

INTRODUCTION

Many severely withdrawn autistic young children, especially those whose symptoms appear early, do not elicit normally emerging mothering responses. This paper describes an attempt to develop the beginnings of such triggering behavior in the child so that reciprocal responsiveness between the mother and such a withdrawn child can unfold. Researchers such as Bell (1974), Lewis and Lee-Painter (1974), Brazelton, Koslowski and Main (1974), Schaffer (1971), and others have concentrated their more recent research on the behaviors of normal infants and mothers and on the processes and transactions that go on between them. These studies clearly highlight the fact that the infant is an active rather than passive participant in these transactions and that the infant's behavior shapes, reinforces and changes the caregiving behavior of the mother. According to Schaffer (1971), the infant stimulates the mother so that she comes into phase with the baby which produces

---

Dorothy Gartner, PhD, is Clinical Associate Professor in the Division of Child and Adolescent Psychiatry at the State University of New York, Health Science Center at Brooklyn.

Nancy M. Schultz, PhD, is in private practice in New York. She is also Adjunct Supervising Psychologist at the Department of Child and Adolescent Psychiatry, St. Luke-Roosevelt Hospital, NY.

affectional bonds between them. Over time the relationship stabilizes so that it is reasonably constant and predictable to both. The infant initiates these transactions with the mother in ways beautifully described by Stern (1979), with eye gaze, head and body movements, crying and fussing. One can see the infant get the mother's attention by staring at the mother, making facial movements as well as body movements and later, sounds, so that the mother is virtually compelled to respond. Similarly, the infant terminates the transaction by head and body movements away from the mother and by shifting gaze. The infant is now signalling that a respite from the stimulation is needed. The mother learns these cues. She gets to know her infant, its temperament and timing. Brazelton et al. (1974) found that most mothers "phase" their responses to the baby in accordance with the baby's attention-inattention cycles. As the mother gets reinforced by the infant's responses, she gains confidence in her mothering abilities and her sense of intimacy with her baby grows.

The mother, too, is initiating interactions in her characteristic fashion with behaviors such as facial expressions, especially mouth and eye movements, cooing and touching. The child comes to know its mother's voice, smell and touch intimately. Thus, what is occurring between baby and a sensitive, aware mother is simultaneous initiating and responding between them. Slowly, a basic fit develops between them so that they can be in and out of contact synchronously. Stern (1979) has stated that this critical process in the infant's development not only makes it possible for the baby to get its needs met and begin to know itself and its mother, but that it is the prototype for all interpersonal exchanges. Similarly, Winnicott (1974) considers the "holding environment," which refers to the responsiveness of a sensitive mother to her infant's needs, as beginning the organization of the infant's ego functions and the modulation of the intensity of its drives. This ensures a positive unfolding of all future development.

When this early process is not set in motion, for various reasons, serious problems develop between mother and baby. Mahler (1968) found that if the infant lacked or lost the ability to utilize the mother during early phases of life then crucial disturbance developed. Robson and Moss (1970) traced the changes in the subjective feelings of attachment of mothers to their babies. They found that if the mother cannot comfort her baby within the first few months of life so that crying and fussing decrease, and if there is no eye-to-eye contact or smiles, there follows a breakdown in the caregiving system. A vicious cycle develops in which the mother's efforts to cope with the crying infant are inadequate and the infant then responds with more crying which causes the mother to withdraw even more. Such mothers often feel angry and hurt. They feel that their baby is rejecting them and that they are, therefore, failures as mothers. The shame and humiliation of this is extremely painful to the mothers who then further withdraw from their babies.

Robson and Moss' findings shed light on the processes that occur between mothers and their autistic infants. Autistic babies are either very non-demanding, "good" babies who stay quietly in crib or play-pen, communicating few cues, or they are babies who are irritable and fussy and not readily comforted. In either case they establish limited eye contact, are not always aware of or responsive to their mother's presence, rarely smile and rarely initiate contact. Unlike normally developing children, they do not communicate readiness to begin or terminate an interaction and thereby hinder their mother's ability to respond sensitively. Because they often find ways of comforting themselves, such as by rocking, twirling or head banging, they frustrate the mother's pleasure in providing her child with comfort and thus prevent feelings of intimacy from developing. As a result of the estrangement and distance between them, the mother's caregiving responses are not evoked nor strengthened. The mother and infant do not establish a fit, and as a result, the synchronous transactions between them do not develop adequately. The mother begins to distrust her observations and responses which further separates her from the child. Attachment, intimacy and reciprocal sending and receiving communications are neither sustained, enhanced nor enjoyed. Rutter (1978) states it succinctly when he says, ". . . firstly, more than anything else, it is the reciprocity of social interchange that is missing in autism." This is a very different point of view from the early one expressed by Kanner (1943) when he hypothesized that autism was caused by the cold and distant mother, sometimes referred to as the "refrigerator mother." This early point of view has caused needless heartache and guilt in generations of mothers, often, unfortunately, reinforced by professionals. It has been observed repeatedly that the mothers of autistic children are normally distributed along the warm to cold continuum or along any other set of variables.

DESCRIPTION OF CHILDREN

Since the autistic child and its mother have missed the essential early stages of reciprocal interactions and have not, therefore, established a natural fit, we are proposing, in this paper, therapeutic interventions that address these processes in severely withdrawn young autistic children. The children discussed in this paper range in age from 2 to 5, male and female. They all met the criteria for autistic disorder in the *Diagnostic and Statistical Manual of Mental Disorders* (DSM-III-R) (American Psychiatric Association, 1987). They lacked expressive and receptive language, were profoundly withdrawn, and exhibited typical autistic features such as twirling, head banging, rocking and stereotypic movements. They were socially isolated, only occasionally establishing eye contact. Some of the children made unintelligible sounds and some tended to shriek piercingly at times. Their histories revealed that they had all developed many of these symptoms before 36 months of age. These were children with a profound lack of responsiveness. They represented the extreme end of the pervasively disordered continuum.

The children were seen in a therapeutic nursery which consisted of 4 or 5 children with two therapists and several trainees, either psychology interns or psychiatry child fellows. The children attended the nursery three times a week for two hours each time. Each child was assigned to a trainee who worked with the child and the mother in the nursery and at home. Every mother was required to attend each nursery session where she would observe the therapist work with her child and also interact with her child as well as the other children. While they participated in the nursery, the mothers would often first become sensitive to the weak cues of other children before they could respond to their own child. This made them more hopeful about their abilities to be able, ultimately, to pick up cues from their own child. Fathers were also encouraged to take part in the treatment of their child. Whenever possible, the therapist worked with the father and child together.

DESCRIPTION OF TREATMENT TECHNIQUES

The essential intent of this technique is to establish the initial stage in the process between the child and the mother that will enable them to begin to interact with each other synchronously and pleasurably so that they can gradually become more intimate and trusting of each other. At first the therapist does with the child what the mother might have done had development proceeded normally. When the child experiences these interventions in a systematic fashion and in the presence of a trained, sensitive therapist who can focus solely on the child's brief, weak cues, the hope is that the child will be more likely to attempt to repeat these behaviors. Simultaneously, the mother is helped to become sensitive to the weak cues the child is beginning to communicate and she is taught to respond to them. The hope here is that the mother will be helped to free her natural responses that had gotten blocked as a result of the pathological interactions between herself and her baby. When this occurs the beginnings of brief moments of fit get established so that new transactions and affectional bonds are experienced and strengthened. These then take on meaning and autonomy. Interest in each other rather than disinterest develops which gives each a sense of each other's presence and intrinsic value; a sense that someone else is there.

Bobby, a 5 year old, very withdrawn autistic child, wandered about the room as though neither people nor objects existed. He was lost in his world, responding to no one. At first the therapist treated him as though he were a very young baby. She sang to him while he sat on her lap, played with his hands and feet by touching them and moving them up and down rhythmically. Systematically his body was touched with soft velvet and coarse nylon, his hands were put into cold and warm water and perfume was used to stimulate his sense of smell. After several months, Bobby began to lift his arms and legs on his own while looking at the therapist for brief moments. Once these weak cues appeared, his mother was helped to do with Bobby what the therapist had done. His mother would hold him, look into his eyes cooing to him and touch him a lot. Gradually, Bobby began to respond by glancing at his mother. As his mother experienced being responded to briefly, she began to free some of her blocked responses and an unfolding of her interactions with her child began. As Bobby began to touch her face, especially her mouth while she sang or cooed to him, she adjusted her singing and smiles to correspond to his cues. Circular interactions slowly began to develop and she became increasingly more spontaneous, now gradually interacting with Bobby more in keeping with her style than the therapist's.

As the child's communications become clearer they become more comprehensible to the mother so that she can respond more accurately and fully. For example, as three year old Joey became more aware of his environment, after several months of therapy, he became unhappy when his mother left the room. He would cry loudly and look at the door. At first the mother seemed surprised. After several such occurrences she realized that it was not by chance that he was crying and that his behavior indicated that an attachment was beginning to develop. She began holding him on her lap more lovingly, less mechanically, and more like he were indeed a person who could respond to her. A similar situation occurred with two year old Jay. The therapist stroked his cheek with a velvet cloth in the course of each session. He then began moving the therapist's hand to his cheek for more. His mother was then brought into the interaction so that now Jay brought the piece of velvet to her when she was in the room. It gave his mother much pleasure to do something for Jay which he asked of her and which he clearly enjoyed.

As the mother and child begin to understand each other a little better, new, and pleasurable moments occur between them. They develop a better fit with each other so that more natural ways of being together evolve. For example, the mother of three year old Anna was taught to help Anna squeeze a handful of playdough for 5 minute periods several times a day. The mother would put her hand over Anna's and squeeze gently. As Anna began responding her mother became more innovative. She began rolling and pounding the dough with Anna, which led to more eye contact and more touching. As Anna responded by smiling and giggling while playing with the play dough, her mother became more responsive. She also became more empathic, comforting the child when she made her frequent piercing cries rather than punishing her.

Another example of the way in which these interventions foster the unfolding of new interactions between mother and child comes from the work with two year old Rosa. When she first came to the nursery she lay on the floor in a ball. Her mother seldom attempted to interact with her. She was encouraged to hold Rosa on her lap humming gently to her. At first Rosa would slide off her mother's lap going back to her position on the floor. The mother was then taught to watch for moments when Rosa seemed a little more able to tolerate being touched. At such moments Rosa would shift her body towards her mother or glance at her for an instant. These were the times the mother was encouraged to touch Rosa more gently than she had in the past and to stroke her face and body. Gradually Rosa began to snuggle into her mother and move her mother's hands to where she wanted them or touch her, especially on the mouth. There followed moments when Rosa lay quietly in her mother's lap while her mother hummed to her. Eventually, Rosa began to make little sounds which triggered more vigorous humming and singing from her mother.

Additional techniques to evoke reciprocal interaction are used. The mother and child are taught to roll a ball or a toy car back and forth to each other; the mother catches her child coming down the slide repeatedly until the child giggles and trusts that the mother will be there; they splash water together or pour water from cups; they make sounds, the mother first imitating the child's sounds and then initiating some of her own. Mirror play is an especially useful technique. For example, Ms. G. would sit in front of the mirror with Paula standing next to her. She would quietly point to Paula's reflection in the mirror for many sessions. Paula began looking in the mirror making her face move and watching intently. Her mother greatly enjoyed watching Paula's interest in herself which led the mother to initiate games. When Paula looked in the mirror her mother would point to Paula's image and say "Paula" and then touch herself and say "ma ma." After this went on for a long time

Paula began looking at her own reflection more carefully. Later she looked and then touched herself. Following that she began to look at her mother's reflection and then touched her mother. This led to new spontaneous responses in Paula's mother. She began talking to Paula, naming parts of the child's body and also naming Paula's actions. Paula moved about more purposefully, made more sounds which produced more playfulness and smiles in the mother.

CONCLUSION

In normal development the mother and child naturally initiate and respond to each other reciprocally. The mother of a severely withdrawn autistic child must learn to do this in spite of the child's withdrawal. The child must learn to emit cues that will trigger and sustain mothering behavior. From our work with mother-autistic child pairs we have observed the budding, the unfolding of such reciprocal interactions in a number of cases. Autism is a pervasive disorder that limits an individual's development. The technique presented in this paper is only one aspect of a multifaceted approach to the treatment of autism. It is seen as a very beginning intervention in the lengthy and complex work with severely withdrawn autistic children and their mothers. Nonetheless, it is an important intervention because it awakens, unblocks and sustains the mother's natural care-giving abilities and it provides the child with social stimulation and intimacy with its mother. Mahler (1968), Schopler and Reichler (1971), and Fenichel (1974), in spite of differences in approach and theoretic orientation, have all concluded that the mother is a vital participant in the therapy.

The daily routines between a mother and child, usually taken for granted under normal circumstances, often do not occur with autistic children. When the mother and autistic child learn to smile and sing together, touch and look at each other, play and enjoy together, even for brief moments, the quality of their lives is vastly enhanced. The mothers become more able to acknowledge that they do have a significant part to play in their child's treatment and thereby contribute to their child's development.

REFERENCES

American Psychiatric Association (1987). *Diagnostic and Statistic Manual of Mental Disorders* (3rd edition, revised). Washington, D.C.: Author.

Bell, R. (1974). Contribution of human infants to caregiving and social interaction. In M. Lewis & L. Rosenblum (Eds.), *The effects of the infant on its caregiver*. (pp. 1-19). New York: John Wiley and Sons.

Brazelton, T.B., Koslowski, B., & Main, M. (1974). The origins of reciprocity: The early mother-infant interaction. In M. Lewis & L. Rosenblum (Eds.), *The effects of the infant on its caregiver.* (pp. 49-76). New York: John Wiley and Sons.

Fenichel, C. (1974). Special education as the basic therapeutic tool in treatment of severely disturbed children. *Journal of Autism and Childhood Schizophrenia, 4*, 177-186.

Kanner, L. (1943). Autistic disturbance of affective contact. *Nervous Child, 2*, 217-250.

Lewis, M., & Lee-Painter, S. (1974). The interaction approach to the mother-infant dyad. In M. Lewis & L. Rosenblum (Eds.), *The effects of the infant on its caregiver*. (pp. 21-48). New York: John Wiley and Sons.

Mahler, M. (1968). *On human symbiosis and the vissitudes of individuation.* New York: International University Press.

Robson, K.S., & Moss, H.A. (1970). Patterns and determinants of maternal attachment. *Journal of Pediatrics, 77*, 976-985.

Rutter, M. (1978). Diagnosis and definition of childhood autism. *Journal of Autism and Developmental Disorders*, 8, 139-161.

Schaffer, H.R. (1971). *Mothering*. Cambridge: Harvard University Press.

Schopler, E., & Reichler, R.J. (1971). Developmental therapy by parents with their autistic child. In M. Rutter (Ed.) *Infantile autism: Concepts, characteristics and treatment.* London: Churchill Livingstone.

Stern, D. (1979). *The first relationship*. Cambridge: Howard University Press.

Winnicott, D. (1974). *The maturational processes and the facilitating Environment*. New York: International Universities Press in Environment.

SECTION V: OPPRESSION

Mothering the Biracial Child: Bridging the Gaps Between African-American and White Parenting Styles

Robin L. Miller
Barbara Miller

Incident

Once riding in old Baltimore,
Heart-filled, head-filled with glee,
I saw a Baltimorean
Keep looking straight at me.

Robin L. Miller is a PhD candidate at the Center for Community Research and Action at New York University, where she received her masters degree in 1988. She specializes in African-American issues, AIDS prevention and sexual health, and quantitative methodology. She has consulted to Planned Parenthood of Bergen County and the Gay Men's Health Crisis (GMHC), and is currently the Coordinator of Evaluation for GMHC's Department of Education.

Barbara Miller, PhD, is Clinical Psychologist in private practice with the Mead Counseling Center in Greenwich, CT. Her clinical specialty areas include ethnic minority concerns and parenting issues. She has consulted to the Colorado Juvenile Justice System, women's health centers in Washington, DC and Vermont, and a number of colleges including Manhattanville and Marymount in NY.

Now I was eight and very small,
And he was no whit bigger,
And so I smiled, but he poked out
His tongue, and called me "Nigger."

I saw the whole of Baltimore
From May until December;
Of all the things that happened there
That's all that I remember.

—Countee Cullen

By the age of six, most African-American children have learned that blackness more often evokes contempt, fear, and derision than it does positive images on the part of mainstream America. As a result, the primary tasks of an African-American parent are to (1) negate dominant cultural messages which undermine self-esteem and efficacy, (2) validate uniqueness, (3) teach strategies for emotional and physical survival in the face of racism, and (4) foster the development of coping mechanisms for dealing with legal and defacto discriminatory experiences.

Many of the survival skills learned by African-Americans over successive generations are largely unnecessary in the socialization agenda of the majority culture. Unfortunately, the majority culture parent in a Black-white marriage needs to be able to teach African-American survival skills to his or her biracial child in order to insure healthy bicultural adaptation.

Socialization processes in African-American families are generally poorly documented in psychological literature. As a result of ethnocentric biases in psychological research and general acceptance by psychologists of normative perspectives, the socialization literature on African-American families has failed to describe how it is that African-American parents raise their children to become competent adults, what the markers of competency are for African-American adults, and what the socialization goals are for African-American parents.

Research on the parenting style of white parents is well documented, in comparison to the availability of sound research on African-American parenting and socialization. Further, research documenting the different parenting styles of African-American and white parents is sufficiently prevalent to draw conclusions about the differing socialization goals of white and African-American parents. Literature relevant to parenting issues for the Black-white couple, however, is almost non-existent; psychological research has provided little in the way of guidance for the African-American or white mother attempting to successfully socialize an interracial offspring.

In this paper we will attempt to fill this gap in the social science literature by drawing on empirical, theoretical, and anecdotal sources of information; it is our goal to highlight some of the issues of particular relevance to raising children of Black-white marriages.

A THEORETICAL FRAMEWORK FOR UNDERSTANDING SOCIALIZATION

Boykin and Toms (1985) offer a conceptual framework for understanding socialization in African-American families that is applicable to the distillation of critical processes within Black-white families. Boykin and Toms' organizing framework for understanding African-American family socialization patterns is called the "Triple Quandary." The "Triple Quandary" basically understands the socialization goals of African-American parents as an exercise in integrating the values of three competing systems: majority values, African-American culture, and a minority group agenda.

African-American families are assumed to be cognizant of and have internalized majority values (e.g., achievement motivation, individualism, etc.) and to understand their instrumental value for success in society. Concurrently, however, African-American parents, as a result of greater distance from the mainstream, promote an African-American cultural behavioral style that is at odds with the valued styles in larger society. Transformed African cultural patterns are present in the behavioral style and in the values of African-Americans (Nobles, 1988; Sudarkasa, 1988), and remain a potent influence on the behavioral models presented to children. African-American culture is described in terms of the different styles that African-Americans possess in the areas of spirituality, harmony, movement, verve, affect, communalism, expressive individualism, oral expressiveness, and time (Boykin & Toms, 1985; Hurston, 1981; Jones, 1986, 1987, 1988a, 1988b; Nobles, 1988; Sudarkasa, 1988).

The third system in the "Triple Quandary" is related to existence as a minority. Minority status requires the development of specific and unique adaptation and coping styles (Holliday, 1985; Spencer, 1987, 1988). As such, African-American children must learn the appropriate behaviors for functioning in the majority community *and* in the African-American community, with the appropriate knowledge of the implications of belonging to a stigmatized group. It is the recognition of minority status and the attainment of socialization outcomes in recognition of that status that acts as a buffer between majority values and African-American behavioral style. For biracial children, it is minority coping skills that mediate the competing value systems of each parent.

Boykin and Toms (1985) have identified four dimensions which impact effective coping with minority status: active-passive, system engagement-system disengagement, system maintenance-system change, and system blame-person blame.

Whether parents engage in an active or passive coping style directly impacts children's ability to perceive themselves as victims of discrimination, as well as their sense of self-esteem and personal worth. In order to establish a protected sense of personal worth and a unified identity, children must be able to model an active coping style for the racially defined incidents that the child will inevitably confront. For example, imagine that a biracial child has been called a "nigger" by a peer in the school classroom. The parent who offers only sympathy is using a passive coping style, while the parent who calls the school and the offending child's parents has used an adaptive active approach to handling the incident. Active coping helps the child correctly perceive racism and teaches how to handle discrimination without feeling personally stigmatized.

System-engagement versus system-disengagement refers to the type of action that parents may take regarding continued involvement in mainstream institutions versus parallel institutions, and through this, whether parents act to maintain the current system or attempt to change it. Parents must balance their behavior as role models along these dimensions in order to teach and promote personal empowerment. For example, actively trying to change racism in the school through PTA sponsored educational initiatives may be a useful form of system-engagement and system-change. Similarly, regular involvement in African-American parallel institutions like churches and social clubs (system-disengagement) can provide a supportive setting for identity development and offer alternative role models to mainstream culture.

System-maintenance and system-change works in a similar fashion to system-engagement and system-disengagement. African-Americans must know how to successfully negotiate mainstream institutions, but must also have the pride and skills necessary to attempt to fight structural racism. The ability to function in mainstream institutions, but not unwittingly maintain institutionalized racism is equally critical for biracial children.

System-blame versus person-blame becomes critical in terms of whether or not African-American children are socialized by their parents to believe that the status of people of color is a function of systems that support and maintain discrimination as opposed to viewing these as the flaws and failures of minority people.

In summary, the Black-white couple, like African-American parents, while attempting to socialize their children to function in mainstream society, must also prepare their children to cope with life as a minority group member along several coping dimensions, and prepare their children for survival in the African-American community by presenting models of behavioral style unique to African-American culture; a minority experience must guide socialization goals and strategies (Scott-Jones & Nelson-LeGall, 1986).

ETHNIC IDENTIFICATION

Ethnic socialization refers to the communication of an ethnic identity, and is a critical piece of a minority agenda in a society where race is a salient feature of life (van den Berghe, 1967) and a criteria for the distribution of social rewards. The necessity of fostering resilience and adaptive coping mechanisms is critical for caste-bound minorities (Ogbu, 1988; Spencer, 1987) who must function in a world of ambiguity (Peters, 1978). Black-white children are fundamentally African-American when dealing with the larger world, although their ethnic/racial classification by their own standards and those of the African-American and mainstream communities can be ambiguous.

Jackson, McCullough, and Gurin (1988) suggest that the family serves two functions in terms of ethnic identification: the family is the locus of personal self-esteem and self-worth and serves to insulate children from the negative consequences of racism. They suggest that the degree of emphasis in the family on African-American socialization is a key determinant of coping skills.

Spencer (1988) has shown that for African-American male adolescents, an African perspective is a critical coping tool. In a study of young adolescents in Atlanta, Spencer discovered that African-American males who were socialized with a Euro-centric perspective had poor coping skills and high reported stress levels, when compared to males who maintained an African perspective. Spencer (1985) has also demonstrated an inverse relationship between mental health and degree of belief in normative values for African-American children. Spencer (1985, 1987) suggests that African-American parents who raise their children without an emphasis on African-American culture are participants in the continuation and dehumanizing effects of racism.

It has been demonstrated that for African-American children achievement and success are not as strongly related to personal strivings or self-perceptions as they are to perceptions of racial and institutional barriers. Spencer (1985) demonstrated that for white children, personal perceptions are predictive of achievement, but that for African-American children the child's perception of how his or her teacher assesses his or her competence predicts achievement. In a study of 22 third, fourth, and fifth grade classrooms, Spencer found that personal characteristics were the most salient predictors of white students' academic achievement, as measured by standardized tests. For African-American children, social interactions in the classroom were most predictive of test scores. There is no evidence to suggest that similar findings would not apply to biracial children.

Recent evidence has shown that homogeneity of environment,

defined as predominantly African-American versus predominantly white, is related to higher levels of self-esteem for African-American children (see, for example, McAdoo, 1985). This research suggests that support for healthy ethnic identification emerges from intensive involvement in the African-American community for African-American children. For the biracial child, therefore, multicultural settings may provide the most healthy environment for the development of positive ethnic identification.

Holliday (1985) studied 44 African-American children in terms of their development of functional life skills, interpersonal skills, and problem-solving skills. It was hypothesized that because African-American children interact with more settings and have more role requirements that are qualitatively distinct than white children, African-American children would need more extensive behavior repertoires and the flexibility to utilize these repertoires. It was also hypothesized that African-American children would demonstrate early maturity as a function of biculturalism and would be either positively or negatively influenced by the fact that they could not easily predict when their efforts would lead to success or failure. Holliday's study revealed that the press to develop functional life skills was greatest in the home; at home, children demonstrated high communication skills, management skills, independence, and caretaking abilities. Interpersonal skills were in greatest demand at school, while problem-solving skills were most demanded in the neighborhood. Thus, the hypothesis that extensive behavioral repertoires were required of the studied children was supported.

Attainment of functional skills at home was unrelated to academic achievement, but perceptions of teacher assessments were predictive of school achievement. It was also shown that children were better distinguished by the stability of use of behavioral repertoires than by absence or presence of sets of skills. One implication of the study is that African-American children are required to assume a varied set of roles and are more or less successful in their interactions to the degree that they can switch from one set of role requirements to another. For the biracial child, multiple roles and repertoires may be even more explicitly required.

Peters (1985) interviewed mothers of African-American children about the impact of race on their socialization goals. Thirty families were observed in their homes for a period of two years. All of the families were middle-class, two-parent African-American families with a child one year of age at the study's onset.

African-American mothers reported that they had a responsibility to teach their children how to cope with prejudice; mothers viewed a positive personal and ethnic identification as critical to the process of teaching survival. Parents also emphasized the role of providing unconditional love to their children as a means of buffering and mediating emotional upset from experiences of prejudice in the outside world. Mothers viewed race issues as a source of emotional stress for themselves, and for their children. Generally, mothers believed that if they could not provide adequate models of how to cope with race-related stressors, then children would experience unnecessary stress. The availability of ethnically self-assertive role models is crucial for the healthy development of biracial children as well.

Overall, existing literature suggests that self-esteem for African-American children is related to personal support and encouragement in the home, but achievement is related to factors outside of the family socialization environment. Others' perceptions of African-American children's potential appear to be the critical determinants of actual success, a relationship that is not equally relevant to majority children. The critical determinant or mediator of the relationship between outside expectations of roles and behaviors and psychological health appears to be the ability to cope with the world from a minority perspective. Development of a minority coping style, as demonstrated by Spencer, is strongly related to the degree of emphasis by parents on African-American socialization; as Peters has shown, African-American parents consider African-American socialization a primary parenting goal.

The experiences of biracial children will be similar to those of African-American children. For African-American and biracial children, minority agendas are the critical mediator between potential isolation and potential lack of mental health. Without some orientation toward a minority agenda, a child cannot reconcile or cope with the conflict between African-American culture and majority culture or place this conflict in a relevant context. Lacking a minority agenda, children are defenseless against social reality. Thus, the balance between majority values and African-American culture struck by the presence of a minority agenda becomes the deciding factor for positive versus negative socialization outcomes and overall mental health.

CONCLUSION

Neither the mother nor father of an interracial child is capable of empathic understanding or role model provision for a mixed-race person, as neither parent is mixed-race her or himself. However, it must be recognized that the interracial child is an ethnic minority, and must therefore acquire coping skills related to a minority existence. Parents must develop the capacity to integrate a minority agenda into their socialization goals, as a result.

The interracial child has both African-American and white heritage, but may never find complete acceptance in either community. It is therefore imperative that these children be provided all of the cultural and historical knowledge necessary to understand the context of his or her identity, as well as be allowed to integrate aspects of both identities into a unique emergent sense of self. Unless a unified perception of the child is maintained, ethnicity can become a stressor (Adams, 1973; Piscacek & Golub, 1973), leading to bifurcation. In effect, parents in a Black-white marriage must foster a bicultural behavioral repertoire in order to guarantee their biracial children's survival.

EPILOGUE

The topic of our article was of particular interest to us as mother and daughter, members of a biracial family, and psychologists. Working on this article presented us with our first opportunity to work together professionally. It has been fun, challenging, and has taken us through a self-discovery process. Through the process of writing this article, we have learned that our family life and extra-familial interactions have been truly enriched by the blending of the best of African-American and majority cultural values.

REFERENCES

Adams, P. L. (1973). Counseling with interracial couples and their children in the South. In J. R. Stuart & L. E. Abt (Eds.), *Interracial marriage: Expectations and realities*. (pp. 63-80). New York: Grossman.

Boykin, A. W., & Toms, F. D. (1985). Black child socialization: A conceptual framework. In H. P. McAdoo & J. L. McAdoo, (Eds.), *Black children: Social, educational, and parental environments*. (pp. 33-52). Beverly Hills: Sage.

Cullen, C. (1925). Incident. In Adoff, A. (Ed.), *I am the darker brother: An anthology of modern poems by Negro Americans*. (p. 85). Toronto: MacMillan.

Holliday, B. G. (1985). Developmental imperatives of social ecologies: Lessons learned from black children. In H. P. McAdoo & J. L. McAdoo, (Eds.), *Black children: Social, educational, and parental environments*. (pp. 53-71). Beverly Hills: Sage.

Hurston, N. Z. (1981). *The sanctified church: The folklore writings of Zora Neale Hurston*. Berkeley: Turtle Island.

Jackson, J. S., McCullough, W. R., & Gurin, G. (1988). Family, socialization environment, and identity development in black Americans. In H. P. McAdoo, (Ed.), *Black families, 2nd edition*. (pp. 242-256). Beverly Hills: Sage.

Jones, J. (1986). *Being black in America: The politics of personality*. Invited address, Division 8, American Psychological Association. 94th Annual Meeting of the American Psychological Association, Washington, D.C.

Jones, J. (1987). Cultural differences in temporal perspectives: Instrumental and expressive behaviors in time. In J. E. McGrath (Ed.), *The social psychology of time: New perspectives*. (pp. 21-38). Beverly Hills: Sage.

Jones, J. (1988a). Racism in black and white: A bicultural model of reaction and evolution. In P. A. Katz & D. A. Taylor, (Eds.), *Eliminating racism: Profiles in controversy*. (pp. 117-135). New York: Plenum.

Jones, J. (1988b). *Piercing the veil: Bicultural strategies for coping with prejudice and racism*. Invited address, University of Alabama.

McAdoo, H. P. (1985). Racial attitude and self-concept of young black children over time. In H. P. McAdoo & J. L. McAdoo, (Eds.), *Black children: Social, educational, and parental environments*. (pp. 213-242). Beverly Hills: Sage.

Nobles, W. W. (1988). African-American family life: An instrument of culture. In H. P. McAdoo, (Ed.), *Black families, 2nd edition*. (pp. 44-53). Beverly Hills: Sage.

Ogbu, J. U. (1988). Black education: A cultural-ecological perspective. In H. P. McAdoo, (Ed.), *Black families, 2nd edition*. (pp. 169-184). Beverly Hills: Sage.

Peters, M. F. (1978). Introduction to special issue. *Journal of marriage and the family, 11*, 655-658.

Peters, M. F. (1985). Racial socialization of young black children. In H. P. Mc-

Adoo & J. L. McAdoo, (Eds.), *Black children: Social, educational, and parental environments*. (pp. 159-173). Beverly Hills: Sage.

Piscacek, V., & Golub, M. (1973). Children of interracial marriages. In J. R. Stuart & L. E. Abt (Eds.), *Interracial marriage: Expectations and realities*. (pp. 51-62). New York: Grossman.

Scott-Jones, D., & Nelson-LeGall, S. (1986). Defining black families past and present. In E. Seidman and J. Rappaport, (Eds.), *Redefining social problems*. New York: Plenum.

Spencer, M. B. (1985). Racial variations in achievement prediction: The school as a conduit for macrostructural cultural tension. In H. P. McAdoo & J. L. McAdoo, (Eds.), *Black children: Social, educational, and parental environments*. (pp. 85-112). Beverly Hills: Sage.

Spencer, M. B. (1987). Black children's ethnic identity formation: Risk and resilience in castelike minorities. In J. S. Phinney & M. J. Rotheram, (Eds.), *Children's ethnic socialization*. (pp. 103-116). Beverly Hills: Sage.

Spencer, M. B. (1988). Address to the Second Biennial Meeting of the Society for Research on Adolescence. Alexandria, Virginia.

Sudarkasa, N. (1988). Interpreting the African heritage in Afro-American family organization. In H. P. McAdoo, (Ed.), *Black families, 2nd edition*. (pp. 27-43). Beverly Hills: Sage.

van den Berghe, P. L. (1967). *Race and racism*. New York: John Wiley and Sons.

Lesbian Parents: Claiming Our Visibility

Sandra Pollack

Very often in discussions and research on lesbian and straight parents, the focus is on the common factor of motherhood and on the ways lesbian parents and straight parents face some of the same difficulties. I would like us to think not so much about these similarities, but to redirect our thinking and focus more on the differences. I want to think with you about why a good deal of the initial research on lesbian mothers focused on the comparisons rather than the contrasts, why that research can have a negative impact on us as feminists, and why we need to encourage and support the research that is now beginning to be done on the differences. What I want to show is that the life situations/life experiences/realities for lesbian parents are not the same as those of heterosexuals and that it is not particularly advantageous to show that we are all the same.

You will notice that I often use the word "parent" rather than "mother." I do that because I believe that the terms parent and parenting are more inclusive and more easily incorporate the role of persons who are not the biological mothers, such as co-parents, step-parents, adoptive parents, and others who are bringing up children. The term mother too often tends to imply only the biological mother. Yet even as I explain this reasoning, I need to add that for lesbians, the whole question of naming and the terms we use to identify ourselves is more complex than it might be for straight

---

Sandra Pollack is Professor of Humanities and Women's Studies at Tompkins Cortland Community College in upstate New York. She has co-edited, with Charlotte Bunch, *Learning Our Way: Essays in Feminist Education*, Crossing Press, 1984 and, with Jeanne Vaughn, *Politics of the Heart: A Lesbian Parenting Anthology*, Firebrand Books, 1987.

women. For while I recognize the importance of using the term parent, I know that at times I intentionally use the term lesbian mother as a way of identifying myself. On the one hand we want a term that reflects the fact that the care of the children is often done by other than the biological mother, and on the other hand, because, in the public mind, the term lesbian and mother are often seen as a contradiction, we intentionally, at times, want to put these two words together.

This perhaps is only one small example of what happens when we focus on the differences rather than the similarities. When we look specifically at a situation from the perspective of the lesbian, we see things that too easily get overlooked when we just look for the ways in which we are the same as straight women.

And yet, when we look at the literature, we see that many studies suggest that lesbian mothers are just like other mothers. While this might seem reassuring at first glance, such a conclusion is dangerous. It makes us once more invisible, and it obscures the radical alternative lesbian lives can model. Uncritical acceptance of such research may also lead us to the false conclusion that we will be accepted by the larger society because we have some of the same problems and concerns as other mothers. Research which focuses on the ways lesbians and their children resemble heterosexual mothers and their children may be important as part of custody courtroom strategy, but it negates the healthy and positive characteristics unique to lesbian parenting. In addition, most of the research on lesbian parents has focused on white lesbians. Yet it is not only the sexual or political, but also the racial differences that must be considered if we are to fully understand the realities of our lives.

Early research on sexual practices, etiology, and "cures," combined with a view of sexual preference as immutable, defined the lesbian mother out of existence. Before 1970, lesbian mothers were virtually invisible in the research on homosexuality, in the early research in women's studies, and in the literature on mothering.

In 1977 I was shocked into recognizing my own complicity in this process. A woman I worked with in organizing for the New York Women's Studies Association incredulously asked, "You are a mother?" While I had been open about being a lesbian during the two years of our work together, I had never mentioned my children.

Suddenly I became conscious of being a "closet mother." I asked others in the room and discovered two other lesbian mothers. The time had come to acknowledge our full identities and to better understand the impact of raising children as lesbians in a patriarchal society.

The fact that we have been ignored in research, and that we, at times, have colluded in that invisibility, adds to the difficulty of knowing just how large a population we are talking about. In spite of this, estimates are that ten to twenty percent of adult women are lesbians, and that twenty to thirty percent of lesbians are mothers, a total of three to four million lesbian parents in the United States. Many might be more open if the legal system were not so weighted against them (Hunter & Polikoff, 1976; Martin & Lyon, 1972; Riley, 1975). As economic heads of households, lesbian parents often remain in the closet because they cannot afford to risk losing their jobs.

We begin to break that pattern of invisibility as we define ourselves. When we consciously claim the labels of lesbian and of parent, we assume the power to decide what we want them to mean in our lives. This self-definition and empowerment should anchor future research, legal defense strategies and work with clients in therapy.

The homophobia that pervades our society exhibits itself in a myriad of myths about lesbian parents— for example, lesbians will molest children, the children will grow up to be homosexuals, lesbians will engage in sexual activity in front of their children, the children will develop psychological problems and be stigmatized and ridiculed by society. Nowhere does this homophobia allow for the recognition that lesbian parenting can be a healthy, wholesome experience for adults and children.

An important link in my thinking about the need to claim our visibility as lesbian parents has been an understanding of lesbian mothers and the law. One of the most publicized lesbian mother custody battles was that of Mary Jo Risher. The 1975 case was covered by the mass media and turned into a prime-time television movie. In a comprehensive summary of this case, Lindsay Van Gelder (1976) showed that public sympathy was aroused (perhaps for the first time) when people saw how a thirty-nine-year-old white

Texas mother lost custody of her nine-year-old son, despite the fact that she was a college graduate, nurse, a former Baptist Sunday school teacher, a P.T.A. President, and a Chaplain of the Order of the Eastern Star who had been living for the past three years in a stable committed relationship with her lover.

Both women had good jobs; they were solid members of their community. There was no question of alcoholism or drugs. They saw themselves as a family with two adults and three children (two boys from Mary Jo's previous marriage and one daughter from her lover Ann's previous marriage). They were each other's insurance beneficiaries, had joint checking accounts, co-owned property. The life Mary Jo and Ann lived was "straight" in most ways except that they were two women loving each other. According to several psychologists, Mary Jo's son had an "exceptionally loving stable family life." However, as one juror said, "We are taking him out of a good home to put him in a better one" (Van Gelder, 1976, p. 72).

Remarried Douglas Risher now had a new baby and a "full-time" wife to stay home with the children. One of Doug Risher's witnesses was a social worker who felt that nine-year-old Richard would be better off in a home "where the mother didn't work." Douglas and his wife could provide the proper father and mother image. This image was more important than the fact that Douglas Risher had a record of drunk driving, had broken Mary Jo's nose, had been accused of getting a nineteen-year-old woman pregnant, and had paid for her abortion.

The mass media coverage of this case may have caused some people to feel sorry for Mary Jo when she was ordered to give up her son on Christmas morning, but it barely began to challenge the assumption that the straight nuclear family is best. The question was never whether or not Mary Jo was a good mother; Mary Jo as a lesbian mother was on trial.

The Risher case is an important example of the futility of seeking safety in the argument that we are "all really the same"—that lesbian mothers and straight mothers are not so different after all.

Obviously I do not wish to imply that only lesbian mothers lose custody of their children. Phyllis Chesler in *Mothers on Trial* (1987) certainly points out many examples of how heterosexual mothers face similar trauma in a male court system where too often the financial and material advantages of the father, or other males, are given precedent over a recognition of the parenting skills of women. The point I do wish to make, though, is that in spite of this shared anguish, there is a difference for lesbian mothers who not only may lose custody of their children in the courts, but who may also lose a sense of self-esteem and validation as they try to argue that their lives are really no different from those of heterosexual mothers.

Lesbians have always raised children in our society, but this fact has only recently come to the attention of the courts. With the consciousness stimulated by the women's liberation and gay liberation movements, more and more women are insisting on their right to be what they are: lesbians and mothers.

While there have been some lesbian mother court victories (Armanini v. Armanini, 1979; Medeiros v. Medeiros, 1982; Miller v. Miller, 1979; Schuster v. Schuster and Isaacson v. Isaacson, 1974), the overwhelming fear among lesbian mothers is that they will lose their children. That fear is based on reality. In a contested custody case, the courts will, in most instances, believe the mother is an unfit parent because she is a lesbian. Going to court is also an enormous psychological, emotional, and financial drain. And custody cases can always be reopened. The homophobic nature of the courts is shown in the child custody orders which grant the lesbian parent custody but include provisions that she is not permitted to live with a lover (Basile, 1974). One can never really feel safe as a lesbian mother.

Judges at times exhibit a voyeurism that belies their claim to objectivity. Such an attitude was evidenced in my own protracted custody case when my ex-husband's lawyer was describing a visit his client made to my house when my lover had been visiting me for the weekend. As the lawyer was reciting the events, the judge burst out with, "Where were they (the adult women) and what were they wearing?" What assumptions did this judge have about homosexuals? Was he assuming we were probably in bed or parading around naked? Would he ask those questions about a heterosexual man or woman? To have to explain that we were sitting in the living room wearing ordinary clothing, that my daughters and my lover's daughter were watching TV, was an insult to our dignity. Yet lesbian mothers are frequently abused in this way. For too many people, the word lesbian or homosexual only conjures up images of sex.

In the words of another judge, "Ma'am, will you explain to the Court exactly what occurs—we talk here generally of a homosexual act. Just what does this entail? What do you do?" And again later, the same judge asked if there was "any potential that the lesbian mother might 'use' her child in sexual activity" (Hitchens & Price, 1978-9, p. 453).

Given the realities that many lesbian mother custody cases are lost, that the legal system is homophobic, and that court battles are long and expensive, the desire for research that would help the lesbian parent in court is understandable. This research though has largely been a reaction—an attempt to answer the fears and myths perpetuated by the very homophobic society we must now try to convince, and the form of that reaction has too often been to show that we are the same as straight mothers rather than dealing with the homophobic assumptions of the courts.

The fact that a mother is a lesbian is often so startling and offensive to a judge's value system that once this issue is brought into the case, it is omnipresent in the judge's mind. In a positive and important study, recognizing the particulars of lesbian custody cases, Donna Hitchens and Barbara Price (1978-79) argue that this problem should be dealt with directly by the mother's attorney, who should know the prejudices to be countered and the evidence to be used. The custody outcome, they state, depends more on the beliefs and attitudes of the judge about homosexuality than on the specific facts of the case.

Court transcripts studied by Hitchens and Price reveal three erroneous assumptions commonly held by judges and mental health professionals called in to testify. The first has to do with the sexual behavior of lesbians. Lesbians are assumed to be promiscuous, liable to sexually harm the children, and sexually maladjusted. The belief, then, is that allowing the mother to be both with her lover and her children would result in undesirable sexual behavior.

The second myth is that children of gay parents will grow up to be gay or will have confused sex-role identification. The third assumption is that the child could be socially stigmatized and therefore seriously harmed if the mother's lesbianism is widely known.

Expert testimony directed at countering these myths rather than focusing only on the general stability of the mother and the mother's parenting ability appears to be essential.

Unlike the important Hitchens and Price research, most of the other early lesbian studies focused on showing how lesbian and straight families have few differences. This simply means that according to these researchers, neither lesbians nor their children have pathological problems that are very different from those of heterosexual single mothers (Golombok, Spencer, & Rutter, 1983; Kirkpatrick, Smith & Roy, 1981; Lewin & Lyons, 1982). It appears to me that an underlying assumption in these studies is that the lesbian mother will be judged on how well she compares to the heterosexual norm.

Demonstrating that we are the same may have seemed to be useful as a legal strategy, but these comparison studies often overlook serious questions and, therefore, present skewed results. For example, to study the ways lesbians and straight mothers rely on relationships with kin, particularly in child care and holiday celebrations, one must also ask questions related to the realities of lesbian life. Do lesbians go home for the holidays alone or with their lovers? Are children free to talk about the women in their mother's life when they are with relatives? What is the relationship between disclosure and employment for lesbian parents?

While the daily lives of both groups of mothers have many similarities, the specifics of the household must be examined to really find out about raising a child in this setting. Are lesbian posters, books, and records around as freely as heterosexual materials would be? Can lesbian conversations take place as freely as heterosexual conversations? Probing these areas will uncover differences that mark lesbian lives more deeply than questions about whom they can turn to for child care, or how to cope with the low salaries all women receive, or the fact that few women get adequate financial support from ex-husbands.

There are differences in the way lesbian and heterosexual women take charge of and plan for their futures—be it in home ownership, self-employment, or life-long planning (Pagelow, 1980). So, too, when we show lesbian and straight mothers functioning as caregivers, the myth that heterosexual mothers are more child-oriented than lesbian mothers comes under serious challenge (Miller, Jacobson, & Bigner, 1981). These differences, rather than the similarities, must be emphasized both in court and in the larger world to show the benefits of lesbian parenting and to reinforce a positive self-image among lesbians.

Some comparison studies focus on the sex roles of children and conclude that the two groups have similar sex-role behavior and attitudes toward ideal child behavior (Kweskin & Cook, 1982). Again, my reservation is the underlying assumption that there are appropriate sex roles for boys and girls. What these studies really examine is whether the children conform to acceptable societal norms. Yet this very assumption of appropriate roles is what feminists are committed to eliminating. The consequences of not conforming weigh heavily, however.

In the Mary Jo Risher case, much was made of the apparent heterosexual orientation of the children. Ann's daughter, Judie Ann, was described as an "especially pretty child, very charming who espoused a traditional feminine role." Mary Jo's son, Richard, said he wanted to be a policeman. Despite all this backward bending, even the slightest deviations were seized upon. Apparently, Mary Jo allowed Richard to appear at the psychologist's office "wearing unsuitable clothing"—a YWCA T-shirt and a jacket that belonged to Judie Ann. Upon cross-examination, the psychologist acknowledged that since Richard was taking a gym course at the Y, the shirt was hardly high drag (Van Gelder, 1976, p. 73). No matter, Mary Jo was a lesbian and therefore should be more sensitive to Richard's appearance.

Researchers often feel it necessary to show that the children are "all right," that they are not contaminated by lesbianism, and that they will grow up to be "proper boys and girls." Kirkpatrick et al. (1981) tested children ages five to twelve and concluded that the gender development of the children of heterosexual and homosexual mothers was not identifiably different. While we might use these studies as a courtroom tactic because the children "do just fine," we must remain aware of the acceptance of sex-role stereotyping on which such an argument is based.

Our strategies would be very different if we chose to emphasize the value of the independent model provided by lesbians (Berzins, Willing, & Wetter, 1978 in Riddle, 1978). Dorothy Riddle says it strongly: "Rather than posing a menace to children, gays may actually facilitate important developmental learning . . . children have the possibility of learning that it is possible to resist traditional sex-role socialization. . . . Children become exposed to the concept of cultural and individual diversity as positive rather than threatening" (pp. 39-50).

Studies that look at the actual lives of the children of lesbians may be more useful than those focusing on sex-role identities. Karen Gail Lewis (1980) encouraged children of lesbians to talk about how their mother's lifestyles have influenced their lives. Lewis concludes that "the children do want to be accepting of their mother's lifestyles, and . . . the gay community and the therapeutic community owe it to the children to provide the opportunity for them to work towards a realistic assessment and acceptance of their feelings" (pp. 198-203).

Lewis raises an important point rarely addressed by the research: the possible benefits of being a child of a lesbian mother. The children of lesbians may become aware (perhaps more so than other children) of their responsibility for themselves and their own choices. So too Marjorie Hill in "Child-Rearing Attitudes of Black Lesbian Mothers" (1987), focuses on the positive aspects of difference. Poet Audre Lorde says it clearly, "There are certain basic requirements of any child—food, clothing, shelter, love. So what makes our children different? We do. Gays and Lesbians of Color are different because we are embattled by reason of our sexuality and our Color, and if there is any lesson we must teach our children, it is that difference is a creative force for change, that survival and struggle for the future is not a theoretical issue. It is the very texture of our lives . . . " (1986, p. 313). This message should be repeated frequently.

We need to convince the courts that the child's interests are often best served by living with a lesbian parent who can be open rather than leading a double and secret life. We need to recognize that concern over the absence of a male model is a bogus issue, that the problem often is not the lack of a male presence, but the lack of a male income. A lesbian parent who can live openly, and who can share income and household expenses with other women, has a better chance of maintaining a standard of living that is beneficial for the child.

While this issue, like the decision of whether we use the term parent or mother to identify ourselves, is more complex than it might be for straight women, I also do not want to imply that if we simply stood up in court and shouted the benefits of lesbian parenting, we would fare much better in the courts. I would like to hope that such may be the direction for the future, and there may be some indications of that in the successful lesbian mother decisions, but it is premature to make too much of these victories. We can though, at this point, at least identify it as an area that needs more research.

When we begin to listen to the voices of lesbians, what kind of call for new research do we hear?

At lesbian parent workshops women say they want a stop to the neutralizing of their lives. They want to portray the positive aspects and specialness of their lives. They want research on the relationship of adolescents to lesbian mothers, as there is little in the adolescent literature that pertains to them. They are concerned with the role of co-parents and with ways to provide their children with skills to counter homophobia. They want help in developing support groups for children. They want to know how to get support for lesbians choosing to have children via alternative fertilization and how to better validate lesbians who do not live with their children. They want to find ways to recognize second-generation lesbians and gay men, individuals whose lives are often kept invisible because their existence feeds into the homophobic fear that children will turn out gay.

When we listen, we hear of the ways in which lesbian parents have issues to deal with that are not generally found in the straight community. Marilyn Murphy shares her pain as she reaches the decision not to attend her son's wedding because she feels the unfairness of an institution that recognizes the love a man and a women share, but not the love two women share. "After all," she says, "what kind of a mother has to stop and think about whether or not to attend her child's wedding? A lesbian mother does" (1987, p. 198).

Our relationships are not recognized in a myriad of ways.

- In many states our relationships are illegal, and it is not against the law to discriminate against us. We have no formal recognition of our unions, our separations, our births, our deaths. This reality has an impact on our families. Our situation is not the same as it is for straight women.
- Our children have been taken from us—by religious doctrine, by the courts, by the pressures imposed upon us to make us choose between our children and our lovers.
- As co-parents we have no assurance that we will be allowed to continue to raise our children at the death of the birth mother.
- Lesbian parents agonize with the internalized oppression that often makes it impossible for them to tell their child that their mother is a lesbian.

While many of the day to day tasks of raising a child may be the same for straight and lesbian women, the reality of prejudice against the family for the parents' sexual orientation is a major difference—lesbians must deal with this with day care workers, teachers, and relatives.

What might this mean to therapists and researchers? Recognizing the differences and the particular stresses they entail may be more helpful to the client than dealing with her as if she were like any other "single mother." Sally Crawford in her essay in *Lesbian Psychologies* (1987) does an important job of identifying some of the particular stresses for lesbians in the family-building process. And as Nancy Polikoff says (1987), "In the courts too often, a lesbian mother must portray herself as being as close to the All-American norm as possible—the spitting image of her ideal heterosexual counterpart—and preferably asexual . . . the necessity of assuming a role that contradicts her identity has important consequences . . . the toll on the client is obviously enormous. She is forced to deny any pride in her lesbianism, any solidarity with other lesbians; she may even be compelled to deny or alter her sexual relationships. There is no guarantee that, at the end of this ordeal, she will be allowed to keep her children."

As a lawyer, Polikoff tells how she has encouraged lesbian mothers not to see themselves as having more in common with heterosexual mothers than with other lesbians. She urges them to resist, in every conceivable forum, the presumption of heterosexuality that attaches to motherhood. "When we constantly assert in the public arena that we will raise our children to be heterosexual, and that we will protect them from the manifestations of our sexuality and from the larger lesbian and gay community . . . we essentially concede it is preferable to be heterosexual, thereby foreclosing an assertion of pride and of the positive value in homosexuality" (p. 326). This sense of pride and positive self-identity may often need to be reinforced in the client's therapy.

The biological mother and the co-parents may need help to stay focused on positive aspects and the specialness of their situation. The co-parent, regardless of her role within the family, can be easily disenfranchised. As therapists, you may be called to testify in custody disputes. We will need help to support our families in an alien legal framework. For example, today, a known sperm donor, who originally intended to remain uninvolved but who later changes his mind can gain full parental rights. A minimally involved father of a child raised by a lesbian couple will almost certainly obtain custody if the legal mother dies. Under the law, after all, he is the sole surviving parent. At present we do not have legal recognition of parenthood for both mothers. But in some states, before sympathetic judges, there may be room to take the offensive and gain this recognition by presenting a positive picture of the role played by the co-parent.

As lesbian parents we are a diverse group. I would hope that you will hear our varied voices. It is our strength to be able to share our differences. Research and therapy that recognizes these differences will be more empowering to lesbian parents than showing that we are the same as, or that it is desirable when we or our children are the same as, heterosexual families.

REFERENCES

Armanini v. Armanini (1979). *5 family law reporter,* 2501 (N.Y. Sup.Ct.)

Basile, R. (1974). Lesbian mothers. *Women's Rights Law Reporter, 2,* 3-5.

Chesler, P. (1987). *Mothers on trial: The battle for children and custody.* Seattle, WA: Seal Press.

Crawford, S. (1987). Lesbian families: Psychosocial stress and the family-building process. In Boston Lesbian Psychologies Collective, (Eds.), *Lesbian psychologies: Explorations and challenges* (pp. 195-214). Urbana: University of Illinois Press.

Golombok, S., Spencer, A., & Rutter, M. (Oct. 1983). Children in lesbian and single parent households: Psychosexual and psychiatric appraisal. *Journal of Child Psychology and Allied Disciplines, 24,* 551-572.

Hill, M. (1987). Child-rearing attitudes of black lesbian mothers. In Boston Lesbian Psychologies Collective, (Eds.), *Lesbian Psychologies: Explorations and challenges* (pp. 215-226). Urbana: University of Illinois Press.

Hitchens, D. J., & Price, B. (1978-9). Trial strategy in lesbian mother custody cases: The use of expert testimony, *Golden Gate University Law Review, 9,* 451-453.

Hunter, N. D., & Polikoff, N. D. (1976). Custody rights of lesbian mothers: Legal theory and litigation strategy. *Buffalo Law Review, 25,* 691-733.

Kirkpatrick, M., Smith, C., & Roy, R. (1981). Lesbian mothers and their children: A comparative study. *American Journal of Orthopsychiatry, 51,* 545-551.

Kweskin, S., & Cook, A. (1982). Heterosexual and homosexual mothers: Self-described sex-role behavior and ideal and sex-role behavior in children. *Sex Roles, 8,* 967.

Lewin, E., & Lyons, T. A. (1982). Everything in its place: The co-existence of lesbianism and motherhood. In W. Paul, J. D. Weinrich & M. Hotvedt (Eds.), *Homosexuality: Social, psychological and biological issues.* Beverly Hills: Sage Publications.

Lewis, K. G. (May,1980). Children of lesbians: Their point of view. *Social Work, 25,* 198-203.

Lorde, A. (1986). Turning the beat around: Lesbian parenting 1986. In S. Pollack, & J. Vaughn (Eds.), *Politics of the heart: A lesbian parenting anthology* (pp. 310-315). Ithaca, NY: Firebrand Books.

Martin, D., & Lyon, P. (1972). *Lesbian/Women.* San Francisco: Glide Publications.

Medeiros v. Medeiros (1982). *8 family law reporter,* 2372 (Vt. Sup.Ct.)

Miller, J. A., Jacobson, R. B., & Bigner, H. J. (1981). The child's home environment for lesbian vs. heterosexual mothers: A neglected area of research. *Journal of Homosexuality, 7,* 49-56.

Miller v. Miller (1979). *405 Michigan reporter,* 809.

Murphy, M. (1987). Mother of the groom. In S. Pollack & J. Vaughn (Eds.),

Politics of the heart: A lesbian parenting anthology (pp. 198-211). Ithaca, NY: Firebrand Books.
Pagelow, M., (1980). Heterosexual and lesbian single mothers: A comparison of problems, coping, and solutions. *Journal of Homosexuality, 5,* 189-203.
Polikoff, N. D. (1987). Lesbian mothers, lesbian families: Legal obstacles, legal challenges. In S. Pollack & J. Vaughn (Eds.), *Politics of the heart: A lesbian parenting anthology* (pp. 325-332). Ithaca, NY: Firebrand Books.
Riddle, D. (1978). Relating to children: Gays as role models. *Journal of Social Issues, 34,* 39-50.
Riley, M. (1975). The avowed lesbian mother and her right to child custody. *San Diego Law Review, 12,* 799-864.
Schuster v. Schuster & Isaacson v. Isaacson (1974) 585 P. 2d 130 (Wash. Sup. Ct.) in R. A. Basile. *Women's rights law reporter.* 2, 3-5.
Van Gelder, L. (Sept. 1976). Lesbian custody: A tragic day in court. *MS.*, 72-73.

Sarah and the Women's Movement: The Experience of Infertility

Dina Afek

INTRODUCTION

One out of every six couples of childbearing age in the United States experiences some kind of difficulty conceiving a child or carrying a pregnancy to term (Menning, 1988). Since there are no statistics about infertility in single and lesbian women who want to have children, we can only assume how many women and men are touched by infertility. Infertility is a medical as well as a social and psychological issue. In this paper, however, I will focus on the psychological impact of infertility, particularly on the subjective experience of women dealing with infertility. Since the beginning of humankind, cultures all over the world have been concerned with fertility. Fertility goddesses are some of the earliest artifacts of ancient cultures. The Old Testament tells us the story of Sarah and Abraham, who were unable to have children. Sarah asked Abraham to take her maid Hagar as a concubine, so she could bear a child for her to raise. "And Sarai said unto Abram: 'Behold now, the Lord hath restrained me from bearing; go in, I pray thee, unto my handmaid; it may be that I shall be builded up through her'" (Genesis 16:2). This might have been the first recorded incident of a surrogate contract. The language of the Bible talks about "barren" women, about bearing children for men. A woman's fertility was equal with her worth in the same way that land was worth something only if it produced crops. Despite all this, it is interesting to note that all four matriarchs, the most important women in the Old

---

Dina Afek has recently received her Master's degree in Counseling Psychology from Goddard College, where she focused on feminist therapy and infertility.

Testament, were infertile at first until God "blessed" them. Rachel addressed the psychological pain of infertility when she said to God: "Give me children or I die!" (Genesis 30:1).

What happens to women today who want to have children and find out they cannot become pregnant or carry a pregnancy to term? My personal interest in infertility was sparked when my husband and I tried unsuccessfully for several years to conceive. After years of treatments and tests, we now have a wonderful two year old daughter. The depth of my wish for a child and the intensity of the pain I experienced surprised me. I wanted to learn more about this issue and focused my graduate studies on the psychological aspects of infertility. I read numerous books and articles on the subject and spent two semesters as a therapist intern in an infertility clinic. I interviewed ten feminists in the local community about their attitudes toward infertility and the new reproductive technologies and talked with many people informally about their experiences with infertility.

Most of mainstream Western society still sees bearing and raising children as the true role of married women. The "Institution of Motherhood" (Rich, 1976) is one of the most prevalent oppressions women endure in patriarchal society. On the other hand, there are more and more people who choose a childfree life; there is a growing concern about overpopulation and women increasingly are beginning careers before becoming mothers. "The ten million Americans whose lives and hopes are touched by infertility are caught between two opposite and powerful social currents . . . In the eyes of the first segment of the population, the infertile couple is seen as an object of pity or even scorn. In the eyes of the second, infertility may be seen as a 'blessing' or, at worst, a minor inconvenience. People who work at achieving pregnancy at a time of world overpopulation have even been called 'immoral'" (Menning, 1988, p. 172).

MYTHS AND REALITY ABOUT INFERTILITY

There are many myths about infertility. Many of them are based on unfounded assumptions that can be very painful for people dealing with infertility.

Myth: Infertility is a "female condition."
Reality: Male factors contribute to infertility as often as female factors. The breakdown of infertility by cause reveals that an estimated 35% of cases involve a female problem, 35% a male problem, 20% a combined problem of both partners and the remaining 10% is unexplained (Menning, 1988).

Myth: Infertility is psychological in origin, an unconscious wish not to have a child or not to become pregnant. Women have been told to seek psychoanalysis, to "just relax," or to adopt in order to get pregnant.
Reality: Most likely there are psychological influences on human fertility, but they seem to play only a small role. Most psychological problems are not the source but the reaction to the crisis of infertility.

Myth: Infertility is untreatable.
Reality: The medical causes for infertility can be diagnosed by an infertility specialist in 90% of cases. Fifty percent of these can be successfully treated (Menning, 1988).

Myth: Infertility is a "yuppie disease," a problem only for the upper middle class.
Reality: Infertile people come from every socio-economic class and from all races and cultures.

Myth: The notion that adoption is preferable to testing and treatment is heard a lot, especially in more radical circles. The argument is that it is more moral to adopt, while there are so many children to be adopted, than to seek to achieve a pregnancy at any cost.
Reality: Today there are far fewer babies available to adopt than 20 years ago because more women either choose abortions or keep their babies. International adoption poses a big financial problem, and the wait for a child is often years. And maybe most importantly, adoption is not for everyone and should be a positive choice rather than a halfhearted alternative.

THE WOMEN'S MOVEMENT

The women's movement has not sufficiently addressed infertility. It seems as if we have been so caught up in helping ourselves and each other break out of stereotyped female roles that we forgot to include women who choose and want to be mothers. The right to safe abortions has been and still is an issue of critical concern. After the fact, when children are already here, we deal with the dilemmas of working mothers, divorced mothers and childcare. It seems as if infertile women have been somehow forgotten.

Or is it more than that? Is wanting children not as legitimate as not wanting them; is this a less than feminist desire? When I searched for material on infertility in women's bookstores, I could not find one single book. The only books I found were about feminist reasons for opposing new reproductive technologies such as donor insemination, in vitro fertilization, embryo transfer and surrogacy. None of these books or articles mentions the suffering of infertility. Most are unsupportive of infertile women, and some are outrightly hostile. The wish for a biological child of one's own is seen as egotistical or a succumbing to societal pressures. The motivation for wanting to have a biological child and the pain of infertility are explained as internalized oppression.

THE NEW REPRODUCTIVE TECHNOLOGIES

Anne Donchin (1986) makes it clear that there is no feminist theory which provides us with a clear direction in terms of the development of reproductive technology. She talks about three possible options that the Feminist Movement has in regards to the new reproductive technologies: (1) We could oppose all use of reproductive technology despite its short-term benefits to some women individually. (2) We could look at the positive options and choices these technologies give women and could unconditionally support them. (3) "We could work to integrate the plurality of feminist positions into an interim policy, commit ourselves to intensified dialogue and attempt to influence the present direction of reproductive innovation in much the same pragmatic way feminists are now participating in forming economic policies . . ." (Donchin, 1986, p. 137).

Even though, or rather, because I can see certain dangers in these techniques, I think the Women's Movement should take a more powerful stand on these issues and adopt Donchin's third option. By bluntly opposing the existing techniques and technologies, as well as future research, we are letting the predominantly male medical establishment indeed keep the monopoly over our bodies and minds, and we are alienating women who deal with infertility instead of supporting them. In light of all the discussion about new reproductive technologies, we forget to see that these are last resort alternatives for only a small minority of women. There are many important medical, social and psychological aspects of infertility that are relevant to all women. I hope that there will be more discussion among feminists on all the issues related to infertility and reproductive choices and alternatives. The recent increase in lesbians seeking donor insemination as a way to become pregnant and have children helps confront the feminist movement with these issues in a positive way.

THE ROLE OF THE FEMINIST THERAPIST

Feminist therapists who see women who suffer from infertility have a special role to play. As therapists, we need to come to terms with our own thoughts and feelings on this issue before we can effectively empower women who struggle with infertility. We need to know about the experience of infertility.

There are psychological reactions specific to infertility and feelings shared in common by most women experiencing infertility. Feminist therapists need to know what these reactions and feelings are. They, of course, have much to do with the specific social, cultural and personal context of a woman's life and need to be acknowledged as such. Feelings of unworthiness, low self-esteem, shame, guilt, anger, depression and grief are very common.

Infertility is like a death. It is the death of a potential child and the death of a dream. For a lot of women it is also the death of a certain innocence about procreation. Many of us grow up taking it for granted that we will have children one day. We just assume that, if and when we choose to have children, our bodies will produce them. Infertility can be worse than death, because there is often no actual object for grief. It is hard to grieve for something that never was. Society does not acknowledge this loss and thus does not help with the grieving process. One does not get much sympathy for being depressed every month when one's period starts. But menstruation often becomes the enemy as the only visible, tangible symbol for many infertile women.

Infertility is an invisible handicap. Not only can nobody tell if someone is or is not infertile, but it is a problem often overlooked in our society, because it is not regarded as a social problem by policy makers and the general public. This leads to a lack of affordable services, insurance policies and adequate research. Harriet Simons (Mazor & Simons, 1983) and others have pointed out that the infertile population is one of the most neglected minority groups in America.

Infertility is paradoxical. On the one hand, everything is public: the tests, the treatments, when you have sex, your innermost organs—all is known to doctors and nurses. If you choose to adopt you come under the scrutiny of social workers and agencies; if you decide on donor insemination, the whole process of conceiving becomes public. On the other hand, there is a lot of pain, a terrible sense of loss, and these nobody knows about or dares to address. This often leads to feelings of total isolation. Often a couple will isolate themselves from family and friends and try to support each other as much as possible. For single women dealing with infertility, this can be even harder if there is no partner with whom to share their pain. For some, the visits to the clinic become the only place to get the needed attention, and the infertility workup itself becomes a substitute for support or even a substitute for a child.

Anger is another common feeling for people dealing with infertility. It is often a reaction to helplessness and loss of control. Being infertile means loss of control over our bodies and our lives. It is almost impossible to be angry at "the situation," so we look for objects on which to focus our anger. And there are many real things to be angry at: the inconvenience of the tests, the physicians' insensitivity, the reactions of family members, the degrading nature of invasive procedures, etc., etc. On the other hand, there are also some more irrational targets of this anger. Many women experience an enormous anger at pregnant women. From my own experience with infertility, I know that I needed this anger to protect myself from the immensity of the pain. Another target for anger is the partner in a couple, whether that person is the fertile or the infertile member of the dyad. This anger is often not acknowledged and is expressed in different forms, such as picking fights over other issues or being emotionally or sexually withholding.

Infertility has a large impact on sexual relations and sexuality in general. Keeping a temperature chart is one of the basic steps in an infertility investigation. You are instructed not only to measure your temperature first thing every morning, thus making you think about infertility right away, but also to note when you have sex. The temperature chart becomes "a third bedfellow" (Menning, 1988). Sex which is public knowledge and sex on demand do not promote a healthy sexual relationship. Most couples who deal with infertility experience some sexual difficulties for a period of time. After infertility is resolved, it may take a long time before sexual intercourse can again be experienced as pleasureable.

These are just some of the issues with which women have to cope when dealing with infertility. The following are a few therapeutic strategies that can help women cope better, and use this crisis as an opportunity for growth. Some of them helped me personally when I went through therapy for infertility related issues.

- —Therapists need to convey sensitivity and warmth in contrast to all the cold, medical interventions.
- —Therapists need to validate a woman's feelings. Family and friends often tell infertile women that their problem is not really that bad, that their pain is not real.
- —Therapists need to let the client grieve for all the actual and potential losses she experiences, the losses that we usually do not talk about such as hysterectomy, abortion, miscarriage, stillbirth . . . When there is unexplained infertility, there is uncertainty about the loss. It is not clear if in fact there is or will be a loss. It is very important to acknowledge this uncertainty. It is helpful to talk about old losses as well, since unfin-

ished feelings around losses that were not grieved for come up during the crisis of infertility.

- Therapists need to know the importance of empowerment. Infertility is the loss of control. Therapists can help women find ways to regain control over their lives. Part of this is to encourage women to think about how far they want to go with the infertility investigation and the tests and to think about alternatives such as adoption or childfree living.
- Even if working with only one partner of a couple, therapists need to recognize that infertility is a family problem and the way in which each partner copes with the problem has tremendous implications for the relationship. Miriam Mazor (1983, p. 33) says that "infertile couples often have to complete in terms of their relationship, what many others postpone until after their children are grown."
- Therapists need to be aware of the importance of encouraging women to build a support system beyond their partners, to talk with other women and/or to join a support group.
- Therapists need to realize that infertility resolution is often a lifelong process. Infertility does not disappear when we become parents. We still grieve for the children we will never have or the children we lost in miscarriage or stillbirth.

CONCLUSION

Infertility is an issue that needs to be addressed by feminists. Therapists have a special role and can help women deal with the effects of infertility. Even women who do have children might have a history of infertility, and some of these wounds might still interfere in these women's lives. Infertility is a serious life crisis that has a profound impact on people. Women—who in patriarchal society are second class citizens—are particularly vulnerable if they experience infertility. As motherhood is denied to infertile women, they need to redefine themselves as women, without the so called "natural" role society has given us. Low self-esteem, shame and guilt can only be alleviated by recognizing the content of the hurt, grieving the losses of infertility and acknowledging internal and external pressures to become a parent.

The Women's Movement has a role to play by supporting women through this crisis with the recognition that motherhood is a positive choice for many, many women and infertility has a big psychological impact. Supporting more research, better insurance coverage and including infertility tests and treatments in women's health centers are some of the things I would like to see. We need to talk more and openly about the dangers and benefits of the new reproductive technologies and work toward policies that take into account all women's experiences.

REFERENCES

Donchin, Anne (1986). The future of mothering: Reproductive technology and feminist theory. *Hypatia: A Journal of Feminist Philosophy*, *1*, 121-137.

The holy scriptures. Philadelphia: The Jewish Publication Society of America.

Mazor, Miriam D., & Simons, Harriet F., Eds. (1983). *Infertility: Medical, emotional and social considerations*. New York: Human Sciences Press.

Menning, Barbara E. (1988). *Infertility: A guide for the childless couple*. New York: Prentice Hall Press.

Rich, Adrienne (1976). *Of woman born*. New York: W.W. Norton and Co.

Sturdy Bridges: The Role of African-American Mothers in the Socialization of African-American Children

Beverly Greene

> . . . from Black mothers . . . we learn
> the possibilities of dignity in a degrading situation.
>
> —Adrienne Rich
> of Woman Born
> 1976

In the context of a general discussion on motherhood, this article examines the legacy of adaptive strengths which African-American mothers have exercised in socializing African-American children in the context of an antagonistic environment; a brief discussion of the potential complications in the socializing process; traditional resources found in African-American families; and psychotherapeutic interventions which maximize the utilization of those resources.

The term "Black" is used in this article to refer to Americans whose ancestors, with some Native American and Northern European admixture, came primarily from the tribes of West Africa and were the primary focus of the United States slave trade. Any at-

---

Dr. Beverly Greene is Clinical Psychologist in private practice in Brooklyn, NY. At the time of this writing, she was Director of Inpatient Child & Adolescent Psychology Services and Clinical Assistant Professor in the Department of Psychiatry, Kings County Hospital and Downstate Medical Center, Brooklyn, NY. She is currently Supervising Psychologist and Clinical Assistant Professor in the Department of Psychiatry and Community Mental Health Center at the University of Medicine and Dentistry, Newark, NJ.

tempt to understand the lives of African-Americans would be incomplete without an understanding of the complexity of their heritage. While there is great diversity within African-Americans as a group, they share constellations of distinct characteristics which have their origins in the values and practices unique to African culture. Underscoring the importance of African cultural derivatives is helpful in understanding the respective contributions of African and American culture to the cultural distinctiveness of African-American persons (Baker, 1988).

In the United States, the devaluation of women and the roles occupied by women contributes to the tendency to selectively devalue and simultaneously glorify the role of mother in American culture. This phenomenon is problematic for many reasons. It fails to take into account the realistic demands of the role of mother under different circumstances, individual and ethnic group differences between women and their reasons for having children, and the effect of other life stresses in conjunction with motherhood. The complexity and difficulty of the tasks required of mothers are popularly portrayed as something which females are "naturally" equipped to manage (Rich, 1976). This implies that no particular skills or abilities are required beyond what one "naturally" knows. This portrayal is juxtaposed against the prominence of "mother blaming" in the psychological literature (Caplan & Hall-McCorquodale, 1985). The irony here is that on the one hand mothers are "blamed" as central figures in their child's development, while on the other hand, the literal tasks of motherhood are devalued.

Bell (1971) writes that motherhood has been an historically important role for Black women, deriving from pre-colonial Africa where children were highly prized and the roles of childbearer and childrearer were taken seriously and valued. Ladner (1971) notes that African women were often considered the founders or mothers of tribes and the primary carriers of the culture. Nobles (1974) points out too that the special bond that has been observed in the relationships between Black women and their children cannot be simply attributed to the fact that in slavery, a Black family was legally defined to include only a mother and her children. Rather, it reflects deep roots in an African heritage and a philosophical orientation which places a special value on children themselves because they represent the continuity of life.

DISTINCT ASPECTS OF BLACK MOTHERS' ROLES

The role of mother is an important one for many Black women and is accompanied by tasks not required by their white counterparts (Collins, 1987; Joseph & Lewis, 1981). Psychotherapists must understand the additional stressors that impinge on Black mothers as well as the effects of various mechanisms of mastery against racism that Black mothers either consciously or unconsciously teach young Black children. It may be helpful to determine which strategies or mechanisms are adaptive or maladaptive, how well the adaptive strategies function, under what conditions they function optimally, and what may undermine or enhance their functioning (Comer, 1988).

Attempts to understand the Black mother's role in and her contribution to the socialization of Black children should not be used to minimize the importance of fathers, siblings, peers, extended family members or teachers. They can all individually and selectively enhance and/or undermine this process. It is essential to understand the role of Black females who are "kin," that is, women who are not the natural mothers but who play a mothering role in raising Black children (Collins, 1987; Hill, 1971; Joseph & Lewis, 1981; Stack, 1974).

Cade (1970) observes that in the Cameroons all women of childbearing age are referred to as "mother." She explains this as a reflection of the African value system which sees children as part of and belonging to a communal network which extends beyond natural parents. It should be noted however that these extended family influences may be less intense and powerful than a natural mother's influence, particularly in the early rather than the later stages of childhood.

It is fair to say that mothers, in this case Black females, are usually charged with the task of socializing Black children. In 1982, 81.9% of Black children who did not live with both parents lived with their mothers, 14.5% lived with neither parent and only 3.6% lived with their fathers (Edelman, 1985). Further, 55.3% of all

Black children are born to single mothers (National Center for Health Statistics, 1982). The term "single mother" should not be understood as a category limited to teenage mothers or the pejorative stereotype of the Black mother on welfare. It is clear that Black mothers are central figures in the socioemotional development of Black children.

Richardson (1981) suggests that sociocultural and racial environments and experiences of mothers can greatly influence their perception of social reality and that their perception will affect childrearing values and behavioral strategies. Richardson (1981) and Collins (1987) write that one major task confronting Black mothers is that of mediating between their children and the hostile external society.

It can be concluded that Black females have and continue to serve important functions in cultural transmission, economic and parenting roles. It would seem logical that a Black child's understanding of what it means to be a Black adult would be heavily influenced by his or her mother's phenomenological understanding of racism and sexism and their respective roles in shaping the mother's own life.

Traditionally, Black women have been blamed for the family ills and stresses which are in fact caused by institutional racism. A disparaging and deficit oriented social science literature then measures Black persons and their family structures against an idealized concept of white families with the view that owing to the Black female's alleged domineering and matriarchal nature, the Black family represents a tangled web of pathology (Moynihan, 1965). Paradoxically, Hill (1971) reminds readers that the Black woman has always represented a strong and competent mother figure as even slaveholders entrusted their white children to her care. It is suggested that this need to pathologize Black persons, in this case Black women, has resulted in a line of distorted research inquiry which focuses on deficits and in doing so overlooks strengths and resources which could be utilized to assist individuals and families when problems occur. Further, this serves the purpose of reaffirming and legitimizing the original racist stereotypes and providing the appearance of a justification for the very racist and sexist practices which blatantly contradict the American ideal of equality and fair play.

Nobles (1975) writes that the task of the Black family is to prepare its children to live among white people without becoming white people, and to mediate between two often contradictory cultures. This process may require an ability to be different people at different times, a duality of socialization, without losing a core sense of self. It is required of Black families that they teach Black children to be aware of and able to imitate the majority culture whether they accept its values or not. The need to be bicultural in an antagonistic environment may produce competing and conflicting developmental tasks and tensions (Baker, 1988; Chestang, 1973; Pinderhughes, 1989). An understanding of what those conflicts are for Black children, how they may be manifested, and how they are or may be successfully negotiated has been inadequately explored.

A special task and added stressor confronting Black parents involves finding ways of warning Black children about racial dangers and disappointments without overwhelming them or being overly protective. Either extreme will facilitate the development of defensive styles which leave a child inadequately prepared to negotiate the world with a realistic perspective. This particular process in its essence may be seen as racial socialization. Allen and Majidi-Ahi (1989, p. 157) write that teaching Black children how to cope with racism represents a socialization issue which "exemplifies all that is distinct about the Black experience in America."

The family may be seen as the traditional buffer between a child and the outside world, and the major source of communicating cultural values and practices. Characteristics of Black families and their childrearing practices are a reflection of derivatives of African culture as well as adaptations to a culture which is both hostile and has different values and practices (Boyd-Franklin, 1989; Collins, 1987; Pinderhughes, 1989). Ferguson-Peters (1985) writes that the supportive childrearing strategies of Black families buffer some of the cruel and demeaning messages Black children receive from the dominant culture.

Parents are usually, but not exclusively, the persons responsible for the nurturance and guidance of a child through its developmental periods into adulthood (Franklin & Boyd-Franklin, 1985). It must be noted that biological parents may not necessarily perform this function or perform it exclusively, particularly in Black families, where extended kinship patterns are prevalent and of cultural significance. A major task of parenting persons is that of interpreting the outside world's messages to a child about who he or she is with respect to Black and White persons, and what his or her respective place in the world is or can be. This must be done in addition to teaching the child the skills he or she may require to survive and negotiate the cognitive, social and, for Black children, the racial tasks of the world.

This is a complex task for any parent; however it is further complicated for Black parents as they must perform it in what may be described as the ubiquitous environment of real or potential racial discrimination and prejudice. McAdoo (1983) writes that racism constitutes a pervasive daily reality for Black families in which the potential for being devalued with its attendant physical or psychological harm is always present and beyond their control. The context of a racist environment further changes and intensifies the meaning and impact of life's normal and catastrophic events, increasing the day to day level of stress (McAdoo, 1983).

The pressure of racism and the varied efforts and methods used by Black parents to minimize its damaging effects on their children can be accurately perceived as a major and additional source of stress not shared by their white counterparts. It is reflected for most Black persons in the amount of energy which must be consumed in and the distraction presented by, the ongoing requirement of coping with the dominant culture's prejudices and barriers.

NONTRADITIONAL BLACK MOTHERS

A delicate balance is required of all Black mothers in socializing Black children in this culture; however, some Black mothers face particularly difficult challenges. Many of these unique challenges will be obscured by rigid adherence to traditional notions about what kinds of women may be mothers. The traditional concept of the family unit as father-mother-child does not apply to many Black and White families, although the cultural significance of extended kinship patterns among Black families renders this view even less useful clinically. The failure to expand this view will result in a failure to take into account a wide range of groups of people who function as and consider themselves a family unit. A few examples are briefly discussed.

The Black adolescent female does not fit traditional views of who may be a mother, nor is adolescence the ideal developmental period in which to become a parent. Nevertheless, Joseph (1984) writes that adolescent mothers are a growing social reality with unique characteristics and needs. Among those characteristics are developmentally appropriate dependency needs, unrest, low frustration tolerance and a general struggle for identity (Joseph, 1984). It becomes all the more important that these young Black mothers have appropriate levels of information and support as they are at increased health and economic risk (Gibbs, 1989; Joseph, 1984). When this is unavailable through their families, communities must develop strategies for providing such supports.

A similar need for strong supportive networks is found in many single mother families. Developmental immaturity is not an operative factor; rather, the need to juggle multiple roles and functions, without respite, frequently in the context of poverty or financial strain is.

Consistent with the diversity within the Black community, Black lesbians may also be found in the role of mother. In addition to the challenges that all Black mothers face in childrearing, Black lesbian mothers must manage the additional stress of coping with the Black and White communities, homophobia which is intensified by the heterosexual and homosexual communities, expressions of racism.

Traditionally, mothers are presumed to be heterosexual. Lesbians are presumed to be inappropriate maternal figures and to correctly reject motherhood for themselves (Crawford, 1987). These fallacious assumptions about lesbians and mothers coupled with dichotomous stereotypes of Black women may leave Black lesbian mothers with particularly difficult challenges in childrearing. Initially, Black lesbian mothers may be required to justify their right or even their desire to have children. In heterosexual women the ubiquitous desire for motherhood is incorrectly presumed. Within Black American culture, motherhood and childrearing are encouraged despite the dominant culture's stereotype of Black women as promiscuous and prolific breeders (Greene, 1986). In this strange context Black lesbian mothers are faced with the need to explain something which in most women, particularly Black women, is assumed as natural and culturally sanctioned. Neither homosexual or heterosexual communities will necessarily understand or support a Black lesbian's desire to bear or raise children. Often, her family of origin may be critical and unsupportive of her choice as well. The aforementioned factors and the presumed rejection of the mother role in lesbians in conjunction with the mammy stereotype in Black women may predispose Black lesbian mothers to inappropriately deny a normal range of ambivalent feelings about being a parent. Further, in this context, the presumed inappropriateness of lesbians as mothers in conjunction with simultaneous idealizing and devaluing stereotypes of Black women as mothers may predispose Black lesbian mothers to deny or minimize a normal range of parent-child difficulties. The reluctance to consciously or unconsciously acknowledge the existence of such problems and parental challenges may have its origins in a fear of confirming pre-existing stereotypes to themselves and others. Psychotherapists must be attuned to the dangers inherent in a Black lesbian mother's perceived requirement to demonstrate a higher level of competence as a parent than that required of her heterosexual or white lesbian counterparts. Other ubiquitous stressors for these mothers include realistic fears of discrimination, child custody challenges, and hostility often associated with disclosure. This may result in further isolation from necessary sources of potential support and validation of their experiences. Finally, realistic fears of hostility and rejection directed at their children resulting from expressions of homophobia compounded by racism increase the stress inherent in childrearing in this context.

THE AT-RISK STATUS OF BLACK CHILDREN

A major responsibility for all Black mothers is that they must prepare their children to become Black adults. Part of that preparation involves communicating to their children the racial dangers and realities of the world that confronts most Black persons, how to make sense of them, when and how to respond to racial dangers if at all. Because of society's devaluing stance toward Black persons, it may be particularly important for Black mothers to provide more positive messages and alternatives to their children to offset the negative reflections they see of themselves in the eyes of the dominant culture. Clearly, if a natural mother is unable to do this, extended or other family members, peers, educational and mental health environments can and often do so.

The involvement of other Black females in Black families in rearing children of their own as well as children of "kin" is an important phenomenon to understand if one is to explore the function and effect of Black mothers in its appropriate context (Collins, 1987; Hill, 1971; Stack, 1974; Troester, 1984). This phenomenon and its adaptive value will be explored in greater detail later in this article.

The failure to mitigate the dominant culture's devaluing message, and rather to reinforce it can be associated with maladaptive adjustments. Historically, Black mothers have displayed resilience, strength and the ability to maximize the use of whatever meager resources were available as they actively encouraged their children to "do better." Reflections of this may be seen in biographies, Black art and literature. Psychotherapists can encourage Black mothers to use these materials in assisting their children in taking pride in and understanding the strengths, uniquenesses and contributions of Black culture and Black persons to American life.

Spencer (1987) writes that a Black child's preparation by parents and other socializing agents to understand and take pride in their own culture can be a major source of resilience and coping and that race consciousness provides a necessary foundation for the coping strategies needed by Black children. Its absence leaves a Black child at additional risk for impaired development. Sanchez (1989) writes that the first time Black children discover that they are Black is usually through a negative experience.

It is important that Black mothers be encouraged to address and raise race and racial questions directly with their children while exploring the positive symbols of Black culture with them (Harrison-Ross & Wyden, 1973; Pinderhughes, 1989; Spencer, 1987).

Good coping skills have been observed in children whose parents were models of resilience and who were available to their children with encouragement, comfort, and reassurance (Anthony & Cohler, 1987). Therefore, black mothers must be aware of their potency as role models for children who will imitate what they see before they can understand much of what is said to them.

The view of childhood as a protected developmental period during which children mature and explore the world unencumbered by many of life's stark and dangerous realities, does not hold true for a majority of Black children, particularly economically impoverished Black children. As Black parents are vulnerable to the insults and barriers of an institutionally racist society, particularly Black mothers who, as women, occupy the occupational and economic ranks of the least well paid, so are their children, and in ways that their parents cannot protect them from. One reflection of this is a 50% poverty rate for Black children compared to a 20% poverty rate for all American children (Edelman, 1985).

Garbarino (1982) defines risk as the impoverishing of a child's world of the basic social and psychological necessities of life, leaving her or him at risk for impaired development. As the context of racism and sexism is antithetical to the optimal development of individual endowments, Black children may be seen as being at greater risk for impaired development than their white counterparts (Powell, 1983; Wyatt, 1985).

The "at risk" status of Black children is reflected concretely in significant differences between Black and White children on a number of dimensions. Black children are six times as likely as their white counterparts to show excess exposure to lead; six times as likely to contract tuberculosis; ten times as likely to die before the age of one year from nutritional deficiencies; and four times as likely to suffer from gastritis and gastrointestinal infections and disorders (Edelman, 1985). Furthermore, Black children are found in correctional facilities at 400 times the rate of their white counterparts and are placed in psychiatric, foster care and health care facilities at a rate 75 percent higher than that of their white counterparts (Edelman, 1985).

Operating in a context where they are frequently double bound, where different standards apply to the same phenomena, Black children may be unable to predict whether certain behavior on their parts will be regarded positively and rewarded, negatively and punished, or simply ignored (Holiday, 1985). Despite this, many Black children do excel in this atmosphere where the opportunity to succeed against the odds may represent an underpinning of exceptional performance. The danger however is that it might just as easily lead to frustration, indifference, hostility (Holiday, 1985), and self destructive behaviors. In this context it is puzzling that theoreticians and behavioral scientists do not frame their research inquiries around the question of why more Black children are not more dysfunctional or more riddled with deficits and what it is that occurs among Black folk which has historically mitigated or worked successfully against that outcome. Day to day survival becomes an ongoing struggle for most Black mothers and their children. It would follow that a major task confronting Black children rests in the challenge to survive in a society where they must incorporate the dominant values of that society, which includes an insidious devaluation of persons of color, while simultaneously incorporating the values of a Black community. Another task involves developing their natural abilities and endowments when a large portion of their creative energy must often be used simply to survive.

THE ROLE OF KINSHIP AND EXTENDED FAMILIES

It is suggested that the socioemotional environment of Black children, an environment in which Black mothers play a key role, represents a major factor contributing to their adaptive development. Franklin and Boyd-Franklin (1985) write that socialization is enhanced in the context of love and support for the child; however it is negatively affected when it occurs in the context of parental contempt, rejection or failure. Mother-child dyads in isolated environments or in the presence of overwhelming or severe maternal stressors or maternal psychopathology, may be at risk for maternal failure. The existence and degree of poverty, marital difficulty, the presence of many young children in the home, particularly infants, illness, and other stressors may also jeopardize the success of this process.

The more a Black mother must be preoccupied with meeting basic survival needs, the more difficult it becomes for her to execute other tasks. This difficulty may be intensified for Black mothers who are isolated from community or family networks of support. When available, the use of these networks and support systems should be actively encouraged and explored. In their absence, developing such networks may be seen as an important part of the therapeutic work.

As Black females are often given responsibility for the care of siblings as well as household tasks at an early age, Hale-Benson (1980) suggests that there is an "early motherhood identification" amongst many of them. This tendency may be reinforced by extended kinship patterns, the role of interdependence and interconnectedness consistent with Black families, the less protected status of Black children by the dominant culture, and the subsequent assumption of higher levels of responsibility for themselves at an earlier age than their white counterparts.

Extended kinship patterns have been recognized as one of the strengths of Black families and can be of adaptive value (Hill, 1971; Joseph & Lewis, 1981; Stack, 1974). This is reflected in the role of "other-mothers." Troester (1984) uses the term "other-mothers" to describe women who are grandmothers, aunts, or cousins connected by "kinship" with the child's natural mother. Because they may live different lives which embody values which differ from a child's biological mother, they may also provide emotional safety, values, sounding boards and alternative role models. Troester (1984) notes that kinship status between other-mothers and children is tempered by a level of emotional distance which may be difficult to obtain within the intensity of the mother-child dyad. She adds that "other-mothers" may provide "affection and gentleness" when the natural mother must be "stern and demanding" (Weems, 1984).

Boyd-Franklin (1989) uses the term "multiple mothering" to describe this phenomenon and discusses its adaptive value across a wide range of situations in Black families. It is common in Black families for grandmothers to raise their grandchildren when their own children are deceased, dysfunctional, attempting to return to school or better their conditions, or are simply overwhelmed. While the children in these families have relationships with and may share a 3 generation household which includes their natural mother, many of them may experience the grandmother as their psychological mother. Many of these children refer to their grandmother as "mother" and if asked who their mother is will refer to their grandmother and not their natural mother (Boyd-Franklin, 1989). This may seem confusing and perhaps pathological to a therapist who is unfamiliar with the cultural norms of Black families. Nevertheless it is a strength of Black families and of particular adaptive value in low income families.

Black mothers have been criticized for what has been seen as a tendency to exercise great strictness and restrictiveness when responding to their child's behavior. This may be attributed to Black mothers' perceptions of double standards for the conduct of Black and White children. This has left many Black mothers with the assumption that a range of misbehavior, normally observed in all children, will be tolerated less when it comes from a Black child (Ferguson-Peters, 1985). This is buttressed by the perception of some Black parents that Black children must outperform their white counterparts to be perceived by the dominant culture as minimally competent (Ferguson-Peters, 1985).

It is fair to say that a predictable range of intensity exists within the context of any mother-child relationship. This range of intensity may be exceeded for Black mothers and their children, as a result of the special things that Black mothers must do to simultaneously protect and prepare Black children for adulthood. This is particularly salient given that Black mothers are aware that the optimal development of Black children will be opposed by the barriers which result from racist and sexist practices. This level of intensity and the protectiveness which may accompany it may be most problematic during adolescence when a predictable level of rebellion occurs between parent and child. Extended kinship patterns previously discussed may be useful in mitigating problems occurring in this area by offering other close relationships to mother and child which may help to buffer their relationships with one another.

SKIN COLOR CONFLICTS AND RACIAL ANGER

In slavery, lighter skinned Black persons, often the progeny of white slave masters, were sometimes given a measure of better treatment than darker skinned slaves. This often meant less overtly abusive treatment or different forms of abuse; nevertheless, jealousies and resentments between darker and lighter skinned slaves were fueled by it. As a result, many Black and White persons developed feelings about skin color preferences and resentments that persist to this day. The most salient aspect of this notion is that lighter skinned Black persons, particularly women, are seen as more attractive and acceptable, and hence, better treated by the dominant group (Greene, 1986, in press; Neal & Wilson, 1989). In this context it is predictable that skin color variations within Black families can be a source of difficulty between family members. Skin colors may vary from extremely light to extremely dark within the same family of origin amongst Black persons (Boyd-Franklin, 1989; Greene, 1986, in press).

Concerns about skin color, hair texture, body size and shape, and facial features are commonly reported by Black women in both individual and group therapies (Boyd-Franklin, 1987, 1989; Greene, 1986, in press; Neal & Wilson, 1989; Pinderhughes, 1989; Trotman, 1984). While many Black women are not negatively affected by this legacy, others, with both light and dark skin, report these concerns in conjunction with feelings of shame, guilt, anger and resentment (Neal & Wilson, 1989). The therapist must allow for and be attuned to the emergence of cues which suggest the presence of these concerns. Whether they are subtly suggested or overtly articulated they should be explored with delicacy and sensitivity as they are often the repository of intense pain.

A relevant line of inquiry is related to the question of whether or not a Black mother is predisposed to be more protective of her darker skinned children either as a result of her own conflict about skin color or perhaps the realistic notion that the dominant culture will be even less hospitable to these children. What impact might this have on the child's development and how might that child perceive his or her level of competence? It is important to raise the question of whether or not the darker skinned children would experience their mother's heightened sense of protectiveness as a lack of faith in their abilities rather than the mother's understanding of the dominant culture's obstacles. It may be difficult to clearly distinguish unconscious maternal racial conflicts in a Black mother from an honest attempt to protect or prepare in some special way what she perceives to be a more vulnerable or at risk child from a rejecting environment. It should be noted that special skill and sensitivity is required of the Black mother who faces this challenge so that her child is not left feeling doubly rejected. However, psychoanalytic theory would support the notion that for some Black mothers, a heightened sense of protectiveness of a child may represent a compensatory defense mechanism against the mother's own unconscious hostility or other negative wishes for that child. This constitutes a reaction formation defense mechanism which is described as one in which outward behavior may provide a "disguise" or unconscious outlet for forbidden or repressed wishes or impulses (Freud, 1936; Goldensohn, 1984; Walrond-Skinner, 1986). This response is not representative of Black mothers. Usually, a Black mother's heightened sense of protectiveness of her child is a realistic and adaptive response to the dominant culture. It has been presented however to make therapists aware and encourage the exploration of a wide range of clinical possibilities.

It must be acknowledged that there are Black mothers who do prefer their lighter skinned children and who scapegoat their darker skinned or different looking children. The therapist must be particularly attentive to subtle indications of this dynamic in a Black mother's polarized images of her children. When presented or suggested, the therapist must be prepared to address this as an important part of the therapeutic work.

There are many different scenarios and outcomes along this line of inquiry. These questions have been raised to suggest a way of organizing and thinking about them and to suggest some of the subtle ways in which parental skin color conflicts may be passed on to the next generation (Boyd-Franklin, 1989).

As the existence and effects of racism have been historically denied, so has the racial pain, hurt and rage which may often result. How a Black mother responds to her own racial pain will influence how she teaches her children to respond to it (Greene, in press; Harrison-Ross & Wyden, 1973; Pinderhughes, 1989). One may need to determine if open acknowledgement of such feelings is acceptable or unacceptable, to whom and why.

Teaching Black children to suppress or repress racial anger or to deny racial pain has and in some situations may continue to be of lifesaving importance, yet it always carries a price. This is particularly true if it is utilized to address a chronic continuous stressor. It is not advisable to teach any child to simply act on angry feelings.

Milner (1983) suggests that it is important to help children understand and accept their angry feelings, in this case, their racial anger. This will leave them with a greater ability to accept negative feelings without being threatened by them and therefore have less of a need to project them onto others, or internalize them.

It may also be helpful to assist a Black mother in planning a discussion with her child about angry feelings in response to racial rejection or hostility. Such a discussion might include assisting a child in setting priorities about what kinds of situations call for a direct or indirect response and why, and in what situations a direct response might be dangerous to the child, as well as exploring alternate ways of expressing or managing angry feelings. This line of inquiry is explored in greater detail in Greene (in press).

It is of additional importance to assist a client in appreciating that as a Black mother, she has added parenting tasks that require particular skill and sensitivity and represent an additional source of stress for her, as well as an additional area of competence, when managed successfully.

THE COST OF SURVIVAL

This emphasis on the adaptive skills and resilience of Black mothers should not encourage the adoption of an idealized view of them. Rather this has been an attempt to present an alternative to prevailing Anglocentric views which have pathologized Black mothers and their roles in childrearing. Hopefully this will contribute to the evolution of a balanced perspective.

In this context it is critical that we do not romanticize the successful struggles of Black mothers by failing to acknowledge and understand fully the psychological and physical costs of their survival.

There are significant internal and external pressures on Black women to exemplify the mythical images of ubiquitous strength and self sacrifice. The need to cope with the realistic demands of being a Black parent whose children are at risk in this society and to live up to the unrealistic image of the always strong and nurturing Black woman is frought with risk. Too often it results in a Black mother's neglect of herself and her own development. This is a significant risk in single parent families; however, it is not limited to them (Boyd-Franklin, 1989).

When these problems occur, the therapist must be prepared to actively facilitate and support a Black mother's mothering role as well as her own need for nurturance, support and personal growth. Boyd-Franklin (1989) suggests that therapists who work with Black women must help them to establish a balance between setting limits on family and extended family demands, developing themselves, and more appropriately and directly expressing feelings while remaining connected to family members.

We must also recognize and understand the failures of what Renita Weems (1984) characterizes as our "less than perfect mothers." In "A Personal Narrative" she writes:

> There are many Black women who have not been able or eager to talk about our less than perfect, our outrageous mothers. It is like playing the dozens on your own self. We have simply sat and nodded while others talked about the magnificent women who bore and raised them and who along with God made a way out of no way. . . . We paid to hear them lecture about the invincible strength and genius of the Black mother knowing full well that the image can be as bogus as the one of the happy slave. . . . I cannot forget my mother Though not as sturdy as others, she is my bridge. For that I am grateful. (pp. 27-28)

A discussion of the strengths observed in Black females in parenting roles despite particular complications they face should not imply that they are naturally endowed or specially suited for motherhood. Many Black females have neither the temperament for nor the interest in being parents and it cannot be assumed that being Black would or should naturally predispose them to do so.

SUMMARY

This article has attempted to examine how Black mothers under most difficult circumstances have been successful at negotiating and mediating a hostile environment for their children while simultaneously teaching them adaptive social and survival skills. It is important that psychotherapists who work with Black females understand the roles of race and racism in complicating the task of parenting for Black mothers and the task of development for Black children.

It is important that we expand the current level of inquiry on the developmental difficulties of the mother child relationship to include the aforementioned areas. This will require further exploration of many hypotheses presented here as they pertain specifically to Black mothers whose enduring connections to their children are reflected in the following passage (Rodgers, 1979, p. 377):

> My mother . . . proud of having waded through a storm, is very obviously a sturdy black bridge that I crossed over on.

While many "sturdy bridges" are required to successfully negotiate the healthy psychological development of a Black child, this bridge called "mother" remains particularly important.

REFERENCES

Allen, LaRue & Majidi Ahi, Shayda (1989). Black American children. In Jewelle Taylor Gibbs & Larke Nahme Huang (Eds.), *Children of color: Psychological interventions with minority youth* (pp. 148-178). San Francisco: Jossey Bass.

Anthony, E.J. & Cohler, B.J. (Eds.) (1987). *The invulnerable child*. New York: Guilford Press.

Baker, F.M. (1988). Afro-Americans. In Lillian Comas-Diaz & Ezra Griffith (Eds.), *Clinical guidelines in cross-cultural mental health* (pp. 151-181). New York: Wiley & Sons.

Bell, R. (1971). The relative importance of mother and wife roles among Negro lower class women. In Robert Staples (Ed.), *The black family: Essays and studies*. Belmont, CA: Wadsworth.

Boyd-Franklin, Nancy (1987). Group therapy for black women: A therapeutic support model. *American Journal of Orthopsychiatry, 57*, 394-401.

Boyd-Franklin, Nancy (1989). *Black families in therapy: A multisystems approach*. New York: Guilford Press.

Cade, Toni (1970). *The Black woman: An anthology*. New York: New American Library.

Caplan, P. & Hall-McCorquodale, I. (July 1985). Mother-blaming in major clinical journals. *American Journal of Orthopsychiatry, 55*.

Chestang, L. (1973). Character development in a hostile environment. *Occasional Paper #3*. Chicago, IL: U. of Chicago Social Services Adm.

Collins, Patricia Hill (1987). The meaning of motherhood in black culture and black mother-daughter relationships. *Sage: A Scholarly Journal on Black Women*, *4*, 3-10.

Comer, J. (1988). *Maggie's American dream: The life and times of a black family*. New York: New American Library.

Crawford, Sally (1987). Lesbian Families: Psychosocial stress and the family-building process. In Boston Lesbian Psychologies Collective (Eds.), *Lesbian Psychologies: Explorations and challenges* (pp. 195-214). Chicago, IL: Univ. of Illinois.

Edelman, Marian Wright. (1985). The sea is so wide and my boat is so small: Problems facing black children today. In Harriet & John McAdoo (Eds.), *Black Children* (pp. 72-82). Beverly Hills: Sage.

Ferguson-Peters, Marie (1985). Racial socialization of young black children. In Harriet McAdoo & John McAdoo (Eds.) *Black children* (pp. 159-173). Beverly Hills: Sage.

Freud, Anna (1936). *The ego and the mechanisms of defense*. New York: International Universities Press.

Franklin, A.J. & Boyd-Franklin, N. (1985). A psychoeducational perspective on black parenting. In Harriet & John McAdoo (Eds.), *Black children* (pp. 194-210). Beverly Hills: Sage.

Garbarino, J. (1982). *Children and families in the social environment*. New York: Aldine.

Gibbs, Jewelle Taylor (1989). Black American adolescents. In Jewelle Gibbs & Larke Nahme Huang (Eds.), *Children of color: Psychological interventions with minority youth* (pp. 179-223). San Francisco: Jossey Bass.

Goldensohn, R. (Ed.) (1984). *Longman dictionary of psychology and psychiatry*. New York: Longman.

Gordon, E. (1989). Ordinary black women. *Readings: A Journal of Reviews and Commentary in Mental Health*, *4*, 12-17.

Greene, B. (1986). When the therapist is white and the patient is black. Considerations for psychotherapy in the feminist heterosexual and lesbian communities. *Women and Therapy*, *5*, 41-65.

Greene, B. (in press). What has gone before: The legacy of racism and sexism in the lives of black mothers and daughters. *Women and Therapy*.

Hale-Benson, Janice (1980). The black woman and child rearing. In LaFrances Rodgers-Rose (Ed.), *The black woman* (pp. 79-87). Beverly Hills: Sage.

Harrison-Ross, Phyllis & Wydew, Barbara (1973). *The black child: A parent's guide*. New York: Wyden.

Hill, R. (1971). *The strengths of black families*. New York: National Urban League.

Holiday, Bertha G. (1985). Developmental imperatives of social ecologies: Lessons learned from black children today. In Harriet & John McAdoo (Eds.), *Black children* (pp. 53-69). Beverly Hills: Sage.

Joseph, Gloria & Lewis, Jill (1981). *Common differences: Conflicts in black and white feminist perspectives*. New York: Doubleday.

Joseph, Gloria (1984). Black mothers and daughters: Traditional and new populations. *Sage: A Scholarly Journal on Black Women, 1*, 17-21.

Ladner, Joyce (1971). *Tomorrow's tomorrow: The black woman*. Garden City, NY: Doubleday.

McAdoo, Harriet (1983). Societal stress and the black family. In Hamil McCubbin & Charles Figley (Eds.), *Stress and the family*. New York: Brunner Mazel.

Milner, D. (1983). *Children and race*. Beverly Hills: Sage.

Moynihan, D.P. (1965). *The negro family: The case for national action*. Washington, D.C.: U.S. Dept. of Labor.

National Center for Health Studies (1982). "Advance report of final natality statistics," 1978 *Monthly Vital Statistics Report*, 31, (18).

Neal, Angela & Wilson, Midge (1989). The role of skin color and features in the black community: Implications for black women and therapy. *Clinical Psychology Review, 9*, 323-333.

Nobles, W. (1974). African root and American fruit: The black family. *Journal of Social and Behavioral Sciences*. Spring.

Nobles, W. (1975). The black family and its children: The survival of humaneness. Unpublished paper.

Pinderhughes, Elaine (1989). *Understanding race, ethnicity and power: The key of efficacy in clinical practice*. New York: Free Press.

Powell, Gloria J. (Ed.). (1983). *The psychosocial development of minority group children*. New York: Brunner Mazel.

Rich, Adrienne (1976). *Of woman born: Motherhood as experience and institution*. New York: W.W. Norton.

Richardson, B.B. (1981). Racism and child rearing: A study of black mothers. *Dissertation Abstracts, 42*, 1:125-A.

Rodgers, Carolyn (1979). It is deep. In Roseann Bell, Beverly Guy-Sheftall, and Betty Parker (Eds.), *Sturdy black bridges* (pp. 377). New York: Doubleday.

Sanchez, Sonia (1989). Sonia Sanchez. In Brian Lanker (Ed.), *I dream a world: Portraits of black women who changed America* (p. 68). New York: Stewart, Tabori & Chang.

Spencer, Margaret Beale (1987). Black children's ethnic identity formation: Risk and resilience of castelike minorities. In Mary Jane Rotheram & Jean S. Phinney (Eds.), *Children's ethnic socialization* (pp. 103-116). Beverly Hills: Sage.

Stack, C. (1974). *All our kin: Strategies for survival in a black community*. New York: Harper and Row.

Troester, R. (1984). Turbulence and tenderness: Mothers, daughters and "othermothers" in Paule Marshall's Brown Girl, Brownstones. *Sage: A Scholarly Journal on Black Women, 1*, 13-16.

Trotman, Francis (1984). Psychotherapy with black women and the dual effects of racism and sexism. In Clair Brody (Ed.), *Women therapists working with women* (pp. 96-108). New York: Springer.

Walrond-Skinner, Sue (1986). *A dictionary of psychotherapy*. London: Routledge & Kegan-Paul.

Weems, Renita (1984). "Hush, mama's gotta go bye bye.": A personal narrative. *Sage: A Scholarly Journal on Black Women*, *1*, 25-28.
Wilson, M. (1989). Child development in the context of the black extended family. *American Psychologist*, *44*, 380-385.
Wyatt, Gail (1985). The sexual abuse of Afro-American and white women in childhood. *Child Abuse and Neglect*, *9*, 507-519.

SECTION VI: RESEARCH

Motherhood and Sex Role Development

Mary A. Halas

There is an ongoing revolution in men's and women's role arrangements within families that traditional theories of sex-role socialization and development cannot explain. These changes are most dramatic among married women with preschool children. There also have been substantial challenges to the traditional sex-role theories from empirical data on childhood development (Maccoby & Jacklin, 1974) and suggestions for further research to reexamine the development of sex roles across the lifespan (Cahill, 1983).

Men and women in increasing numbers are leading complex lives for which their sex-role socialization did not prepare them, since traditional theories are the dominant U.S. cultural norms (Bernard, 1976) and provide the underlying rationale for parental childrearing styles (Block, 1978), education (Baumrind, 1972; Block, 1976;

Mary A. Halas, PhD, is Licensed Psychologist and counselor in full-time private practice in Alexandria, VA. She specializes in women's issues, sex-role development for men and women, working with survivors of sexual and emotional abuse, and premenstrual syndrome. She has lectured and published articles on both sexism in medical care, and treating adolescents suffering from PMS.

Neugarten, 1972), and counseling and psychotherapy (American Psychological Association, 1975; Broverman, Broverman, Clarkson, Rosenkrantz & Vogel, 1970; Holroyd, 1976; Robbins, 1983). The high rates of separation and divorce and the numbers of couples seeking marital therapy indicate the need for therapy and education to focus on the social revolution in marriage now under way (Cowan & Cowan, 1981).

This study grew out of my desire, as a feminist therapist, to understand this revolution and to assist those who are caught up in its pressures and strains. It attempts to document where we are at the present time. This article presents a study of mothers having second children and a theory developed from that study. It concentrates on four areas: (a) *socialization for sex roles*—and how it continues through the lifespan, (b) *motherhood as one critical agent/occasion* of sex-role socialization, (c) *description of development*—an orderly and consistent pattern to changes in sex roles and gender concepts in a direction toward androgyny, and (d) *prescription or evaluation*—evidence of advantages of higher levels of development.

METHOD

To study development, I needed to have a passage of time; therefore, I chose a longitudinal method. To maximize change, I wanted to observe a critical event that might stimulate change; therefore, I studied second-time motherhood.

I interviewed 22 middle class mothers in their homes two times during the last trimester of their second pregnancies and two more times four months after their deliveries. I used the method of ethnographic research outlined by Spradley (1979) and conducted according to the theories of Guba (1978).

Research with this qualitative method discovers categories of meaning important to a group or culture such as, in this study, "reasons for who does what" in role divisions. Ethnographic research is a process of discovery and description of a segment of a culture. It generates theories but does not test them. Ideally, in order to provide empirical validation of qualitative research, it is followed by experimental research that asks about incidence, cause and effect, etc.

Following the second and fourth interviews, couples filled out two instruments: the Lockwood Wallace *Marital Adjustment Scale* (Locke & Wallace, 1959), and a modification of Cowan and Cowan's (1981) *Who Does What Scale.* These quantitative instruments provided additional data and a partial validity check on the ethnographic method.

PRE-BIRTH AND RETROSPECTIVE RESULTS: A TYPOLOGY

Four distinct groups of women emerged, based on their sex-role arrangements and attitudes: conformist, mainstream, egalitarian and androgynous (see Table 1). Distinctive themes appeared at each of the four levels:

1. Conformist: husband dominance, consistency with models from the past, and failures of communication.
2. Mainstream: reactions to their background and emulation of the current culture, plus interplay of husband dominance and wife assertiveness.
3. Egalitarian: inner-directedness and individuality, with an increase in mutuality with husbands and positive attitudes toward stereotypic male and female tasks.
4. Androgynous: transcendence of sex-roles, balancing of personalities and family togetherness, change and fluidity in roles.

A fifth group included mothers from five *couples in disequilibrium,* in which the husband and the wife within each couple were at different sex-role developmental levels.

Conservative Mothers

The title for this group of mothers came from its desire to conserve what its members perceived as the values of the past. Throughout interviews, they referred to their own growing up experiences as models for mothering and to a selection of conservative experts to justify their opinions ("Mr. Burton White says part-time help is fine").

TABLE 1. Typology of Couples

	CONSERVATIVE	MAINSTREAM	EGALITARIAN	ANDROGYNOUS
CONFORMITY	past is model	conform to up-to-date ideal	own preferences are source of choices	personal role choices continually changing
CHANGE OVER TIME	value consistency, minimal change	change in adolescence; little since marriage	continues through negotiation of conflict	ongoing growth responding to situations
CROSS-SEX BEHAVIOR	very little	husbands do a few cross-sex tasks they prefer	multiple for both spouses	family tasks seen without sex distinctions
TOLERANCE FOR DIFFERENCES	there are absolutes; a right way to do things	ambivalence; search for a right way to do things	tolerance for choices of others	comfort w/ their own and others' choices

AWARENESS OF SEX-ROLE	sex roles seen as biologically determined	sex roles seen as part of evolving culture to emulate	aware that present choices conflict with background	freeing selves fr. background spouses help each to develop
SOCIALIZATION OF CHILDREN	sex-role differences emphasized	some egalitarianism; tend sex-type children	aware of subtle sexism	conscious efforts to make both sexes androgynous
ATTITUDE TOWARD EQUALITY	husband is dominant	portray selves as equal & don't acknowledge	fairness is major concern	sex-linked roles not relevant
HANDLING OF CONFLICT	tends to remain unresolved	more tools to resolve; also use denial	productive resolutions also can live with unresolved	ease and humor in working out differences

These mothers were very aware of the cultural context in which they lived and expressed feelings of aloneness and isolation. The employed wives and day care centers in their neighborhoods felt to these women like a criticism and a threat to their way of life and values. Conservative women performed very little if any cross-sex behavior and expected none from their husbands—even during the early childrearing years when they faced an overload of housework and childcare work.

Conservative mothers believed there are absolutes of right and wrong ways of doing things. Those who do not follow the right way of behaving can expect to have undesirable outcomes in their children's behavior, personality or achievement. For example: "Children in day care aren't as talkative or as friendly as my son. There's something they just aren't getting."

For conservative women, the explanation for differences in the sexes' roles is biological. Biology is the source of instinctual mother love, the mother's desire to stay at home, differences in male and female disciplinary styles, and the natural behavior differences between boys and girls.

Husband dominance was another theme. "He did say we could take a vacation," said one conservative wife. These women endured frequent denigration of their opinions, interests and contributions to running of the family, plus critiques from their husbands on their childrearing techniques. Conservative women's conflicts with their husbands tended to remain unresolved, primarily because they had difficulty empathizing with each other's perspectives. The other person when s/he disagreed wasn't holding a different view; s/he was wrong.

From a clinical perspective, conservative mothers raised some concern, largely due to their difficulties in achieving empathic communication on their differences with their husbands. Factors that appeared to support conservative women in succeeding with the sex roles and values of the past were homogeneity of background with their husbands, high income, and a local community with many young families and child-oriented services.

Mainstream Mothers

Ten mothers in the study operated at a mainstream level of sex-role development. Four of these had conservative husbands whom they were pressuring to change. Mainstream mothers were aware of the changing nature of U.S. middle class culture and wanted to be up-to-date. Their ideal included a husband whose primary responsibility was to provide income but who was significantly involved at home, plus a wife who cared primarily for house and children but had significant achievements outside the home.

Mainstream mothers typically accepted both same-sex and cross-sex activities more out of a sense of duty than preference, because these were "what was left to be done." These mothers felt pressure to meet two sets of social expectations—the ideals of the traditional mother at home and of the modern woman employed at a paying job. They expressed painful guilt for not meeting either (or both) of these ideals. One mother chose to compromise her own needs but not her child's by doing her part-time typing job at home during her child's naps.

Mainstream mothers worked hard to educate themselves on the current U.S. middle class parenting culture. They read childrearing manuals extensively and enrolled in various parenting courses. These women talked about the ideal of socializing boys and girls to be equal, in areas such as toy selection. They were unaware, however, of treating their boys and girls differently in emotional and behavioral areas.

Women at the mainstream level were more assertive with their husbands than were conservative women. Their repeated efforts to get their husbands more involved in childcare yielded some favorable results. One mother said: "At first I felt like I was at home all day and he deserved to go out running when he got home . . . Now I tell him, there are times you cannot have your run because it is not feasible."

Overall, mainstream women enjoyed two distinct advantages over conservative women. First, the mainstream conformity to a model accepted in the current U.S. culture provided both practical and emotional support for its members' role arrangements and a means of responding to cultural change—continued conformity as the norm changes. Second, mainstream couples' cooperative communication made it easier for them to adapt to new situations as they arose.

Egalitarian Mothers

Equality in marriage was the ideal for egalitarian mothers. They made role choices based on their own inclinations rather than conforming to outside norms. They were aware of and comfortable with how their choices diverged from the mainstream U.S. culture. In egalitarian couples, both spouses performed multiple cross-sex behaviors, and husbands and wives bargained and figured so that their workload would be equal and fair.

For the first time in the developmental sequence, egalitarian women had and got respect for their activities in work and education even when they did not generate any money. For example, one woman writer spent more money on babysitting while she wrote than she earned for her published works, but her writing was respected as a family priority. Egalitarian women were able to exercise more choices than conservative and mainstream women, because their husbands responded to their wives' assertiveness and made conscious choices to limit their own careers. Three of their husbands had flexible work schedules, including a grammar school teacher, a graduate student, and a veterinarian with short hours.

Egalitarian couples had more tolerance for differences. They also could see and present evidence that contradicted their personal convictions. One of these mothers said that she felt her children got the best care through her staying at home. She volunteered, however, that "I had to laugh" at the realization that the children of her friends who did not stay at home were turning out "about the same" as her own child.

In socializing their daughters, egalitarian women expressed concern about subtle socialization agents in choices and cultural pressures on girls and boys. They wanted to socialize their daughters in a more androgynous model than the mainstream culture. These women experienced conflict in working out with their husbands what equality means, but they had several ways to work things out.

They were able to tolerate conflict because they expected it would result eventually in productive resolutions to which each partner had contributed.

Androgynous Mothers

Androgynous mothers expressed an even greater freedom from the need to match any norm from the past or present. They had an informed, educated distrust of many childrearing manuals used as parenting bibles by mainstream women. For the first time in the typology, women had husbands who encouraged their wives' sex-role development. One mother said, "Jim at first was ahead of me as far as feminist philosophy."

Androgynous mothers saw all house and childcare tasks as family work without sex-linked distinctions, and without fixed assignment of roles. For example, husbands got up at night to participate in feeding even when wives were breastfeeding. They were the only husbands in the study actively to seek out a major role in house and childcare, even when the wife was not employed. Both mothers and fathers were free to do cross-sex or same-sex stereotyped activities depending on what worked best for them as a couple, as individuals, and in the particular situation. Housework was not a big issue, and they both did it.

For the first time in the typology, concern for the socialization of boys appeared. One mother said, "I get the feeling that most boys are not raised to be sensitive to other people's feelings or to understand about their own emotions, so we talk about that a lot."

Overall, androgynous mothers had many alternative routes to work out differences with their spouses, and showed less stress than women at other levels. They seemed to achieve their distinctive level of enjoyment and relatively low stress in the midst of the rigors of early parenting by their focus on the family unit and togetherness. For example, every workday of the year, one couple had a picnic lunch with their daughter. The househusband father packed his daughter in a back carrier and walked to his wife's office.

POST-BIRTH FINDINGS

The findings from the two post-birth interviews with mothers supported the theory that there is a sex-role developmental process that extends into adulthood. Those individuals who changed from before to after the birth of a second child did so in a consistent direction – toward androgyny.

Sex roles of mothers and fathers at the conservative level were quite distinct both before and after the births of second children. For couples in the mainstream and disequilibrium groups, in contrast, there were shifts from fairly separate to slightly more fluid divisions of labor between spouses following the births of second children. Shifts were in response to the strain on the old roles which the increased and unpredictable workload of two children created.

As a result of having learned from previous childrearing, mothers were more confident and at ease in handling their new babies. Second-time parenting also made substantial changes in the self-concepts of many. Changes among mothers in the study were: (a) more assertiveness in getting their husbands to share in homemaking; (b) increases in inner-directedness and greater control over children; (c) deepening appreciation of femaleness; (d) enhanced sense of competence, achievement and endurance (also decreased incidence of postpartum depression); and (e) increased self-nurturing and appreciation of their own rights and needs.

Wife Assertiveness – Behavioral Changes

One critical factor in sex-role growth or lack of it in every group in the study was couple communication. That is, wife assertiveness and husband receptivity in most cases was the *sine qua non* for sex-role development. A key element was what value a woman put on her own activities, whether paid or volunteer. One woman was at home full time, yet she was more assertive and successful in getting her husband to increase his involvement at home than was one highly paid scientist who relied on dramatic, aggressive emotionality in attempting to get her husband to discuss how they divided tasks.

Nonassertive wives, who did not have the same sense of value in their own self-fulfillment, had negative outcomes from the increased demands of first and second children. Rather than face the conflict of negotiating, two employed wives and one stay-at-home wife gave up things that were important to them, such as exercise and athletic activity.

Changes in Self-Concept and Emotions

The sense of physical achievement for some women of improving on the previous experience of childbearing through carrying a pregnancy to term, or having breastfeeding go more smoothly or having an easier delivery deepened their positive feelings about being women. The enhanced self-esteem about being female appeared in all groups of the typology. One androgynous woman's feminist philosophy previously had included a sexist definition of equality in the workplace. She described the process of her emotional change related to having her second child:

> I used to feel that women who leave work early to do something with their kids or take off to take kids to the doctor are not going to be considered serious professionals. Now I wouldn't take a job in which that wouldn't be part of the agenda. We were both able to go to Johnny's picnic Friday.

Cross-sex changes mothers made following the births of their second children were in traditionally male areas of attributing competence to themselves. They transferred feelings of being strong and enduring in managing two children competently to other areas of their lives such as employment. One mother decided she had the "right stuff" to handle graduate school, because, "I have learned [that] school is possible because having two kids is possible . . . I've been tested."

Some women from each group in the typology increased their self-nurturing as a protective reaction to the increased demands of mothering two children. Some mothers found they no longer could follow the stereotyped female role of meeting all their children's and husbands' needs ("I don't have to be a martyr to be a mother."), and they made more choices based on their own preferences and rights.

QUANTITATIVE RESULTS AND DISCUSSION

Analysis of the quantitative data attempted to answer two questions: (a) Can the existence of distinct sex-role developmental levels be validated by an objective instrument? and (b) Is the evaluation that it is better to be at higher levels of sex-role development supported by objective evidence about role and marital satisfaction among mothers?

Support for Sex-Role Developmental Typology

The quantitative data from the *Who Does What Scale* (WDW) supported the couple typology, showing distinctive profiles of the couples' role arrangements in five task areas of housework, family decisions, work and education, care of the first child and care of the second child. Scores above 0 indicated fathers took greater responsibility in an area, scores below 0 indicated mothers took greater responsibility.

As Figure 1 illustrates, wives in every group of the typology did a greater proportion of childcare than did their husbands, and husbands had a greater commitment to employment. At each successive level, however, the trend was for more balance between husbands' and wives' participation in specific tasks. The curve gets flatter at each successive level, a trend especially notable in the two childcare areas. Husbands participated more at each successive level and approached 50-50 sharing of childrearing in the androgynous group.

What the equal-sharing quantitative data cannot show in decisions and housecare areas is that even when mothers and fathers reported equal levels of work and decision-making, these were in separate arenas among conservative and mainstream couples. The women made daily decisions about food brands and children's clothing, and the men decided where to live and what car to buy. Figure 1 also confirms ethnographic findings on specific features of various couple types. Conservative husbands responded to the increased pressures and responsibilities of second-time parenting with increased work on the job rather than at home. Their levels of childcare decreased after the second birth. Wives in disequilibrium pressured their husbands to do more at home, and the slight rise in

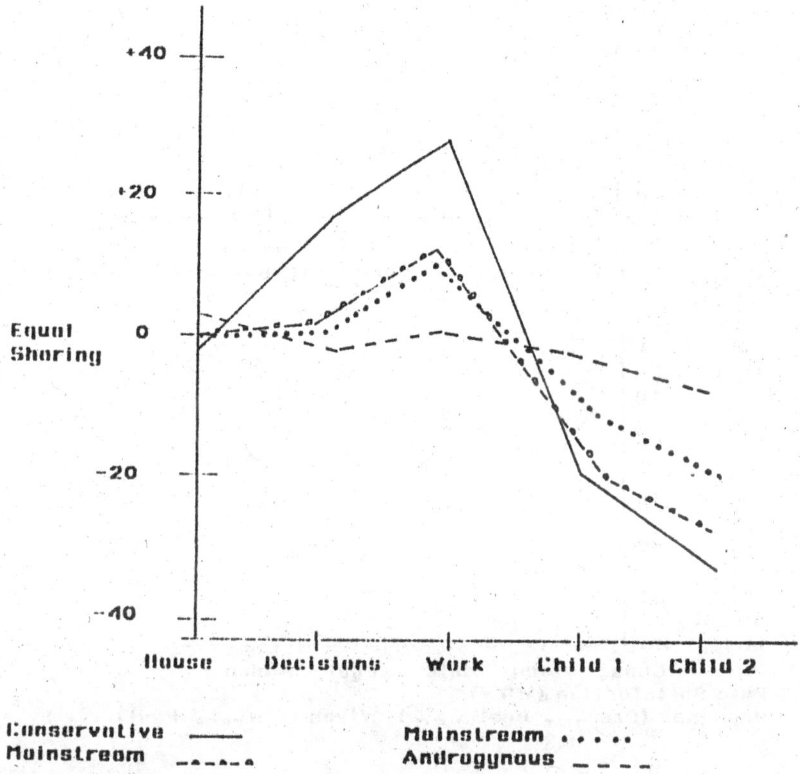

FIGURE 1. Task Performance of Four Sex-Role Groups on the Who Does What

husbands' scores after the second birth on four of five tasks shows the effectiveness of wives' efforts.

Support for Advantages of Higher Developmental Levels

Figure 2 presents data that support the theories of Bem (1978), Block (1973) and Rebecca, Hefner and Oleshansky (1976) that higher levels of sex-role development are desirable. In the first graph, couple marital satisfaction rises in the later stages in sex-role development, with conspicuous dips in the groups known to be in

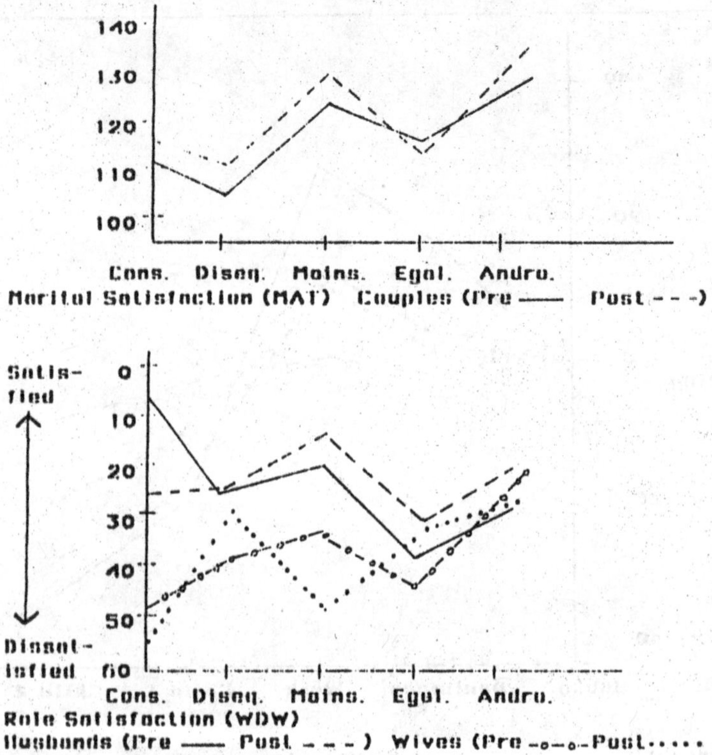

FIGURE 2. Satisfaction Pre and Post Second Births for Five Sex-Role Groups of Couples

conflict over transition to later stages (disequilibrium and egalitarian).

The second graph in Figure 2 also supports feminist theories about the desirability of androgynous sex-roles for men and women. Conservative, disequilibrium and mainstream men were more satisfied with their roles than were their wives. At the egalitarian and androgynous stages of sex-role development, husbands' role satisfaction was slightly lower, but wives' satisfaction rose to levels close to their husbands'.

For feminist advocates concerned about equality between the

sexes, this graph gives strong support. Men's role satisfaction may go down slightly when they are sharing more equally in family responsibilities with their wives than when they are dominant. But their satisfaction never sinks to the levels at which women's start when their husbands are dominant and are not participating much in home responsibilities other than income production.

INTERPRETATIONS

Four main interpretations emerge from the study of mothers having second children:

1. Sex-role attitudes and behaviors continue to change throughout early parenting in adults. In addition, a substantial number of adults have developed sex roles far different from the ideal described in traditional sex-role theories. There is strong support for feminist theories that androgyny is rare, but attainable in behavior and attitudes.
2. There are discernible steps in the sex-role developmental process, and the direction of growth is from a sex-linked division of labor and personality attributes at the earlier levels, toward a transcendence of sex-linked attribution in personality and behavior at the later levels.
3. Having a first child changes women's and men's lives in a sex-stereotyped direction. Having a second child provides a challenge to which many receptive mothers and fathers respond with sex-role development toward androgyny.
4. Sex-role developmental levels at the later end of the continuum are more desirable. They present lower risk for individual, couple and family dysfunction than those at earlier levels. The fluidity of sex-role arrangements and the greater variety of emotional and behavioral capabilities in both men and women at later levels tend to result in higher satisfaction and more flexible responses to crises than is possible at earlier levels.

IMPLICATIONS FOR THERAPY AND EDUCATION

Each of the groups in the typology has certain issues around which conflict revolves. A primary therapeutic issue for conformist women would be to assist them and their spouses to see and hear each others' points of view, moving past the conviction that a spouse's disagreement means s/he is wrong.

For mainstream women, counseling and education could focus on balancing and integrating home-related and work-related activities to help mothers, in particular, move out of the guilt-ridden "supermom" trap. Egalitarian mothers' overly active sense of democracy and respect for the inner direction of individuals puts them at risk for failures of discipline with their children, an imbalance in need of correction. Both egalitarian and androgynous women can benefit from support and creative problem-solving in meeting the challenges the current society poses (through inadequate childcare resources and sexism in employment, to their preferred style of functioning).

The findings also suggest that sex-role growth is a desirable goal for counseling and education. Each successive level in the typology involved increased flexibility and mutuality in relationships and increased capability for satisfaction in response to the challenges of second-time parenting.

Therapists and educators who are aware of the belief systems of women at different sex-role developmental levels can fine-tune their messages promoting sex-role growth so that clients and students can more easily assimilate them. For example, in working with women who are having difficulty exercising appropriate controls over their children's behavior, a therapist might cite the nationally known childrearing authorities in dealing with a conservative woman, and cite the importance of equal rights for parents as persons in working with an egalitarian mother.

REFERENCES

American Psychological Association. (1975). *Report of the task force on sex bias and sex-role stereotyping in psychotherapeutic practice.* Washington, D.C.: APA.

Bem, S. L. (1978). Beyond androgyny: Some presumptuous prescriptions for a liberated sexual identity. In F. L. Denmark & J. Sherman (Eds.) *Psychology of women: Future directions of research.* New York: Psychological Dimensions.

Baumrind, D. (1972). From each according to her ability. *School Review, 80,* 161-195.

Bernard, J. (1976). Change and stability in sex-role norms and behavior. *Journal of Social Issues, 32,* 207-223.

Block, J. H. (1973). Conceptions of sex role: Some cross-cultural and longitudinal perspectives. *American Psychologist, 28,* 512-526.

Block, J. H. (1976). Issues, problems, and pitfalls in assessing sex differences: A critical review of *The Psychology of Sex Differences. Merrill-Palmer Quarterly, 22,* 283-308.

Block, J. H. (1978). Another look at sex differentiation in the socialization behaviors of mothers and fathers. In F. Denmark & J. Sherman (Eds.) *Psychology of women: Future directions of research.* New York: Psychological Dimensions.

Broverman, I., Broverman, D., Clarkson, F., Rosenkrantz, P., & Vogel, S. (1970). Sex-role stereotypes and clinical judgments of mental health. *Journal of Consulting and Clinical Psychology, 34,* 1-7.

Cahill, S. (1983). Reexamining the acquisition of sex roles: A social interactionist approach. *Sex Roles, 9,* 1-15.

Cowan, C. P., & Cowan, P. A. (April 1981). Couple role arrangements and satisfaction during family formation. Paper presented at the Biennial Meeting of the Society for Research in Child Development. Boston, MA.

Guba, E. G. (1978). *Toward a methodology of naturalistic inquiry in educational evaluation.* Los Angeles: Center for the Study of Evaluation, UCLA.

Holroyd, J. (1976). Psychotherapy and women's liberation. *Counseling Psychologist, 6,* 22-27.

Locke, H. J. & Wallace, K. (1959). Short marital adjustment and prediction tests: Their reliability and validity. *Marriage and Family Living, 21,* 251-255.

Maccoby, E. E. & Jacklin, C. N. (1974). *The psychology of sex differences.* Stanford, CA: Stanford University Press.

Neugarten, B. (1972). Education and the life cycle. *School Review, 80,* 211-215.

Rebecca, M., Hefner, R., & Oleshansky, B. (1976). A model of sex-role transcendence. *Journal of Social Issues, 32,* 197-206.

Robbins, J. H. (1983). Complex triangles: Uncovering sexist bias in relationship counseling. *Women & Therapy, 2,* 159-169.

Spradley, J. S. (1979). *The ethnographic interview.* NY: Holt, Rinehart and Winston.

